TRADE YOUR WAY
TO FINANCIAL FREEDOM

TRADE YOUR WAY
TO FINANCIAL FREEDOM

VAN K. THARP

McGraw-Hill

New York   San Francisco   Washington, D.C.   Auckland   Bogotá
Caracas   Lisbon   London   Madrid   Mexico City   Milan
Montreal   New Delhi   San Juan   Singapore
Sydney   Tokyo   Toronto

Library of Congress Cataloging-in-Publication Data

Tharp, Van K.
    Trade your way to financial freedom / by Van K. Tharp.
       p.   cm.
    "Dr. Van Tharp's secrets to: how to find the Holy Grail in the
market and how to design a winning system that fits you."
    Includes bibliographical references.
    ISBN 0-07-064762-3
    1. Finance, Personal. 2. Stocks. I. Title.
HG179.T452 1998
332.024—dc21   98-18356
                                             CIP

McGraw-Hill

A Division of The McGraw-Hill Companies

1 2 3 4 5 6 7 8 9 0 DOC/DOC 9 0 3 2 1 0 9 8

ISBN 0-07-064762-3

The sponsoring editor for this book was Stephen Isaacs, the editing supervisor was John M. Morriss, and the production supervisor was Suzanne W. B. Rapcavage. It was set in Palentino by Terry Leaden of McGraw-Hill's Professional Book Group composition unit.

Printed and bound by R. R. Donnelley & Sons Company.

McGraw-Hill books are available at special quantity discounts to use as premiums and sales promotions, or for use in corporate training programs. For more information, please write to the Director of Special Sales, McGraw-Hill, 11 West 19th Street, New York, NY 10011. Or contact your local bookstore.

 This book is printed on recycled, acid-free paper containing a minimum of 50% recycled de-inked fiber.

This book is dedicated to my wife, Kalavathi Tharp.
Kala provides a very special spark in my life.
Without that spark and her tremendous love,
this book would not be possible.

CONTENTS

PART TWO:

CONCEPTUALIZATION OF YOUR SYSTEM

Chapter 4

Steps to Developing a System   61

Chapter 5

Selecting a Concept That Works   81

Chapter 13

FOREWORD

The title of Chapter 1 of this book is: "The Legend of the Holy Grail." "The Holy Grail" is a phrase you often hear in some trading and investment circles. Most people believe that it refers to some mysterious trading system out there that is going to make them millions with little or no risk. It's not that at all.

But before I tell you about the Holy Grail, let me tell you a little about who I am and why Dr. Tharp asked me to write the Foreword to his book. I started managing other peoples' money in 1992 and in just 5 years those assets have grown from about $3 million to about $50 million. That has happened partially because my hedge fund has compounded by better than 40 percent per year, net to investors, over the last 5 years. We were up 61 percent net to investors in 1996 and 53 percent net to investors in 1997. Since I met Dr. Tharp, my net worth has grown many times over, and I do believe that it comes from adopting many of the Holy Grail secrets contained in this book. I think that Dr. Tharp understands and teaches those secrets better than anyone else I have ever met. Let me tell you why:

When I was a young boy, I remember dreaming that I would become a millionaire by the time I reached 25 years of age. I reached that goal through real estate development in 1981, but only briefly and then it all came tumbling down around me. I was devastated, but I picked myself up and started again. My next attempt at real success was in the investment field.

Yet I almost had a similar type of crash in my fortunes. I remember the day clearly. I was sitting in my office in Naples, Florida, in late 1992. It was a typical south Florida autumn day. I was watching the palm trees sway in the breeze outside my window, wondering why my trading had become more difficult since I began managing money for others. I wasn't about to crash at the time, but I had the same sort of feeling in my gut that I had had before my first crash.

My interests in investing began in 1967, when I would make regular trips to the local public library to devour every book I could find on investing. I'd also study biographies of successful businesspeople. I certainly wish I had been aware of Dr. Tharp's modeling work back then, because it would have saved me so much time and so many heartaches.

In 1969, at the age of 13, I talked my reluctant parents into opening a brokerage account for me at the local Merrill Lynch office in Toledo, Ohio. The conditions of the account: I had to fund the account myself from lawn mowing and odd jobs, and every trade had to be confirmed by my mother since it was a Unified Gift to Minors Act account. Once open, my father would occasionally give me a little money to put into the account, as long as I didn't tell my mom.

As I looked out the window, I realized how fortunate I was. I now lived in a tropical climate. I had probably again achieved my childhood dream of success doing something I loved to do. Twenty-two years had gone by since I made my first trade; only now I was doing it successfully. Yet, somehow, I was now beginning to find trading difficult.

That nervous feeling helped me open up to whole new levels of success—way beyond those of my first childhood dreams. That feeling was the key to what was going on, and the key to my success, but I didn't know what that key was— not yet at least.

A few days later, I notice a magazine ad about Dr. Van Tharp. I had read about him in Jack Schwager's book *Market Wizards*, so I decided to give him a call. That call was the start of a close professional and personal relationship that would end up affecting my life, my family, and even my business interests and associates. I already understood many of the secrets contained in this book. However, through my association with Dr. Tharp, I now understood the ultimate aspect of the Holy Grail secret—the part that Dr. Tharp so eloquently describes in Chapter 1.

The Holy Grail is not what you would expect it to be. It is something that is different for each person. It's a hidden secret that you have to discover for yourself, but it is obvious once it is realized.

I must admit that when I first learned what Dr. Tharp was going to write about in this book, I was concerned. He was giving away too many of our secrets! However, I'm not concerned any more because I now realize that those secrets are so personal. My Holy Grail is not the same as your Holy Grail. In addition, many of you will just let those secrets pass by you, so I urge you to be careful. Read this book carefully. Indeed, pay particular attention to:

- Understanding the psychological biases against good system development (Chapter 2)
- Setting objectives for what you are trying to accomplish (Chapter 3)
- Understanding expectancy and R multiples (Chapters 6 through 10)
- Realizing that the golden rule of trading is created by how you get out of the markets, not by picking some magic stock (Chapters 9 and 10)
- Understanding the importance of position sizing (Chapter 12)

And pay special attention to the meaning of the Holy Grail as described in Chapter 1. Until you've mastered yourself, you'll always struggle with the market. I wish all of you could integrate that meaning into your being and then truly apply it to your trading.

The material that Dr. Tharp presents in this book, in his *Market Mastery* newsletter, in his home-study courses, and in his seminars will change your life if you are open to them. I urge you to take the first step today and open yourself up to the material found in this book. Enjoy the journey. It's a great one!

David Mobley, Sr.
Naples, Florida
February 1998

ACKNOWLEDGMENTS

This book is a product of 15 years of thinking about markets, studying hundreds of great traders and investors, and coaching many more to greatness by helping them apply some of the principles you'll find in this book. If this book helps hundreds more, even if I never meet you, it will have been worth the effort.

During those 15 years, numerous people have helped shape the thinking that has gone into this book. I can only acknowledge a few of those people by name. However, everyone who contributed in any way has my deepest thanks and appreciation.

I'd like to acknowledge Ed Seykota for showing me very early on the importance of simplicity and creative money management. Ed has presented at three of my early seminars, and I'm deeply indebted to his wisdom.

Tom Basso has been a great contributor to my thinking and my life. Tom was a guest speaker at more than a dozen of my seminars and several of our professional trader schools. Tom has also contributed several sections to this book. Thank you, Tom.

Ray Kelly was one of my earliest clients. I've watched him evolve from a tough floor trader—whose favorite saying used to be "My way or the highway!"—into someone who would freely give his time to inner-city high school kids just to convince them to start to take responsibility for their lives. Ray is one of the best traders I know and a great teacher as well. He's presented at many of my seminars and has written the arbitrage section of this book.

Chuck LeBeau helped me make the link from the famous trader's axiom—"Cut your losses short and let your profits run"—to the importance of exits. Think about it. Cutting losses short is all about aborting losses—exits. Letting profits run is all about exits as well. The entire axiom is all about exits. Chuck's persistence in driving home this point has been very valuable to me. Chuck is now a guest speaker at my advanced systems seminar and has also contributed a section to this book on fundamental analysis.

I would also like to acknowledge a very special person in my life—David Mobley, Sr. I've probably done more consulting with David than any other trader. I've also worked with most of his family. I've watched them all grow tremendously over the last 6 years since we've been close, but especially David. Thus, it is with great pleasure that I asked David to write the Foreword to this book. David's company, Maricopa, was one of our first graduating companies.

Kevin Thomas, Jerry Toepke, and Louis Mendelsohn all contributed great sections to the concepts chapter (Chapter 5). Their work is very insightful and helpful. I deeply appreciate your contributions.

I'd also like to acknowledge our first graduates—Webster Management. Three key people at Webster met at my school for professional traders. They have achieved tremendous success by understanding the key components necessary for investment and trading success—expectancy and money management. I'd particularly like to acknowledge the contributions to my thinking from Paul Emery, Rob Friedl, Parker Sroufe, and Paul Rusnock.

Chuck Branscomb has been a great model for me of how to adopt these principles. When he first came to my seminars, he thought he had a great system—when he really had no system at all, just some entry signals. He's attended all my system seminars (except for one held in London) and most of the other seminars. I've watched him evolve into a very knowledgeable systems trader. He's also a great example of how solid "intuition" about the market evolves out of solid systems trading. Chuck is the editor of our newsletter, *Market Mastery,* and several excerpts from Chuck's work were put into this book. In addition, Chuck helped tremendously in generating some of the graphics in this book.

John Humphreys is the senior developer of Athena Money Management software used in this book. John has incorporated all my suggestions about money management into the software to the point where one can now begin to see the millions of possibilities that exist in money management, which I call "position sizing" throughout this book. I knew position sizing was critical when the project started, but now that I can actually see the results of using the software I know that its importance is beyond anything that I had imagined.

I'd like to thank everyone in my supertrader program. Several of them—William Curtiss and Rolf Sigrist—who continually bounce their great, creative ideas off me, have helped shape my thinking tremendously through their education process. I'd also like to thank Loyd Massey and Frank Gallucci for their tremendous suggestions in reviewing the manuscript. I'd also like to thank Bruce Feingold, Sir Mark Thomson, Dennis Ullom, Willard ("Buddy") Harper, Andreas Pfister, Corky Dobbs, and Jim Hetherington for the tremendous insights I've gained from working with them.

Some very special teachers in my life deserve a special mention. These include Connierae Andreas, Deepak Chopra, Robert Dilts, Todd Epstein, John Grinder, Tad James, Robert Kiyosaki, John Overdurf, James Sloman, Enid Vien, and Wyatt Woodsmall. Your contribution to my personal evolution has been tremendous.

I'd like to thank my editors at McGraw-Hill for their wonderful help. Stephen Isaacs miraculously appeared when I needed a publisher and John Morriss was very helpful throughout the production process.

Lastly, but not least, I'd like to thank my staff at I.I.T.M., Inc. for their support in completing this book. Cathy Hasty has been a great help in laying out the book and with the graphics. Annette French has always "been there" to assist me with whatever was necessary.

My deepest thanks go to all of you and to the many people who also contributed, but were too numerous to mention.

PREFACE

A number of my clients have asked me not to include certain sections in this book, with the admonishment of "You're giving away too much." Yet my job is to coach traders and investors to achieve peak performance. Every available tool is important in attempting to do that, because so much misinformation is available in the literature that the average person will constantly be led astray.

Most of the misinformation is not deliberate. People want to be led astray. They constantly ask the wrong questions, and those selling information get rewarded by giving them the answers they want. For example:

- What's the market going to do now?
- What should I buy now?
- I own XYZ stock. Do you think it's going to go up? (If you say no, then they'll ask someone else until they find a person who agrees with their opinion.)
- Tell me how I can get into the market and be "right" most of the time.

In April 1997, I did a 2-day seminar in Germany. Toward the end of the seminar, I gave the participants the choice of doing an exercise dealing with self-sabotage (which all of them needed) or asking me questions. They took a vote on what to do. Guess what the first question asked of me was? "Dr. Tharp, what's your opinion about what the U.S. stock market will do for the rest of 1997?" This was despite my best efforts over the past two days to explain to them why such questions were unimportant.

When people move beyond questions of "what" to buy into questions about "how," they still ask the wrong questions. Now the question becomes something like:

What criteria should I use to enter the market in order to be right most of the time?

There is a large industry available to give you the answer to such questions. Hot investment books are filled with entry strategies that the authors claim to be 80 percent reliable or to have the promise of big gains. A picture tends to be worth a thousand words, so each strategy is accompanied by a graph in which the market just took off. Such "best-case" pictures can sway a lot of people and sell a lot of books.

At an investment conference in 1995, a well-known speaker on the futures markets talked about his high-probability entry signals. The room was packed as he carefully explained what to do. Toward the end of the talk, one person raised his hand and asked, "How do you exit the market?" His response, albeit facetiously, was, "You want to know all my secrets, don't you?"

At another conference about a year later, the keynote speaker gave an hour talk before 600 people on high-probability entry techniques. Everyone listened eagerly at every word. Nothing was said about exits except that one should keep a tight stop and pay close attention to money management. After the talk, this particular speaker sold $10,000 worth of books in about a half-hour period, because people were so excited that such high-probability entry techniques were the answer.

At the same conference, another speaker talked about money management—the key factor in determining one's profits. Thirty people listened to the talk, and about four of them purchased a book having to do with that particular topic.

People gravitate toward the things that don't work. It's human nature. You'll learn why this occurs and what to do about it in this book.

Such stories could be told about conference after conference. Everyone will flock to a talk on high-probability entry signals, and less than 1 percent will learn anything significant. However, talks featuring the most important keys to making real money will have few people in attendance.

Even the software products dealing with the markets have the same biases built into them. These products typically are loaded with indicators that can help you perfectly understand why markets did what they did in the past. Why wouldn't they? Those indicators are formed from the same past data about which they are predicting prices. If you could do that with future prices, the software would be wonderful. However, the reality is that you cannot predict prices in this manner. But it does sell a lot of software.

I have over 15 years of experience as a coach for traders. I have worked with some of the top traders and investors in the world and have completed thousands of psychological evaluations on all sorts of traders and investors. As a result of my background and experience, I have filled this book with the kind of information that will help you really improve your performance as a trader or investor.

During that research period, many of my own beliefs about the market have been shattered. I expect many of your most "sacred" beliefs about trading or the market (or perhaps even your beliefs about yourself) will be shattered before you finish this book. The reason is that you can learn the real "secrets" to the market only if you pay attention to what really works. If your attention is elsewhere, you are not likely to find any secrets. However, this book simply contains my beliefs and opinions. Explore its contents with an open mind and you will take a giant leap forward in your ability to make money consistently.

I have divided this book into three primary parts: Part One is about self-discovery and moving yourself to a point where it's possible for you to do market research. I've included a chapter on the essence of successful trading, a chapter on judgmental heuristics, and a chapter on setting your personal objectives in this section. I've deliberately made this a short section, so you won't get too impatient with me for not giving you what you probably think is the "meat" of the topic of system development. However, this material is critical to your success!

Part Two deals with my model for system development. It covers concepts behind trading or market systems, and I've invited various experts to write the sections behind those concepts. Part Two also deals with expectancy—one of the key ideas that everyone should understand. Few people who are actively involved in the markets even know what expectancy means. Even fewer people understand the implications of designing a system around expectancy. Thus, you may find it important to study this section carefully.

Part Three involves the various parts of a system. These

include setups, entry or timing techniques, stop-loss exits, profit-taking exits, and one of the most critical chapters in the book, position sizing. I've also included a concluding chapter on all the other important topics that had not yet been addressed.

Van K. Tharp, Ph.D.
June 1998

The Most Important Factor in Your Success: YOU!

The objectives of this book are twofold:

1. To help you in your search for the secrets of the "Holy Grail"
   And at the same time,
2. To help you in your search for a winning trading system that's right for you

There is a critical assumption in both of those objectives: that you are the most important factor in your performance. Jack Schwager, after writing two books in which he interviewed some of the world's top traders, concluded that the most important factor in their success was that they each had a trading system that was right for them. I'd like to take that assumption one step further: You cannot design a system that is right for you unless you know something about yourself.

As a result, the first part of this book is about self-discovery and moving yourself to a point where it's possible for you to do market research. I've included a chapter on the psychological essence of successful trading, what the Holy Grail is really all about; a chapter on judgmental heuristics; and a chapter on setting your personal objectives.

CHAPTER 1

The Legend of the Holy Grail

We have only to follow the thread of the hero's path, and where we had thought to find an abomination, we shall find a god. And where we had thought to slay another, we shall slay ourselves. Where we had thought to travel outward, we will come to the center of our own existence. And where we had thought to be done, we will one be with all the world.

Joseph Campbell[1]

Let me tell you a secret about the market. You can make big money by buying breakouts that go beyond a normal day's range of price movement. These are called "volatility breakouts." One trader is famous for making millions with volatility breakouts. You can do it, too! You can make a bundle! Here's how you do it.

First, you take yesterday's price range. If there's a gap between yesterday and the day before, then add the gap into the range—that's called the "true range." Now, take 40 percent of yesterday's true range and bracket today's price by that amount. The upper value is your buy signal and the lower value is your sell signal (i.e., for selling short). If either value is hit, get into the market and you'll have an 80 percent chance of making money tomorrow. And over the long run, you'll make big money.

Did that particular pitch sound interesting to you? Well, it has attracted thousands of speculators and investors alike. And while there's some truth to the pitch—it can be a basis for making big money in the market—it's certainly not a magic secret to success. Many people could go broke following that advice, because it's only part of a sound methodology. For example, it does not tell you:

- How do you protect your capital if the market goes against you?
- How or when do you take your profits?
- How much do you buy or sell when you get a signal?
- Which market is the method designed for or does it work in all markets?

Most importantly, you must ask yourself, when you put all those pieces together, does the method fit you? Is it something you'd be able to trade? Does it fit your investment objectives? Does it fit your personality?

This book is intended to help traders and investors make more money by learning more about themselves and then designing a methodology to fit their own personality and objectives. It is intended for both traders and investors, because both of them attempt to make money in the markets. The trader tends to have a more neutral approach—being willing to both buy and sell short. The investor, in contrast, is looking for an investment that can be purchased and held over a longer period of time. Both of them are looking for a magic system to guide their decision making—the so-called Holy Grail system.

The journey into finding the profits available in the markets usually starts another way. In fact, the typical investor or trader, in preparing to trade, goes through an evolutionary process. At first he gets hooked on the idea of making a lot of money. Perhaps some broker gives him a pitch about how much money he can make playing the market. Here's one I've heard in a radio advertisement in North Carolina that goes something like this:

> Do you know where real money is made year after year? It's all in the agricultural sector—people have to eat. And when you consider the weather we've been having lately, there's likely to be a shortage.

And that means higher prices. And for just a small investment of $5,000, you can control a lot of grain. You'll make a small fortune if grain moves just a few pennies in your favor. Of course, there are risks in this sort of recommendation. People can and do lose money. But if I'm right about what I'm saying, just think how much money you can make![2]

Once the trader has committed his initial $5,000, he's hooked. Even if he loses it all—and in most cases he will—he will still retain the belief of: "I can make big money playing the markets. Didn't Hillary Clinton turn $1,000 into $100,000? If she can do it, then I certainly can do it."[3] As a result, our investor will spend a great deal of time trying to find someone to tell him what to buy and sell—determine what the hot prospect is going to be.

I don't know many people who have made money consistently following other people's advice—be it the advice of brokers or investment advisors. The one major exception to this consists of the people who have bought good stocks on someone's advice since 1982 and have held onto them. Even this scenario could change dramatically and quickly. There are other exceptions—but they are very rare. Generally, most people either lose all their capital or get discouraged and drop out of the picture.

A few people miraculously move on to the next phase, which is "Tell me how to do it." Suddenly, they go on a wild search for the magic methodology that will make them a lot of money. This is what most people call the "search for the Holy Grail." During this search, traders are looking for anything that will provide them with untold riches because it unlocks the secrets to the universe. Typically, people go to lots of seminars in which they learn about various methods, such as:

> Now this is my chair pattern. It consists of at least six bars in a congestion range followed by a seventh bar that seems to break out of the congestion. Notice how it looks like a chair facing to the left? See what happens on this chart after a chair pattern occurred—the market just zoomed up. And here's another example. It's that easy. And here's a chart showing how much profit I made with the chair pattern over the last 10 years. Look at that—$92,000 profit each year from just a $10,000 investment.

Somehow, when the typical investor tries to use the chair system, that $10,000 investment turns into large losses. You'll learn the reasons for these losses later in this book. The important point, however, is that the investor simply goes looking for another system. And this process could go on forever—until our investor either goes broke, gives up, or really learns the meaning behind the Holy Grail metaphor.

THE HOLY GRAIL METAPHOR

In trading circles, one frequently hears: "She's searching for the Holy Grail." Typically this means that she's searching for the magic secret of the market that will make her rich—the secret rules that underlie all markets. But is there such a secret? Yes, there is one! And interestingly enough, *when you really understand the Holy Grail metaphor, you will understand the secret of making money in the market.*

Several books deal with the topic of the Holy Grail metaphor.[4] Few people have ever read the Grail romances, but most Westerners instantly recognize the Grail quest as a very significant quest. Scholars interpret the quest as everything from a blood feud to a search for everlasting youth. Other scholars consider the Grail quest as a search for perfectionism, enlightenment, unity, or even direct communion with God. The investor's search for the Holy Grail could take on an entirely new meaning when framed within the context of those quests.

Most investors believe that there is some magic order to the markets. They believe that a few people know about it, those who make vast fortunes from the market. Consequently, these people are constantly trying to discover the secret so that they too can become wealthy. Such a secret exists. But few people know where to find it, because the answer is where they would least expect it to be.

As you complete more and more of this book, you'll really understand the secret of making money in the markets. And as that secret is revealed, you'll begin to understand the real meaning of the Grail quest.

One of the more interesting Grail accounts is based upon a war in heaven between God and Satan. The Grail was placed in the middle of the conflict by neutral angels. Thus, it represents a spiritual path between pairs of opposites (i.e., such as profits and losses). The land (or at least the territory of concern) had become a wasteland. Joseph Campbell[5] claims that the wasteland symbolizes the inauthentic life that most of us lead. Most people typically do what other people do, following the crowd and doing as we're told. Thus, the wasteland represents the lack of courage to lead one's own life. The Grail consequently becomes the symbol of leading one's own life—the attainment of the ultimate potential of the human psyche.

If you follow the crowd as an investor, you might make money during long trends, but overall you'll probably lose. Instead, investors make money by thinking independently and by being unique. For example, most investors ask others for advice (including their neighbors). Yet money is made by developing your own ideas and following a method that is designed to fit you. Most investors have a strong desire to be right about every trade, and so they find some hot entry technique that gives them a feeling of control over the market. For example, you can require that the market totally do your bidding before you enter it. Yet real money is made through intelligent exits—which allow the trader to cut losses short and let profits run. This

> People make money in the markets by finding themselves, achieving their potential, and getting in tune with the market.

requires that the trader be totally in tune with what the market is doing. In summary, people make money in the markets by finding themselves, achieving their potential, and getting in tune with the market.

There are probably hundreds of thousands of trading systems that work. But most people, when given such a system, will not follow it. Why not? Because the system doesn't fit them. One of the secrets of successful trading is finding a trading system that fits you. In fact, Jack Schwager, after interviewing enough "market wizards" to write two books,[6] concluded that the most important characteristic of all good traders was that *they had found a system or methodology that was right for them.* So part of the secret of the Holy Grail quest is in being unique and following your own way—and thus finding something that really fits you. But there is still a lot more to the Holy Grail metaphor.

Life starts out in the neutral position between profits and losses—it neither fears losses nor desires profits. Life just is, and that's represented by the Grail. However, as a human being develops self-awareness, fear and greed also arise. But when you get rid of the greed (and the fear that comes from lacking), you reach a special unity with all. And that's where great traders and investors emerge.

Joseph Campbell, the great scholar and leading expert on myths, says:

> Suppose the grass were to say "Well, for Pete's sake, what's the use if you keep getting cut down this way?" Instead, it keeps on growing. That's the sense of the energy at the center. That's the meaning of the image of the Grail, of the inexhaustible fountain of the source. The source doesn't care what happens once it gives into being.[7]

One of the Grail legends starts out with a short poem that states: "Every act has both good and evil results." Thus every act in life has both positive and negative consequences—profits and losses, so to speak. The best we can do is accept both while leaning toward the light.

Think about what that means for you as an investor or trader. You're playing the game of life. Sometimes you win and sometimes you lose, so there are both positive and negative consequences. To accept both the positive and the negative, you need to find that special place inside of you in which you can just be. From that vantage point, wins and losses are equally a part of trading. That metaphor, to me, is the real secret of the Holy Grail.

If you haven't found that place in yourself, then it's very hard to accept losses. And if you cannot accept the negative consequences, you'll never succeed as a trader. Good traders usually make money on less than half their trades. If you can't accept losses, then

> To accept both the positive and the negative, you need to find that special place inside you in which you can just be. From that vantage point, wins and losses are equally a

you are not likely to want to get out of a position when you know you are wrong. Small losses are more likely to turn into giant ones. More importantly, if you cannot accept that losses will occur, then you cannot accept a good trading system that will make a lot of money in the long run but might lose money 60 percent of the time.

WHAT'S REALLY IMPORTANT TO TRADING

Almost every successful investor that I have encountered has realized the lesson of the Holy Grail metaphor—that success in the markets comes from internal control. This is a radical change for most investors. Internal control is not that difficult to achieve, but it is difficult for most people to realize how important it is. For example, most investors believe that markets are living entities that create victims. If you believe that statement, then it is true for you. But markets do not create victims; investors turn themselves into victims. Each trader controls his or her own destiny. No trader will find success without understanding this important principle at least subconsciously.

Let's look at some facts:

- Most successful market professionals achieve success by controlling risk. Controlling risk goes against our natural tendencies. Risk control requires tremendous internal control.
- Most successful speculators have success rates of 35 to 50 percent. They are not successful because they predict prices well. They are successful because the size of their profitable trades far exceeds the size of their losses. This requires tremendous internal control.
- Most successful conservative investors are contrarians. They do what everyone else is afraid to do. They have patience and are willing to wait for the right opportunity. This also requires internal control.

Investment success requires internal control more than any other factor. This is the first step toward trading success. People who dedicate themselves to developing that control are the ones who will ultimately succeed.

Ingredients of Trading

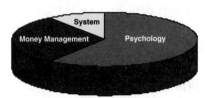

Figure 1–1 Ingredients of trading

Let's explore internal control, the key to trading success, from another perspective. When I've had discussions about what's important to trading, three areas typically come up: psychology, money management (i.e., position sizing), and system development. Most people emphasize system development and de-emphasize the other two topics. More sophisticated people suggest that all three aspects are important, but that psychology is the most important (about 60 percent), position sizing is the next most important (about 30 percent), and system development is the least important (about 10 percent). This is illustrated in Figure 1–1. These people would argue that internal control would fall only into the psychological sector.

Ed Seykota once told me that he taught a college course in trading (in the late 1970s) that lasted 10 weeks. He spent the first week of class teaching basic information about trading. He then spent another week teaching the class Donchin's 10–20 moving-average crossover system. However, he needed the remaining 8 weeks of the class to convince people to use the system that he had taught—to get them to work on themselves enough to accept the losses that it (or any other good trading system) would generate.

I've argued for a long time that trading is 100 percent psychology, and that psychology includes position sizing and system development. The reason is simple: We are human beings, not robots. To perform any behavior we must process information through the brain. Behavior is required both to design and to execute a trading system. And to duplicate any behavior one must learn the ingredients of that behavior. That is where the science of modeling comes into play.

MODELING MARKET GENIUSES

Perhaps you have had the experience of attending a workshop conducted by an investment expert who explains his success secrets. For example, I just told you about a class that one of the world's greatest traders taught on trading in the early 1970s. He spent 2 weeks teaching them a method that would have made them very rich (at the time) and then required 8 more weeks to get them to the point where they were willing to apply it.

Like the people in the class, you may have been impressed in some workshop you attended by the expert's presence and skills. You may have left the workshop full of confidence that you could make money using his methods. Unfortunately, when you tried to put his secrets into practice, you may have discovered that you weren't much wiser than you were before the workshop. Something didn't work or somehow you just couldn't apply what you had learned.

Why does this occur? The reason is that you do not structure your thinking in the same manner as the expert. His mental structure, the way he thinks, is one of the keys to his success.

When others teach you how they approach the markets, chances are they only superficially teach you what they actually do. It's not that they mean to deceive you. It's just that they really do not understand the essential elements of what they do. And even if they did, they would probably have trouble transferring that information to someone else. This leads you to assume that perhaps you must have a certain "gift" or type of talent to be successful in the markets. Many people, as a result, become discouraged and leave the markets because they believe that they do not have the talent. But talent can be taught!

> ...if at least two people can do something well, then that skill can be taught to most other people.

I believe that if at least two people can do something well, then that skill can be taught to most other people. Over the last 20 years, the science of modeling has emerged almost as an underground movement. That movement comes out of a technology developed by Richard Bandler and John Grinder, called Neuro-Linguistic Programming (NLP, for short).

NLP seminars usually just cover the trail of techniques left behind by the modeling process. For example, when I give a seminar, I usually just teach the models I've developed from modeling top traders and investors. However, if you take enough NLP classes, you eventually begin to understand the modeling process itself.

I've modeled three primary aspects of trading and investing and am in the process of modeling a fourth. The first model I developed consisted of *how to be a great trader/investor* and master the markets. Essentially, the steps to developing such a model involve working with a number of great traders and investors to determine what they do in common. If you attempt to model one person, you will find a lot of idiosyncrasies that are unique to that person and probably fail in the modeling process. But if you model the common elements of a number of good traders and investors, then you will find what's really important to the success of all of them.

For example, when I first asked my model traders what they did, they told me about their methodology. After interviewing about 50 traders, I discovered that none of them had the same methodology. As a result, I concluded that their methods were not a secret to their success except that their methods all involved "low-risk" ideas. Thus, one of the ingredients that all these traders had was the ability to find low-risk ideas. I'll define a low-risk idea later in the next chapter.

Once you discover the common elements to what they do, then you must discover the real ingredients of each common task. What are the beliefs that enable them to master the markets? How do they think so that they can effectively carry out those tasks?

The last step in determining if you've successfully developed an accurate model is to teach the model to others and determine if you get the same results. The trading model I've developed is part of my home-study Peak Performance Trading Course.[8] We also teach the model in our Peak Performance Trading Workshop. And we've been able to create some amazingly successful traders, thus verifying the model.

The second model I've developed is *how great traders and investors learn their craft and how they do their research.* That's the topic of this book. Most people consider this to be the *nonpsychological* part of trading. The surprise is that the task of finding and developing a system that is right for them is purely a mental one. Most people have many biases against doing it well. In fact, I generally find that the more therapeutic work an individual has done, the easier it is for that individual to develop a system.

One of your primary tasks in beginning the search for the right trading system is to find out enough about yourself so that you can design a system that will work for you. But how do you do that? And once you find out enough about yourself, how do you find out what will work for you? Those are some of the topics we'll be explaining.

The third model I've developed is *how great traders manage their money or determine their position size throughout a trade.* The topic of money management is talked about by every great trader. There have even been a few books on money management, but most of them talk about one of the results of money management (i.e., risk control or getting optimal profits) rather than the topic itself. Money management is essentially that part of your system that determines your position size—that answers the question "how much?" throughout the trade. I've chosen to call this topic "position sizing" throughout the remainder of this book to eliminate possible confusion that might arise from the term "money management."

Once again, most people are doomed to do all the wrong things in terms of position sizing because of psychological biases that they have. For example, as I'm writing this, I'm on a speaking tour of eight Asian cities. In each city, it is clear that most of the audience does not understand the importance of position sizing. Most of them are institutional traders and yet many of them don't even know how much money they are trading. Many of them don't even know how much they can lose without losing their jobs. Consequently, they have no way to adequately determine how big or small their positions should be.

As a result, I've had my audience play a game to illustrate the importance of position sizing. Even so, no one has asked me, "Dr. Tharp, what should I do in terms of position sizing in my situation?" Yet almost all of them could make great strides in their trading by asking that question and getting an appropriate answer.

You'll learn the key elements about position sizing in this book because it is an essential part of system development.

The last model is one I'm still working on, although we know enough about it to give some excellent seminars on the topic—*the acquisition of wealth.* One of the biases that most people have that keep them from adequate position sizing is the fact that they don't have enough money to hold even a single position as a low-risk idea. As a result, I designed seminars to help them acquire money in ways other than trading. Once again, most people seem to be psychologically wired to do all the wrong things.

One of the principles of wealth acquisition, for example, is to put the power of compound interest on your side. For example, someone who is 20 years old and puts aside a dollar each day into a tax-free account paying 15 percent interest will be a millionaire many times over by the time he or she reaches retirement. Yet the average American family has revolving credit card debt—meaning that the average family has the power of compound interest working against it. It's estimated that 65 million American families— about 200 million people—have revolving credit card debt amounting to $7,000 per family. They are paying as much as 18 percent interest on that debt, so they certainly have compound interest working against them.

The topic of wealth, however, is slightly different from the topic of this book. But I think it's important for you to know that this book is written from the perspective of someone who understands all these vital topics—especially the psychological issues involved.

SUMMARY

Investors and traders usually go through two stages before they find the essence of the "holy grail." First, they need to find someone to tell them exactly what to buy and sell in the market. Second, they search for someone to tell them how to do it! When neither of those two processes works, the few remaining survivors move on to the final stage—putting themselves into a state of mind so they can find a trading system that is right for them.

The "Holy Grail" is not some magical source that is the key to the markets, as most people believe. The metaphor of the "Holy Grail," according to scholars like Joseph Campbell, is all about finding yourself. Similarly, the "Holy Grail" in the markets—the key to unlocking profits—is all about finding yourself.

To unlock the "Holy Grail," you need to appreciate your own ability to think and be unique. People make money by finding themselves, achieving their potential, and getting in tune with themselves so that they can follow the flow of the market.

Getting in tune with yourself means finding an inner peace inside. It means finding a balance between profits and losses. The Holy Grail is not a magical trading system; it is an inner struggle. Once you've discovered that, and resolved the struggle, you can find a trading system that will work for you.

Once you have reached a place inside yourself where you can just be, you'll understand the keys to this book: (1) the importance of exits to your profits and your losses; (2) the importance of position sizing to your equity; and (3) the importance of discipline to making it all work.

I've been modeling four keys to making money in the market: (1) the process of trading; (2) the process of doing trading research; (3) the process of making position sizing work; and (4) the process of becoming wealthy. All of these processes are very psychological. This again illustrates that the search for the "Holy Grail" in the markets is a journey inside of yourself. You must understand this concept in order to complete the journey. You will always have an external struggle with the markets and with systems until you master the internal struggle within yourself. This is the key to the search for your personal Holy Grail trading system.

NOTES

1. Joseph Campbell (with Bill Moyers). *The Power of Myth*. New York: Doubleday, 1988, p. 51.
2. These words are my best recollection of the text of the commercial, but the actual words were probably somewhat different.
3. My comments about the first lady's trading simply reflect my opinion. You can decide for yourself if our first lady really was so "lucky" when you read Chapter 5 on position sizing.

4. Malcolm Goodwin, *The Holy Grail: Its Origins, Secrets, and Meaning Revealed* (New York: Viking Studio Books, 1994). The book discusses the mythology of nine different myths about the Holy Grail which appeared in a 30-year span between AD 1190 and 1220.
5. Joseph Campbell (with Bill Moyers). *The Power of Myth.* See the Recommended Readings in Appendix I for details.
6. Jack Schwager, *Market Wizards.* See the Recommended Readings in Appendix I for details.
7. Campbell, see endnote 4, p. 274.
8. Van Tharp, *The Peak Performance Course for Traders and Investors.* See the Recommended Readings in Appendix I for details.

CHAPTER 2

Judgmental Biases:
Why Mastering the Markets
Is So Difficult for Most People

We typically trade our beliefs about the market and once we've made up our minds about those beliefs, we're not likely to change them. And when we play the markets, we assume that we are considering all of the available information. Instead, our beliefs, through selective perception, may have eliminated the most useful information.

Van K. Tharp, Ph.D.

You now understand that the search for the Holy Grail system is an internal search. This chapter will help you in that search by learning about what might be holding you back. It is your first step: becoming aware of what holds you back. When you have such awareness, you also have the ability to change.

Overall, a basic source of problems for all of us is coping with the vast amount of information we must process regularly. French Economist George Anderla has measured changes in the rate of information flow with which we human beings must cope. He concluded that information flow doubled in the 1,500 years between the time of Jesus and Leonardo DaVinci. It doubled again by the year 1750 (i.e., in about 250 years). The next doubling only took about 150 years to the turn of the century. The onset of the computer age reduced the doubling time to about 5 years. And, with today's computers offering electronic bulletin boards, CD ROMs, fiber optics, the Internet, etc., the amount of information to which we are exposed currently doubles in about a year.

Researchers now estimate that humans, with what we currently use of our brain potential, can only take in 1 to 2 percent of the visual information available at any one time. And for traders and investors the situation is at an extreme. A trader or investor, looking at every market in the world simultaneously, could easily have about a million bits of information coming at him or her every second. And since there are usually some markets open around the world at all times, the information flow does not stop. Some misguided traders actually stay glued to their trading screens, trying to process as much information as possible for as long as their brain will permit.

The conscious mind has a limited capacity to process information. Even under ideal conditions, that limited capacity is between 5 and 9 chunks of information at a time. A "chunk" of information could be 1 bit or it could be thousands of bits (for instance, a chunk could be the number 2 or a number like 687,941). For example, read the following list of numbers, close the book, and then try to write them all down:

6, 38, 57, 19, 121, 83, 41, 917, 64, 817, 24

Could you remember all the numbers? Probably not, because we can only consciously process 7 plus or minus 2 chunks of information. Yet we have millions of bits of information coming at us every second. And the current rate of information availability is now doubling every year. How do we cope?

The answer is that we generalize, delete, and distort the information to which we are exposed. We generalize and delete most of the information—"Oh, I'm not interested in the stock market." That one sentence takes about 90 percent of the information available on the markets, generalizes it as "stock market information," and then deletes it from consideration.

We also generalize the information we do pay attention to by deciding, "I'm only going to look at the daily bar charts on markets that meet the following criteria...." We then have our computers sort the data according to those criteria so that an incredible amount of information is suddenly reduced to several lines on a computer screen. Those few lines are something we can process in our conscious minds.

Most traders and investors then distort the generalized information that remains by representing it as an indicator. For example, we don't just look at the last bar. Instead, we think the information is much more meaningful in the form of a 10-day exponential moving average, or a 14-day RSI, or a stochastic, etc. All these indicators are examples of distortions. And what people trade are "their beliefs about the distortion"—which may or may not be useful beliefs.

Psychologists have taken a lot of these deletions and distortions and grouped them together under the label "judgmental heuristics." They are called "judgmental" because they affect our decision-making process. They are called "heuristics" because they allow us to sift through and sort out a lot of information in a short period of time. We could never make market decisions without them, **but they are also very dangerous to people who are not aware that they exist.** They affect the way we develop trading systems and make decisions about the market.

The primary way most people use judgmental heuristics is to preserve the status quo. *We typically trade our beliefs about the market, and once we've made up our minds about those beliefs, we're not likely to change them. And when we play the markets, we assume that we are considering all the available information. Instead, we may have already eliminated the most useful information by our selective perception.*

Interestingly enough, Karl Popper points out that **progress in knowledge results more from efforts to find fault with our theories, rather than prove them.**[1] If his concept is true, then the more we tend to realize our beliefs and assumptions (especially about the market) and disprove them, the more success we are likely to have making money in the market.

The purpose of this chapter is to explore how such judgmental heuristics or biases affect the process of trading or investing. First, we'll cover biases that distort the process of system development. Most of the biases covered fall into this category. However, some of them affect other aspects of trading as well. For example, the gambler's fallacy affects trading system development because people want systems that don't have long losing streaks, but it also affects how the system is traded once it is developed.

Next, we'll cover biases that affect how you test trading systems. For example, one gentleman, when exposed to some of this information, claimed that it is full of controversy and that key elements were left out. Those statements, however, were just projections coming from him. There is no conflict within the material presented in this book—it's just information. Thus, if you perceive such controversy, it is because that controversy is coming from you. In addition, some steps that most people do in system development are left out, but they are left out intentionally because my research shows that they are not important or are more of a hindrance (than a help) to the development of a good system.

Lastly, we cover a few biases that might affect how you trade the system you've developed. Although this is a book about doing trading system research, the biases included here are important because you need to consider them when you are doing your research—before you actually start trading. I've deliberately kept this part of the chapter to a minimum, however, because these biases are covered in much more detail in my home-study course for traders and investors.

BIASES THAT AFFECT TRADING SYSTEM DEVELOPMENT

Before you think about trading systems, you have to represent market information in a way that your brain can cope with the available information. Look at the chart in Figure 2–1. It illustrates a typical bar chart—which is how most of you think about the market. A daily bar chart, as shown in the illustration, takes a day's worth of data and summarizes it. That summary includes, at most, four pieces of information—the open, the close, the high, and the low. Japanese candlesticks make the information a little more obvious

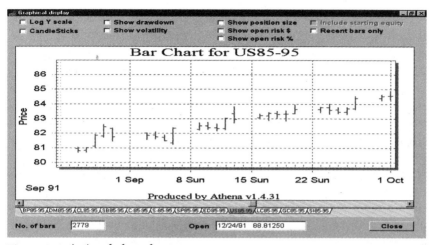

Figure 2–1 A simple bar chart

and also give you visual information about whether the market generally moved up or down.

Representation Bias

That daily bar chart is a good example of the first heuristic, which everyone uses, called the "law of representation." What it means is that **people assume that when something is supposed to represent something, it really is what it is supposed to represent.** Thus, most of us just look at the daily bar and accept that it represents a day's worth of trading. In reality, it's just a line on a piece of paper—no more and no less. Yet you probably have accepted that it is meaningful because:

- You were told it was meaningful when you first started studying the markets.
- Everybody else uses daily bars to represent the markets.
- When you purchase data, the data are typically in daily bar format.
- When you think about a day's worth of trading, you typically picture a daily bar.

Each bar on the chart in Figure 2–1 only shows you two things. It shows the range of prices that occurred throughout the day. And it says a little bit about how prices moved—they moved from the open to the close (plus some variation for the high and the low).

What doesn't a typical daily bar show you? A daily bar doesn't show you how much activity occurred. It doesn't show you how much activity occurred at what price. It doesn't show you when during the day the underlying commodity or equity was at a given price (except at the beginning or the end). Yet this information might be useful to traders or investors. You can get some of this information by lowering your time frame and looking at 5-minute bars or tick charts. But wait! Wasn't the purpose of the daily bar chart to reduce the information flow so you are not overwhelmed?

There is a lot of other information that might be useful to traders that is not shown in the daily bar chart. In the case of futures, did the transactions involve opening up new contracts or closing out old ones? What kind of people were doing the trading? Did a handful of floor traders trade with each other all day long—trying to outguess and outmaneuver each other? How much of the activity was in the form of a single unit (100 shares of stock or a single commodity contract)? How much of the activity was in large units? How much was bought or sold by large investors ? And how much was bought or sold by large money managers or portfolio managers? How much was bought or sold by hedgers or big companies?

And there is a third class of information that is not represented in the daily bar chart—who's in the market. For example, how many people are currently holding long or short positions? What is the size of their positions? That information is available, but it is generally not easily accessible. The various exchanges, with the kind of computers there are today, could store and report information like this each day:

The price moved from 83 to 85. There are 4,718 investors holding long positions, and the average position size is 200 units. During the day, long positions increased by a total of 50,600 units. There are 298 investors holding short positions with an average position size of 450 units. Short positions increased by 5 units. The top 100 positions are held by the following people, and their position is…[followed by a listing].

Perhaps, you're saying, "Yes, I'd like to know who owns what and how large their positions are." Well, if you had that information, would you know what to do with it? Would it be any more meaningful? Probably not—unless you have some beliefs that would allow you to trade it.

The daily bar chart also does not give you any statistical probabilities—given that X happens, what is the likelihood of Y? You can use historical data to determine the likelihood of Y, but only if variable X (and Y, for that matter) is contained in your data. But what if X or Y is interesting and not contained in your data?

Finally, there is another, critical type of information that is not included in a simple daily bar—psychological information about people's beliefs and emotions. That information involves the strength of conviction of the long positions and the short positions. When would various traders be likely to liquidate and at what price? How will they react to various news items or price movements? And how many people are sitting outside of the markets with the belief that it is going up or the belief that it is going down? Are they likely to convert those beliefs into market positions and under what conditions? And if they did, at what price and how much money are they likely to have to back their positions? But do you have beliefs that would help you make money from this information?

> The scary thing is that a daily bar, which is at best summary information, is typically the raw data that you manipulate to make your decisions.

Until now, you've probably thought that a daily bar chart really was the market. Remember, all you're really looking at is a single line on your computer or chart book. You are assuming that it represents the market. You might call it a generalization about the market's activity on a given day, but that is the best you can call it. **The scary thing is that a daily bar, which is at best summary information, is typically the raw data that you manipulate to make your decisions.**

I hope that you're beginning to understand why judgmental heuristics are so important to you as a trader. Yet all I've given you is one example of one heuristic—the tendency we have to assume that a bar chart really represents a day's worth of market activity.

You could just trade bar charts. But most people want to do something with their data before they trade, so they use indicators. Unfortunately, people do the same thing with market indicators. They assume they are reality, rather than attempts to represent something that might occur. RSI, stochastics, moving averages, MACD, etc., all seem to take on a reality, and people forget they are just distortions of raw data that are assumed to represent something.

For example, think about the technical concept of support levels on a chart. Originally, technicians observed that once prices dropped to a certain area on the chart, they seemed to bounce back. That area was then assumed to be a level at which a lot of buyers were willing to buy and thus "support" the price of the stock. Unfortunately, many people treat words like "support level" and "resistance" as if they were real phenomena rather than simply concepts that represent relationships that people have observed in the past.

I've previously talked about the representation bias in the sense that **people tend to judge something by what it "looks like" as opposed to what its probability rate is.** This is especially important in terms of using a trading system or trading signal. Have you considered probability rate information in developing your trading system or assessing the validity of your signals? That is, do you consider the percentage of time that your predicted outcome follows your signal? Probably not, because I don't know one trader in 1,000 who does that—even though I tell people about it constantly. What this means is that most people don't even test their systems or know the expectancy of their systems (see Chapter 6).

Now let's discuss a few more biases. We'll determine what these additional biases might do to your thinking about the markets and to your trading system development.

Reliability Bias

A related bias to the representation bias is to assume our data are reliable—that they really are what they are supposed to be. With respect to the daily bar chart, we just commonly assume that it represents a day's worth of data. It looks like a day's worth of data so that's what it must be. However, many data vendors combine day

T A B L E 2–1

A Personal Story from Chuck Branscomb

"I trade a portfolio of 16 futures markets using a system of my design. I use portfolio trading system software to run my system code against daily data to generate orders each night. The basic entry/exit rules are programmed into a real-time software program so that I am alerted whenever I have taken a position in a market.

"On July 10, 1995 I had correctly placed all of my entry and exit orders for the portfolio prior to the open. Shortly after the Chicago currency markets opened, the real-time software alerted me to a long entry in the Canadian dollar. I was shocked since I hadn't even generated an order for the Canadian dollar that day. I just stared at the screen for a few seconds in disbelief. Having mentally rehearsed being shocked by an unexpected market occurrence, I automatically fell into my rehearsal scenario: take a deep breath, relax all my muscles from forehead to toe while exhaling, and create a systematic process of checking for errors from highest to lowest probability.

"It took just a couple of minutes to find that the low for the previous day was different between the data I had downloaded for my portfolio software to run against versus that collected by my real-time software. A quick check of the previous day's tickdata confirmed my suspicion: the data the portfolio system used was invalid. I quickly edited the database manually and reran the program. It now generated an entry order. I glanced at the screen to see that the market had now rallied well above my entry point. I had feelings of frustration running through me, but I calmly inputted the information from the program into my portfolio manager spreadsheet to size the position. Looking at the screen, I saw the market up yet another 5 ticks now that I had the order ready. My reaction at that point was totally automatic and focused: I called my trade desk and placed an order to enter the position at the market.

"This whole process consumed about 10 minutes time during which the Canadian dollar rallied further and further away from my intended entry price. Fortunately, mental rehearsal saved me from second guessing what to do. My trading objectives include not **ever** missing a trade entry, since I have no idea when a monster move may be evolving. Missing out on a substantial winning trade is far worse than simply taking a small loss. When I knew I should be in that market already, the phone call was an automatic, focused response. For the type of trading that I do, it was the right thing to do. I have no use for *hoping* the market will come back to the entry point or second guessing whether to follow through on the entry.

"This occurrence marked the need for me to create a procedure that would force a disciplined checking of daily data for each futures contract. Up to that point, I thought that I did a sufficient job of screening daily data. I had caught many errors in the past, but I now knew that I needed to create yet more work for myself each day to ensure that I can trade my business plan as designed."

Source: *Market Mastery,* July 1996, vol. 1(2), pp. 2–3.

data and night data, so is it really a day's worth of data? And what about the accuracy of the data?

Seasoned traders and investors know that data reliability is one of the worst problems that traders can have. Most data vendors are fairly accurate with respect to daily bar charts, but when you start using tick data, 5-minute bars, 30-minute bars, etc., accuracy goes out the window. *Thus, if you are testing a system based on 5-minute bars, most of your results (good or bad) could have to do with inaccurate data rather than real expected results.*

Look at the story in Table 2–1 about the problems one can have with data. It's a personal story from editor Chuck Branscomb that appeared in one of our newsletters.

Now that you've read the story, you can understand how most people accept a lot more about the market than is true. All is not as one would expect. And when you think you have a good system, you could simply have poor data. Conversely, you might think that you have a bad system when what you really have are poor data.

But let's assume that you are accepting the fact that daily bar charts really do represent the market. You wish to accept that generalization and trade it. That's fine, but let me show you how many more biases probably creep into your thinking.

Lotto Bias

The lotto bias relates to the increased confidence people have when they, in some way, manipulate data—as if manipulating the data is somehow meaningful and gives them control over the market. Now that you've accepted the daily bar chart as your way of representing the market, you must either trade daily bars or manipulate them in some way until you feel confident enough to trade them. But of course the data manipulation itself often can and will give you this increased confidence.

A perfect example of how this illusion of control works is the state-run lottery game called **lotto.** When you play lotto, you get to pick some numbers (usually six or seven of them), and if you happen to hit all of them, you become an instant millionaire. People really like to play the lotto game (even logical people who understand the odds). Why? Because the prize is so big and the risk is so small (a dollar ticket is small compared with the size of the prize) that people are drawn to play. It doesn't matter to them that the odds are so stacked against them that if they bought a million tickets (each with different numbers) they still would not be likely to win. Your chance of winning a million dollars in a state-run lottery is about 1 in 13 million (and the odds are much greater if you expect to win more).

The big prize for such a small amount of money is also a heuristic, but it's not the lotto bias. The lotto bias is the **illusion of control** that people get when they play the game. *People think that because they get to pick the numbers that their odds of success are somehow improved.* Thus, some people might suspect that if they picked the numbers in their birthday and their anniversary, it might improve their chances for winning. For example, about 10 years ago a man won the jackpot in the Spanish national lottery. He won it because of his interpretation of his dream. It seems that he dreamt about the number 7 for 7 straight nights. Since he thought that 7 times 7 was 48, he selected a ticket with the numbers 4 and 8 on it.

Others, rather than using their dreams, consult with psychics or astrologers. In fact, you can purchase all sorts of advice to help you win the lotto. Some people, who have analyzed the numbers thinking they can predict subsequent numbers, are quite willing to sell you their advice. Others have their own lotto machines and believe that if they generate a random sequence of numbers, it might just correspond to what the state-controlled lotto machine might select. They are also willing to sell you advice. And if some guru or astrologer claims to have several jackpot winners (a distinct possibility if the person has enough followers), then many more people will be attracted to that person. People will do anything to find the magic numbers.

If this seems a little familiar, it should be. This is exactly what occurs in speculative markets. People believe they can make a quick dollar by picking the right numbers. Picking the right numbers, in the case of speculators and investors, means that they simply want to know what to buy and when. The most important question the average person wants to know is what should I buy right now that will make me a fortune. Most people would rather have someone tell them what to do.

People do everything they possibly can to figure out what to do right now. They buy software that picks numbers and analyzes tendencies. Brokers have found that if they help people pick numbers, by reading off entry points on radio and televisions shows, thousands of people will want their advice. If you are known to publicly give advice, no matter how accurate (or inaccurate) that advice is, people will consider you an expert. In addition, there are plenty of gurus who are good at promoting and are more than happy to tell people in their newsletters what to buy and when. And, of course, astrologers and fortune-tellers also play a role in this process.

Some people get the notion that perhaps they would be better off on their own. Consequently, they become fascinated by entry signals that they perceive to be synonymous with a complete trading system. You get a sense of control with entry signals because the point at which you choose to enter the market is the point at which the market is doing exactly what you want it to do. As a result, you feel like you have some control, not just over your entry, but over the market. Unfortunately, once you are in a position in the market, the market is going to do whatever it wants to do—you no longer have any control over anything except your exits.

I'm amazed at what people consider a trading system! For example, one gentleman visited me from Australia several years ago. He'd been talking with various experts all over the United States about what kind of trading systems work. At dinner one night, he told me what he'd learned and showed me the "guts" of the various systems he'd discovered so that I could give him my blessing. He had some great ideas. Yet all of his trading systems, as he relayed them to me, had to do with entry techniques. In fact, the only thing he described about each trading system was the entry. My comment was that he was on the right track, but if he'd now spend at least as much time working on his exits and position sizing, then he'd really have a good system.

Most people believe that they have a trading system if they have some sort of entry point that makes them money. As you'll learn later in this book, there are as many as 10 components to a professional trading system and the entry signal is probably the least important. Nevertheless, most people just want to know about entry.

I was a speaker at an international conference on technical analysis of futures and stocks in Malaysia in 1995. There were about 15 speakers from the United States, and we got rated on our performance. The speakers with the highest ratings talked mostly about entry signals. And the one speaker I heard who talked about the various components of a trading system, and gave a very valuable talk, received much lower rankings.

I attended one of the more highly rated talks. The speaker was a brilliant trader who was up about 76 percent in his account in 1994 with only a 10 percent drawdown. Yet what he talked about were mostly signals for picking changes in a trend. He presented six to eight such signals in his talk and mentioned something about exits and money management when people asked him. Later, I asked him if he traded all those signals. His response was, "Of course not! I trade a trend-following signal. But this is what people want to hear, so I give it to them."

One of my clients, upon reading this, made the following observation:

> I have always felt that this "lotto" bias is a way of dealing with the anxiety of not feeling in control. Most people would rather pretend to be in control (and be wrong) than fear the anxiety of having no control over the environment in which they must exist. The big step is in realizing that "I have control over my actions." And that is enough!

This bias is so powerful that people frequently do not get the information they need to get to prosper in the market. Instead, they get what they want to hear. After all, people typically make the most money giving people what they want rather than giving them what they need. This book is an exception to that rule. And, I hope, there will be a number of such exceptions in the future.

Bias of the Law of Small Numbers

The pattern shown in Figure 2–2 could represent another bias for some people. There are 4 days in which the market does nothing (within the first 5 days shown), followed by a big rise. If you peruse some chart books, you might find four or five examples like that. The law of small numbers says that it doesn't take many such cases for you to jump to a conclusion. For example, let's enter the market when we have 4 days in a narrow range followed by a big jump in prices.

Figure 2–2 Sample pattern that tends to attract people to the market and to entry signals

In fact, my observation is that most people trade by following the patterns they observe in a few well-chosen examples. If you see a pattern like the one shown in Figure 2–2, followed by a large move, then you assume that the pattern is a good entry signal. Notice that all four biases discussed so far have entered into this decision.

The following quote from William Eckhardt really describes this bias well:

> We don't look at data neutrally—that is, when the human eye scans a chart, it doesn't give all data points equal weight. Instead, it will focus on certain outstanding cases, and we tend to form our opinions on the basis of these special cases. It's human nature to pick out the stunning successes of a method and to overlook the day-in, day-out losses that grind you to the bone. Thus, even a fairly careful perusal of the charts is prone to leave the researcher with the idea that the system is a lot better than it really is.[2]

Scientific research knows about this kind of bias. Even the most careful researcher will tend to bias the result toward his or her hypothesis. That's why scientists have double-blind tests—tests in which the experimenter does not know which group is the experimental group and which group is the control group until the experiment is over.

Conservatism Bias

Once we have a trading concept in mind, the conservatism bias takes over: We fail to recognize, or even see, contradictory evidence. The human mind is quick to see the few outstanding examples of moves that work while avoiding or ignoring examples that don't work. For example, if you looked at a lot of data, you might find that the pattern in Figure 2–2 was followed by a large move 20 percent of the time. The rest of the time nothing significant happened.

Most people totally ignore the contradictory evidence, despite the fact that it is overwhelming. However, after seven or eight losses in a row, they suddenly begin to be concerned about the validity of their trading system without ever determining how many losses could occur.

If the move that occurs 20 percent of the time is large enough, then it is still tradable, but only if you are careful to cut losses short during the 80 percent of the moves when nothing happens. But, of course, that points out the importance of the lotto bias. If you just concentrate on the pattern, you probably won't make money.

The implication of this bias is that people search out what they want, and expect, to see in the market. Most people, as a result, are not neutral with respect to the market, and they cannot go with the flow. Instead, they are constantly searching for what they expect to see.

Randomness Bias

The next bias influences trading system development in two ways: First, people tend to assume that the market is random—that prices tend to move according to random chance. Second, people make erroneous assumptions about what such randomness, if it exists, might mean.

One reason people like to pick tops and bottoms is that they assume the market can, and will, turn around at any time. Basically, they assume that the market is random. Indeed, many academic researchers still hold the belief that the market is random.[3] But is that assumption correct? And even if the assumption is correct, could people trade such a market?

The market may have some characteristics of randomness, but that does not mean it is random. For example, you can generate a series of bar charts using a random number generator. When you look at those bar charts, they look like bar charts. But this is an example of the representativeness bias, and "looking like" random is not "being" random. These kinds of data are unlike market data because *the distribution of prices in the market has extreme tails that you could never predict from normally distributed random prices.* Why? When you look at market data, the sample variability just gets larger and larger as you add more data. The 80-point drop in the S&P that occurred on October 19, 1987, within a decade of the inauguration of the S&P contract, would be difficult to predict from a random number series. It might occur once in 10,000 years, but that event occurred in our lifetime. Moreover, it could occur again within a decade. On October 27, 1997, the S&P had a drop of 70 points, and on the next day, it had a daily range of 87 points.

The fact that market price distributions tend to have an infinite variance, or nearly so, suggests that more extreme scenarios than you might imagine are right around the corner. As a result, any derived estimate of risk will be significantly underestimated. And unfortunately, most people take way too much risk in the market. When market wizards like Ed Seykota and Tom Basso claim that risking as much as 3 percent of your equity on a single position is being a "gunslinger," it suggests that most people are really crazy in the amount of risk they take.

Even if the markets were random, people fail to understand randomness. When a long trend does occur in a random sequence, people assume that it is not random. They develop theories to suggest that it is something other than a long series in a random sequence. This tendency comes from our natural inclination to treat the world as if everything were predictable and understandable. As a result, people seek patterns where none exist and assume the existence of unjustified causal relationships.

One consequence of the randomness bias (and the lotto bias) is that people tend to want to pick tops and bottoms. We want to be "right" and have control over the market, and we project our ideas onto the market. The result tends to be a belief that we can pick tops and bottom. This seldom occurs in the life of a trader or an investor. Those who attempt to do it are doomed to many experiences of failure.

Need-to-Understand Bias

The "need-to-understand bias" enters into how most people develop trading systems. They totally ignore the randomness element. In fact, they don't even consider position sizing as part of their system.

One of my clients, Joe, claimed that he had the most difficulty with the market when he got into a position and didn't understand what was going on. As a result, I asked him a number of questions. "How often are your positions winners?" His response was that he was right about 60 percent of the time. "When you don't understand what's going on, how often do you come out a winner?" This time his response was that he almost never came out a winner when he didn't understand. I then said, "Since your system isn't much above chance, you probably don't understand that much about the markets anyway. But when you clearly are confused, you should just get out." He agreed it was probably a good idea.

When you think about Joe's trading system, however, he really didn't have one. Why? Joe was so concerned about understanding that he didn't have clearly defined exit signals that told him (1) when he should get out to preserve his capital and (2) when he should take his profits.

Most people still need to make up elaborate theories about what is going on in the markets. The media are always trying to explain the market even though they know nothing about the market. For example, when the Dow Jones Industrials plunges over 100 points, the next day the newspapers are filled with numerous explanations. For example, here's what you might read in your local paper:

> A late Wednesday warning from federal reserve that it might raise interest rates unnerved investors Thursday. Stocks plunged, especially technology companies, on fears of an industry-wide earnings slow-

down. Stocks are at historically high PE ratios and investors seem to be particularly nervous whenever they think interest rates might rise.

Investors are also concerned about the impact of the Asian economic crisis. Any sign that the Asian troubles might move over here makes investors start to get very nervous.

The next day the Dow Jones Industrials might go up more than 100 points. You'll probably read something like the following:

Wall Street, which was getting nervous over a potential interest rate hike, shook off the rumor and plunged into the market again as the Dow Jones Industrials rose over 100 points. R. P. Jinner, of H. P. Moranthal Securities commented that: "earnings have been so high that investors seem to easily shrug off potentially damaging news."[4]

The need-to-understand bias becomes even more elaborate when it comes to trading system design. People manipulate daily bars in any number of strange ways and then develop strange theories to explain the market based upon those manipulations. The resulting theories then take on a life of their own but have little basis in reality. For example, what is the rational basis for the Elliot Wave Theory? Why should the market move in three legs one way and two legs the other?

Are you beginning to understand why the task of trading system development is so full of psychological biases? My experience is that most people will not be able to deal with the issues that come up in trading system design until they've solved some of their personal psychological issues. In fact, if you are reading this section, give yourself a pat on the back. The natural tendency of most people is to skip psychological sections like this one and go straight to the qualitative aspects of system development. However, the psychological aspect is the foundation—of system development and every other aspect of trading and investing.

BIASES THAT AFFECT HOW YOU TEST TRADING SYSTEMS

Our next set of biases affect the testing of trading systems. Most people never encounter these biases because they never get to the point of testing systems. Actually, the conservatism bias (given later in this chapter) would stop most people from ever testing a system. And more importantly, most people never get to the point where they even have a testable system. However, for those who do get to this point, the result of these next biases can be insidious.

Degrees-of-Freedom Bias

A degree of freedom is a parameter that yields a different system for every value allowed. For example, a moving average based on 10 days will yield different results from a moving average based on 24 days. Thus, the length of a moving average represents one degree of freedom. People tend to want as many degrees of freedom as possible in their systems. The more indicators you add, the better you can describe historical market prices. The more degrees of freedom you have in a system, the more likely that system will fit itself to a series of prices. Unfortunately, the more a system fits the data upon which it was developed, the less likely it will be to produce profits in the future.

System development software (most of it, that is) encourages the degrees-of-freedom bias. Give a system developer enough leeway and that person will have a system that perfectly predicts the moves in the market and makes thousands of dollars—on paper with certain historical markets, that is. Most software allows people to optimize to their heart's content. Eventually, they will end up with a meaningless system that makes a fortune on the data from which it was obtained, but performs miserably in real trading.

Most system development software is designed because people have this bias. They want to know the perfect answer to the markets. They want to be able to predict the markets perfectly. As a result, you can buy software now for a few hundred dollars that will allow you to overlay numerous studies over past market data. Within a few minutes, you can begin to think that the markets are perfectly predictable. And that belief will stay with you until you attempt to trade the real market instead of the historically optimized market.

No matter how much I mention this bias, most of you will still give into it. You'll still want to optimize your systems as much as possible. As a result, let me give you several precautions in such optimization. First, understand the concept you are using so well that you will not even feel that you need to optimize. The more you understand the concept you are trading, the less need you have to do historical testing.

I would strongly suggest that you think about various mental scenarios that might happen in the market. For example, you might imagine the next war, the advent of a nuclear terrorist attack, the adoption of a common currency in Europe, the adoption of a common currency in Asia, China, and Japan joining together as a common power, an unemployment report that jumps 120 percent, etc. Some of these ideas might seem wild, but if you can understand how your system concept would handle these events if they actually happened, then you understand your concept very well.

No matter how much traders and investors learn about the dangers of overoptimization, they still want to optimize. Thus, I strongly recommend that you not use more than four or five degrees of freedom in your system. So if you use two indicators (one degree of freedom each) and two filters in your complete system, that's probably all you can tolerate.

Postdictive Error Bias

People use postdictive errors when they use information in their testing that would only be available after the fact. This kind of error is very common in system testing. It is easy to make. For example, in some software, unless you are careful, you can use today's data in your testing—which is always a postdictive error. For example, imagine the value of being able to use today's close to predict what prices will do today. That's a postdictive error.

Sometimes these errors are quite subtle. For instance, since the highest prices in your data are nearly always followed by lower prices, it's quite possible to sneak high prices into a trading rule so that the rule works great—but only postdictively.

When you are testing data, if your results seem too good to be true, they probably are. You probably got those results through postdictive errors.

Bias of Not Giving Yourself Enough Protection

When you design a system, your goal should be to design one that produces low-risk ideas. **My definition of a low-risk idea is:**

A methodology with a long-term positive expectancy and a reward (overall return) to risk (maximum peak-to-trough drawdown) ratio with which you can live. That methodology must be traded at a risk level (usually based upon percentage of equity) that will protect you from the worst possible conditions in the short run while still allowing you to achieve the long-term expectancy.

The bias that most people have is that they do not trade at a risk level that is low enough to protect them from such worst-case scenarios in the short run. Most people cannot, and do not, anticipate all possible situations that might happen to affect their systems. Consequently, in any worthwhile trading or investing methodology, you must have all kinds of backups to protect you when you're in a bad trade.

If you ask the average person, "How will you get out of a bad trade if it really goes against you?" he or she has no idea. Most people just don't have the backup protection they should have. More importantly, they trade at way too high a level. If you have $50,000 and are trading five or more different commodities simultaneously, then you are probably trading at too high a risk level. That risk level may get you high rates of return, but it will eventually bankrupt your account. Think about the protection bias. Paying attention to this bias alone could preserve much of the equity that you currently have in your account.

BIASES THAT AFFECT HOW YOU TRADE YOUR SYSTEM

Let's assume that you have gone through a system, thoroughly tested it, and determined it to be something you can trade. Unfortunately, there are still more biases—biases that tend to cause people to override their systems.

People want maximum performance, so there is always a temptation to override your trading system. The few times you do something to override your system and improve your performance, that work really stands out in your mind. However, you tend to forget the times that don't work and the day-in, day-out slippage (i.e., the cost of trading) that affects your bottom line.

If you don't have a trading system, then numerous biases affect your trading. However, several key biases come into play even when you have the best of systems. Let's take a look at these biases that tend to cause people to override their systems.

Bias of the Gambler's Fallacy

The gambler's fallacy is a natural consequence of the randomness bias. The gambler's fallacy is the belief that when a trend is established in a random sequence (or in the market, for that matter), the trend will change at any time. Thus, after four consecutive up days in the market we expect a down day. Even people who are well-respected researchers of the market suffer from this bias. For example, Larry Williams, in my opinion, shows this bias in the following quote: "After you have had three or four losing trades in a row, the probability of the next trade being not only a winner but a substantial winner is way in your favor."[5]

When you understand what's involved in winning, as do professional gamblers, you'll tend to bet more during a winning streak and less during a losing streak. However, the average person tends to do exactly the opposite: to bet more after a series of losses and less after a series of wins.

Ralph Vince once did an experiment with 40 Ph.D.s.[6] They were asked to play 100 trials of a simple computer game in which they would win 60 percent of the time. They were each given $1,000 in play money and told to bet as much or as little as they wished on each of the plays. None of the Ph.D.s knew about money management (i.e., the effect of bet size) on the performance of such a game.

How many of them made money? Only 2 of the 40 participants had more than their original $1,000 at the end of the game— or 5 percent. Yet if they had bet a constant $10 per bet, they would have ended up with about $1,200. And if they had bet optimally for achieving the maximum gain (which was to risk 20 percent of their new equity each time—an approach not advocated by this author), they would have ended up with about $7,490 (on average).

What happens? The participants tend to bet more after an adverse run and less after a favorable run. Let's say the first three bets are losers and you bet $100 each time. Now you are down to $700. You think, "Since I've had three losses in a row and the odds are 60 percent in my favor, I'm sure it's time for a win." As a result, you bet $400. But you suffer another loss. Your stake is down to $300 and your chances of making it back are almost nonexistent.

The gambler's fallacy bias enters into how most people develop trading systems, how they size their positions, and how they trade. They totally ignore the randomness element. They look for certainty and trade their systems as if they had it, not giving themselves enough protection. Thus, they don't even consider position sizing as part of their system.

Conservative-with-Profits-and-Risky-with-Losses Bias

Perhaps the number one rule of trading is to cut your losses short and let your profits run. Those who can follow this simple rule tend to make large fortunes in the market. However, most people have a bias that keeps them from following either part of this rule.

Consider the following example in which you must pick one of two choices:

> Which would you prefer: (1) a sure loss of $9,000 or (2) a 5 percent chance of no loss at all plus a 95 percent chance of a $10,000 loss?

Which did you pick, the sure loss or the risky gamble? Approximately 80 percent of the population picks the risky gamble in this case. However, the risky gamble works out to a bigger loss (i.e., $10,000 * 0.95 + 0 * 0.05 = $9,500—which is larger than the sure $9,000 loss). Taking the gamble violates the first part of the key trading rule—cut your losses short. Yet most people continue to take the gamble, thinking that the loss will stop and that the market will turn around from here. It usually doesn't. As a result, the loss gets a little bigger and then it's even harder to take. And that starts the process all over again. Eventually, the loss gets big enough that one becomes forced to take it. Many small investors go broke because they cannot take losses.

Now, consider another example:

> Which would you prefer: (1) a sure gain of $9,000 or (2) a 95 percent chance of a $10,000 gain plus a 5 percent chance of no gain at all?

Did you pick the sure gain or the risky gamble? Approximately, 80 percent of the population picks the sure gain. However, the risky gamble works out to a bigger gain (i.e., $10,000 * 0.95 + 0 * 0.05 = $9,500—which is larger than the sure gain of $9,000). Taking the sure gain violates the second part of the key rule of trading—let your profits run.

People, once they have a profit in hand, are so afraid of letting it get away that they tend to take the sure profit at any sign of a turnaround. Even if their system gives no exit signal, it is so tempting to avoid letting a profit get away that many investors and traders continue to lament over the large profits they miss as they take sure small profits.

These two common biases are well stated in the old saying: "Seize opportunities, but hold your ground in adversity." The good trader had better use the adage: *"Watch profit-taking opportunities carefully, but run like a deer at the first sign of adversity."*

Bias That "My Current Trade or Investment Must Be a Winner"

What makes all these problems come to the forefront is the overwhelming desire of human beings to make current positions (those you have right now) work out. What happens? First, when you have a losing position, you'll do anything to nurse it along, hoping it will turn around. As a result, losing trades tend to become even bigger. Second, profits are taken prematurely in order to make sure they remain profits.

Why? People have an overwhelming desire to be right. Over and over again, I hear traders and investors tell me how important it is for them to be right when they make a market prediction or, even worse, when they invest their money in the market.

I once worked with a client who publishes a daily fax that gives predictions for a particular commodity. Big traders all over the world subscribe to his fax because his accuracy is outstanding. He's known worldwide for his accuracy. However, despite the fact that his accuracy is outstanding, his ability to trade that commodity is rather poor. Why? Because of the need to be right. Once a person makes a prediction, the ego becomes involved in it, making it difficult to accept anything that happens in the process of trading that seems to differ from your prediction. Thus, it becomes very difficult to trade anything that you publicly predict in any way.

S U M M A R Y

The amount of information to which the average individual is now exposed doubles every year. Consciously, however, we can only process about seven chunks of information before it is lost. As a result, we have developed a number of shortcuts or heuristics to help us cope with the vast amount of information to which we are exposed. These heuristics are useful under most circumstances, but their implications for traders and investors are so strong that my belief is that the average person has no probability of making money in the markets unless he or she deals with them.

I've divided this chapter into three types of biases that are summarized below:

Biases That Affect Trading System Development

- **Representation bias.** People assume that when something is supposed to represent something, that it really is what it is supposed to represent. Thus, we assume that the daily bar chart is the market or that our favorite indicator is the market. Instead, it is just a shortcut for representing a lot of information.

- **Reliability bias.** People assume that something is accurate when it may not be. For example, market data that you use in your historical testing or that come to you live are often filled with errors. However, unless you assume that errors can and do exist, you may make lots of mistakes in your trading and investing decisions.

- **Lotto bias.** People want to control the market, and so they tend to focus on entry, where they can "force" the market to do a lot of things before they enter. Unfortunately, once they enter, the market is going to do what the market is going to do. *And the golden rule of trading—"Cut your losses short and let your profits run"—has nothing to do with entry and everything to do with exits.*

- **Law-of-small-numbers bias.** People tend to see patterns where none exists, and it only takes a few well-chosen examples to convince someone that a pattern has meaning. When you combine this bias with the conservatism bias (below), you have a very dangerous situation.

- **Conservatism bias.** Once you believe you have found a pattern and become convinced that it works (by means of a few well-chosen examples), you will do everything you can to avoid evidence that it does not work.
- **Randomness bias.** People like to assume that the market is random and has many tops and bottoms that they can trade easily. Yet the markets are not random. Distributions of prices show that markets over time have infinite variance, or what statisticians call "long tails" at the end of the bell curve. Furthermore, people fail to understand that even random markets can have long streaks. As a result, top and bottom fishing is the most difficult type of trading there is.
- **Need-to-understand bias.** We attempt to make order out of the market and find reasons for everything. This attempt to find order tends to block one's ability to go with the flow of the markets, because we see what we expect to see rather than what is really happening.

Biases That Affect How You Test Trading Systems

- **Degrees-of-freedom bias.** We want to optimize our systems, and we believe that the more we manipulate the data to fit history, the more we know about trading well. Instead, you are much better off understanding how your concept (that you are using to trade or invest) works and only doing a minimum amount of historical testing.
- **Postdictive error bias.** We can inadvertently use data in system development that, in real-life trading, will not have yet occurred. For example, if you factor today's close into your analysis, then you will probably do very well in your testing—especially when you tend to exit before the close.
- **Not-giving-yourself-enough-protection bias.** People fail to consider that position sizing and exit strategies are a key part of trading. Consequently, they often put too much of their capital at risk in a given trade.

Biases That Affect How You Trade Your System

- **Gambler's fallacy bias.** People assume that the probability goes up for a win after a losing streak or up for a loss after a winning streak.

- **Conservative-with-profits-and-risky-with-losses bias.** People want to take profits quickly and give their losses some room. This gives them the illusion of being right, but what they are really doing is "cutting their profits short and letting their losses run."
- **My-current-trade-or-investment-must-be-a-winner bias.** This bias may be at the root of all other biases. Yet being right has nothing to do with making money.

NOTES

1. Karl Popper, *Objective Knowledge: An Evolutionary Approach* (Oxford: Clarendon Press, 1972).
2. Jack Schwager, "William Eckhardt: The Mathematician," *The New Market Wizards: Conversations with America's Top Traders*, p. 114. See the Recommended Readings in Appendix I.
3. Burton G. Maikiel, *A Random Walk Down Wall Street* (New York: Norton, 1996).
4. These news stories were made up, but they are typical examples of what you might read to explain the action of the market.
5. Larry Williams, *The Definitive Guide to Futures Trading*, Vol. II (Brightwaters, N.Y.: Windsor Books, 1989), p. 202.
6. Ralph Vince, "The Ralph Vince Experiment," in Lucas and Lebeau, eds., *Technical Traders' Bulletin*, March 1992, pp. 1–2.

CHAPTER 3

SETTING YOUR OBJECTIVES

The crowd, the world, and sometimes even the grave, step aside for the man who knows where he's going, but pushes the aimless drifter aside.

Ancient Roman saying

Now you understand that the search for the Holy Grail is an internal search. In addition, you should have some idea of what might be holding you back. Now it's time to decide what you want. Sam wanted a 10-minute consultation with me because he just couldn't seem to get results he was happy with. As a result, we met at O'Hare Airport in Chicago at the end of one of my business trips. The conversation went something like this:

What can I help you with, Sam?
Well, I just don't think my trading results are on track?
What does "on track" mean?
I'm not happy with my results.
What are your goals for trading in the market this year?
Well, I really don't have any goals.
What would you like to accomplish in the markets this year?
(*After a long pause*) I'd like to buy my wife a car out of my trading profits.

**Okay. What kind of car are we talking about? A Rolls
Royce? A Mercedes? A Lexus? A pickup truck? What do
you want to buy her?**

Oh, an American car—one that sells for about $15,000.

Great. When would you like to buy this car?

September. In about 3 months!

**Fine. How much money do you have in your trading
account?**

About $10,000.

**So you want to make 150 percent in your account in about 3
months?**

Yes, I guess that's right.

**Do you realize that 150 percent return in 3 months is
equivalent to an annual rate of return of almost 1,000
percent.**

No, I didn't.

**How much are you willing to lose in your account in order
to make that much?**

I don't know? I really haven't thought about it.

Are you willing to lose $5,000?

No, I couldn't do anything like that. That's way too much.

Are you willing to lose $2,500? That's 25 percent.

No, that's still too much. Maybe 10 percent.

**So you want to make 150 percent in the market in 3 months
and you're only willing to take a 10 percent risk in the
process.**

Yes.

**Do you know of any trading method that will consistently
give you a reward-to-risk ratio of 15 to 1?**

No.

**I don't know of any either. Three-to-one is usually a very
good reward-to-risk ratio.**

Although there are many trading and investing methods that
make good money, I don't know of any that meet those require-
ments. However, most beginning traders and investors with small

amounts of money are constantly giving themselves similar expectations—expectations that they are unlikely to meet.

Why is it wrong for most traders to enter the market with too little money? One of the biases discussed in the last chapter was the "not-giving-yourself-enough-protection" bias. You can trade with small amounts of money if you do it in such a way as to not guarantee your probable ruin. Most small traders cannot do that.

DESIGNING OBJECTIVES IS A MAJOR PART OF YOUR SYSTEM WORK

I once worked with a man whose job was to give money to budding CTAs. Part of his job was to assess the various systems that these CTAs had developed, and many people considered him to be one of the world's experts in system development.

One day I said to him, "If you could give any particular suggestion to traders who are trying to come up with a new system, what would it be?" His response was, "To spend at least 50 percent of the system development time working out objectives." He said that objectives were a critical part of any system, and yet few people bother to spend time working on them. If you're going to develop a system for trading or investing in the market, then decide exactly what it is you want to accomplish before you begin. Until you know where you want to go, you can never get there.

Your objectives are a critical part of your system. How can you develop a trading system if you have no idea what it's supposed to do? You just can't do it. So you need to decide what you want to accomplish first. Once you've done that, you can decide if your goals are realistic. If they are, you then can develop a trading system to accomplish those goals.

I took my friend's advice to heart when we did our first seminar, "How to Develop a Winning Trading System to Fit You." A major portion of that seminar was devoted to objectives. However, so many people grumbled over including objectives as part of the seminar that we now require seminar participants to complete the objectives section prior to the seminar.

Typical comments included: "What does this have to do with trading in the markets." "This is private material. I don't want to spend class time talking about my equity or anything like that." None of the participants seemed to realize that if they didn't spend time on their objectives, they wouldn't really be able to develop a system that "fit" them. They needed to assess themselves for strengths and weaknesses; for time, resources, capital, and skills; and for what they were trying to accomplish. What kind of returns did they want to make? What kind of drawdowns were they willing to tolerate in order to make those returns? This is one of the real keys in our search for the Holy Grail.

TOM BASSO ON OBJECTIVES

Tom Basso was a guest speaker at the first three system development seminars that we did. During those seminars, I frequently interviewed him on his objectives in order to demonstrate how one should approach this portion of the task. Tom was kind enough to volunteer to do another of those interviews for this book.

Tom Basso is the president of Trendstat, Inc., located in Scottsdale, Arizona. He is a professional money manager who is qualified both as a CTA and as a registered investment advisor (RIA). He is also a private investor in that he invests his own money in his funds.

Tom was interviewed by Jack Schwager in his book *The New Market Wizards* at my suggestion. Schwager then named him "Mr. Serenity" and considers him his best personal role model out of all the market wizards he interviewed. Basso is also one of the most logical, organized people I have ever met. As a result, I thought you might like to learn how Tom thinks about trading system development.

The first part of the objectives exercise involves taking a self-inventory of your time, money, skills, and other resources. Tom's answers are in italics.

> **Tom, how much capital do you have?**
> *We currently have about $95 million under management.*[1]
> **How much money do you need to live on each year?**
> *About $80,000.*
> **How much of that must come out of your trading profits?**
> *None of it. I get a salary through Trendstat.*

I ask that question in order to determine what percentage of one's trading capital the person needs to make in order to just survive. This is important just to determine if it's reasonable. For example, those who need to make 30 percent or more just to survive are putting themselves in a rather untenable position, plus giving little opportunity for the trading capital to grow.

I frequently get people who have about $100,000 of trading or investment capital, but they need about $50,000 to live on each year. In my opinion, they are putting themselves in a very difficult position. They might believe they can make 100 percent every year, and perhaps they can. But if they start out with a 30 percent drawdown—which is quite possible—their situation becomes very tenuous at best. That's why it's best to think about these situations before you get into them.

Obviously, none of these things is a problem for Tom Basso.

Part I: Self-Assessment

Tom, how much time during the day do you have to devote to trading? This is important because the amount of time you have available almost dictates the kind of trading system you must develop. Those who have a full-time job and just look at the markets in the evening must, quite obviously, find a fairly long term system to use.

I've got about 6 hours each day, but that time is mostly involved in managing our trading business.

When you are trading, how many distractions can you expect to have?

Many.

So obviously, you need a trading methodology that allows you to deal with those distractions.

Yes.

How much time do you expect to devote to developing your trading system, to doing your personal psychological work, and to working on your business plan for trading?

In my case, I've already put in a lot of time over the last 20 years.

However, we're always planning and doing research. I put in however much time it takes.

What are your computer skills? What skills did you need before you began this trading venture?

I'm very good with computers. I custom-programmed all of Trendstat's early models myself. However, at this time I have a fully automated office and a staff of full-time programmers. My job is simply to look for inefficiencies and see to it that the staff takes care of them.

What do you know about statistics?

I understand and can use simple statistics. In addition, I'm familiar with some multivariate statistics.

How would you rate your market knowledge? Here you should include what you know about trading mechanics, what moves the markets, how to execute orders effectively at low cost, which trading indicators you might need, etc.

I have extensive experience in options, futures, stocks, bonds, mutual funds, cash currencies. I am very familiar with trade mechanics and low-cost execution. I also have my own perception of how the markets work.

What are your psychological strengths and weaknesses, especially in terms of trading system development?

I am very strategic and patient, which I believe is useful in developing long-term strategies for trading. I'm self-confident, which gives me a lot of psychological strength in trusting the systems we develop. In terms of weaknesses, I guess I'm always trying to get a lot done—perhaps too much. Sometimes that can distract me from my primary mission as a trader.

How about your strengths and weaknesses in terms of personal discipline?

I am fairly good at discipline. I have no problems following a system.

Do you tend to get compulsive (i.e., get caught up in the excitement of trading), have personal conflicts (i.e., have a history of conflicts with your family, at your job, or during past trading experience), or have any emotional issues that constantly crop up, such as fear or anger?

*I certainly don't think of myself as compulsive. I don't find trading
exciting at all. It's just a business to me. I look at trading as an
interesting brain tease.*

*I don't think I have any conflicts. My family life is reasonably
stable. In addition, I rarely get angry or frustrated.*

*I used to get tense from time to time. But I learned something in
one of your seminars about what happens first when I get tense. In
my case, my fingers got tense first. As soon as I became conscious
of it, I automatically went into a relaxation state as soon as I
noticed it. And now it's so automatic for me that I don't even
notice it.*

**Based upon your personal inventory, what did you need to
learn, accomplish, or solve prior to beginning trading?
How did you do that?**

*I think my personal inventory was and is quite strong. I'm able to
trade well.*

I hope, for those of you who have a lot of things to overcome,
this inventory will be an eye-opener. You really need to think about
all these things before you start developing a trading system. Why?
Because the essence of a good trading system is to find one that best
fits you!

Part II: Define Your Objectives

This section is probably the most important part of developing a
trading system. Until you know where you want to go, you can
never get there. As a result, a major portion of the time you spend
in developing a trading system should be in terms of developing
objectives.

Objectives probably should be treated differently for individual traders and investors versus those who are managing money.
Since Tom fills both roles, I asked him both sets of questions. First,
here are the questions for individual traders and investors.

A. Objectives for Individual Investors and Traders

**What is your advantage or edge in trading? What is the
particular concept that you are trading that gives you an**

advantage? If you don't know, various concepts are discussed in detail in Chapter 5.

Strategic thinking is our edge, because so many people don't do that. We also have an edge in terms of patience and detachment. Most people are neither patient nor detached. Computer programming is also an edge. Most people don't take it to the level that we do. Long-term automated trend following is the outflow of the edge.

How much money do you have personally? How much of that money could you afford to lose? For example, most funds stop trading at 50 percent. How about you? How much risk can you afford to take on a given trade?

I have several million dollars and I could afford to lose 25 percent of that comfortably. All of my money is in our trading program, and we're only risking between 0.8 to 1.0 percent per trade. However, if I were trading on my own, I'd go to 1 percent to 1.5 percent. I think 2–3 percent risk would push the envelope for me, partially because I could be in up to 20 markets at a time.

How much money do you need to make each year? Do you need to live off that money? What if you don't make enough to live off? Can you make more than you need to live off so that your trading capital can grow? Can you stand regular withdrawals from your trading capital to pay your monthly bills?

My income comes from my salary at Trendstat, so I don't need anything from my trading income. Trading income is simply a second income for me.

I know this doesn't pertain to you, but I'll ask it anyway because it's one of the standard questions under objectives. Are you being realistic, or are you expecting to trade like the best trader in the world? For example, suppose you have a very good system that is right half the time and gives you profits that are twice as large as your losses. In that system, just by chance, you could still easily have 10 losses in a row. Your system is still working as expected, but you could easily have 10 losses in a row. Could you tolerate that?

I think I'm quite realistic about the returns and the risk. I also know about 10 losses in a row. I've gone through that in the past, so I know that it is to be expected.

Do you have the time to trade short term?

I have about 6 hours each day to devote to trading. The rest of my time is devoted to specific business or personal commitments. I don't plan to trade short term so that's not a problem.

How much social contact do you need?

I don't need much, but I do enjoy it.

Can you work by yourself day after day? Do you need one or two other people around, or do you need a lot of other people around? How much do those other people influence you?

I have a full staff of people at Trendstat, but I don't need that. I can easily work by myself. Those people didn't influence me at all in terms of the early development of our trading models.

In summary, what do you expect to make each year as a percentage of your trading capital?

About 20 percent to 40 percent.

What risk level are you willing to tolerate in order to achieve that?

About half the potential gain, so the maximum loss would be 20 percent in a year.

What is the largest peak-to-trough drawdown you are willing to tolerate?

About 25 percent.

How will you know your plan is working, and how will you know when it's not working? What do you expect from your system in various kinds of markets? Trending? Consolidating? Highly volatile?

I plan everything. I set up worst-case scenarios, and we run through them just as an exercise. I have specifications on the best case and the worst case for each scenario. Thus, when something comes along, I have usually planned for it and have a range of expectancy. If the results fall within that range, then I know everything is as planned. If the results fall outside that range, then

I know that something needs to be fixed. We'll then step in and study what went wrong.

Generally, I expect a 40 percent return at the best and a 10 percent return at the worst, with average returns of 15 to 25 percent. We also expect worst-case drawdowns of 25 percent.

I remember one year I had a return greater than 40 percent. I'm glad that happened because I was outside the extremes of our parameters. What it told me is that our risk was too great and that we could also be outside the range on the downside. As a result, we went in and cut down our risk so that the worst case on the downside couldn't happen.

B. Objectives for Trading Advisors

Now let's do the objectives for you as a trading manager. What kind of clients do you want? Retail clients? A few good friends? Several pool operators placing money with you? Very sophisticated investors?

We want balanced clients that have reasonable objectives. My objective here is to remain one of the top 100 firms by size, so we'll take the kinds of clients who'll get us there. We have both retail and institutional clients. In some ways they are different and in other ways they are the same, but both types are fine with us.

What are your clients like? What are their goals? What kind of service do you provide for them? For example, by putting their money with you, are they attempting a special type of diversification?

Our clients are definitely looking for diversification. We provide that with four different programs that strive for returns in the 10–20 percent range with lower drawdowns. We're looking for returns of 20 percent with 10 percent drawdowns. Our clients know that, so that's what they're getting in terms of their goals.

Since you are trading clients' money, how much risk can they tolerate? When would they be likely to withdraw their money?

They expect risk in the 5–10 percent range. Any drawdown that is over 15 percent or that lasts over a year is deadly—lots of clients would fire us.

For that matter, how much gain can they tolerate before they get too excited?

Gains over 25 percent definitely get noticed. We don't want to be too high or clients tend to draw a straight line to the moon and then expect that kind of performance to continue.

What kind of fees do you charge? In other words, what is the total amount extracted from the client's account each quarter or month? What kinds of returns will you have to make in order to be able to satisfy a client who is subject to those fees?

We charge a management fee of 2 percent and an incentive fee of 20 percent. Our clients are happy with those fees as long as they can make their 15–20 percent returns after fees and they are not too uncomfortable with the drawdowns.

What is your trading capacity? How do you expect to achieve it? What do you expect to do when you achieve it? How will that change your trading?

Our capacity is about $1 to $2 billion. We expect to achieve it by our current policy of marketing to banks, large pool operators, and high-net-worth individuals. When we reach it, we'll simply turn away new money. As we grow, our trading needs to be continually consolidated at fewer trading desks.

What's the worst thing that can happen in terms of your client relationship? How can you prepare for that so that it will not occur?

The worst thing that can happen to a client is a surprise. We make sure that doesn't happen by educating our clients. I even wrote a book to prepare them, Panic Proof Investing.[2]

How will you handle a large infusion of new capital or a large withdrawal?

A large infusion of new capital is planned in our programs. Large withdrawals are easily handled by the software we've developed.

As you can tell, Tom Basso has carefully planned every little detail of his trading program. That's why an exercise like this one is so important. It gets you thinking about issues you probably would not have thought about had you not done the exercise.

Part III: Trading Ideas

The last section goes more specifically into how you want to trade. It has to do with ideas about markets, entry, exit, and money management—the specifics of your trading plan.

Tom, what kind of markets do you want to trade? Is it appropriate to specialize? Do you want to trade only liquid markets, or are there some illiquid markets you'd like to trade?

I'm a generalist, not a specialist. There are 20 futures markets that I trade, 15 cash currency markets, and 30 mutual funds. All of them are very liquid, because I only concentrate on liquid markets. If I didn't concentrate on these liquid markets, then we'd have a very small capacity—not the several billion dollars we're shooting toward.

What beliefs do you have about entering the markets? How important do you believe entry to be?

Entry is probably the least important component of my trading. I want to enter the market when there is a change of trend. At that very instant—when the trend changes—the reward-to-risk ratio is the best it will be for the rest of the trade.

Given your goals in terms of returns and drawdowns, what kind of initial risk stop do you want? If it's close, will you be able to get right back into the market so that you will not miss a move?

Stops, in my opinion, should be a violation of the reason why I wanted to get into the trade in the first place. And, yes, I always have a way to get back into the trade.

My stop is a function of the market and what it's doing. It's only indirectly related to risk—unless the risk is too big for me to even take a position. I control risk as part of my money management, which I suspect you'll ask about later on in this interview.

How do you plan to take profits? Reversal stops? Trailing stops? Technical stops? Price objectives? Contrary to popular opinion, much of your emphasis should be in the area of stops and exits.

I don't limit the amount I can make in a trade. My philosophy is to

*let my profits run. If I ever find a trade that keeps going in my
direction so that I never have to get out, great!*

*I use trailing or technical stops. Once those are hit, I'm out of the
position.*

**What do you do in terms of money management (which I
call "position sizing" in this book)?**

*I set up a portfolio of instruments to be traded at set risk and
volatility limits as a percentage of equity. I monitor the amount of
initial risk and volatility and keep them at set limits. In addition, I
keep the ongoing risk and volatility at fixed percentages of my
equity. As a result, I always know how much fluctuation can occur
in my portfolio overnight and it's well within my sleeping limits.*

Perhaps now you can understand why planning your objectives is so important to developing a trading system. If you do, then
I've done my job in this chapter. I cannot overemphasize the importance of establishing system and trading-related objectives. They
are the foundation upon which all successful trading (that I know
about) is built. They are also the most easily neglected area.

SETTING YOUR OWN OBJECTIVES

Now is the time for you to walk this same path to successful investing or trading. Reread the questions and Tom's answers a number
of times. Take your time and enjoy the process. Write your answers
down on paper. Give them a lot of thought. What is critical is to
really take the time to think about the issues raised by these questions. That's why this section should be 50 percent of the task of
preparing to trade. When you've finished, you will have developed
the foundation for a successful investing or trading business—a
foundation that very few people bother to build.

Don't expect easy answers that just pop out at you. If you
don't give this area some serious thought, then you have no business working on trading system development. Remember that
thinking about your objectives is about 50 percent of the task of
developing a trading system.

How will you know when you have psychological issues
related to trading system development for these questions? The

questions will not tell you that directly. You'll know that more by your emotional response to the questions. The emotions you feel when answering the questions will be a big clue for you.

If you don't want to answer the questions and put off doing so, then you have some psychological issues. If you get angry or disturbed at some questions, then you probably have some psychological issues. However, keep working at these questions until you are finished and have answers you can live with. Part of the reason for doing the questions is to find out about the most important part of your trading—you.

You might also ask if the questions are telling you that you should not trade. If you have not completed the questionnaire, or have not completed it to your satisfaction, then you are not ready to trade. I would not recommend that you do so until you thoroughly understand each question and your own response to it. Of course, once you've done that, you must still develop a trading system that fits the criteria you've developed for yourself.

Lastly, you might ask how the questions will guide you in system development. What the questions do is allow you to establish boundaries around which you must design your trading system. I'd recommend that you answer the questions, read the book thoroughly, and then reanswer the questions. When you've done that, then you will understand what you need to do in terms of developing a system that fits you.

NOTES

1. Since this interview was finished, Trendstat's assets under management have grown to over a half billion dollars.
2. Tom Basso, *Panic Proof Investing*. New York: John Wiley & Sons, 1994.

PART TWO

Conceptualization of Your System

The purpose of Part II is to help you conceptualize your system and then build the groundwork necessary to construct it. Part II consists of three chapters. Chapter 4 presents the critical tasks that are necessary for developing a system that fits you. It represents years of work studying the world's best traders and investors to determine exactly how they do their research.

Chapter 5 presents a synopsis of some of the various concepts that you might use in your trading system. I've asked some extremely knowledgeable people to contribute to this chapter, plus I've added my own section. Read through the different concepts and determine which concept appeals to you the most. You might even adopt several of them.

Chapter 6 presents the concept of expectancy. Expectancy refers to how much you will make with your trading system per dollar risked. Few traders or investors really understand expectancy, and yet it is one of the most important topics in this entire book.

CHAPTER 4

Steps to Developing a System

> There must be a map or model of the data which shows the zone to
> be navigated and upon which is marked the best route.
>
> *David Foster, Ph.D.*

It's very useful to believe that if several people can do something
well, then the same skill can be copied, or modeled, and taught to
someone else. This is what NeuroLinguistic Programming, or the
science of modeling, is all about. To develop a good model, you
need to find several people who can do the task well. You then need
to interview those people to find out what they do in common.
These are the key tasks involved in the model.[1] It's very important
to find out what they do *in common*. If you don't, you'll simply discover the idiosyncrasies of the people involved, which usually are
not that important.

I've worked with hundreds of outstanding traders and
investors in a coaching role over the past 12 years. During that
time, I've had the opportunity to learn how to do trading research
from these experts. The steps are quite clear and easy to do. This
chapter is a synopsis of the 12-step model I've developed through
this association.

1. TAKE AN INVENTORY

The first key step is to take an inventory of yourself—your
strengths and weaknesses. To have market success you must

develop a system that is right for you. In order to develop such a system, you must take such a self-inventory—of your skills, your temperament, your time, your resources, your strengths, and your weaknesses. Without taking such an inventory, you cannot possibly develop a methodology that's right for you.

Among the questions you need to consider:

- Do you have strong computer skills? If not, then do you have the resources to hire someone who does or who can help you to become computer proficient?
- How much capital do you have? How much of that is risk capital? You must have enough money to trade or invest with the system you develop. Lack of sufficient funds is a major problem for many traders and investors. If you don't have sufficient funds, then you cannot practice adequate position sizing. This is one of the essential ingredients of a successful system and yet it is one that most people ignore.
- How well can you tolerate losses?
- How are your math skills?

There are many important issues that you should contemplate. For example, consider what time constraints you have. If you have a full-time job, think about using a long-term system that only requires you to spend about a half hour each night looking at end-of-day data. Stop orders are then given to your broker for the next day. Trading such a system doesn't take much time, so it's quite appropriate to use if you don't have much time. In fact, many professionals, who spend all day with the markets, still use long-term systems that only use end-of-day data.

Let's look at another issue you should consider. Are you going to be in the market with your own money or someone else's? When you trade for other people, you have to deal with the impact of their psychology on your trading, which could be quite substantial. For example, in any kind of situation in which you are managing other people's money, the net results are a function of the psychology of the people who give you money plus your own psychology.

Say you are a money manager, and after two losing months, your client withdraws her money. You then have three winning months and the client decides to reinvest in your system. After you have another two losing months, she again withdraws. She decides to wait until you get really hot in the markets, and after five winning months, she puts her money back in. You have, again, two losing months. The result of all this is a client who is continually losing while you, as a money manager, made a lot of money. But the wear and tear that she'd have experienced would affect both you and your trading.

You should spend a lot of time thinking about the questions asked in the self-inventory in Chapter 3 on managing client money. And more importantly, think about your answers! Did you just give a quick answer or did you give an accurate assessment of what you believe and feel? In addition, did you just answer the questions or did you put a lot of thought into each answer before you put it down on paper? Compare your answers with Tom Basso's answers, so you can compare yourself with a top professional money manager.

2.   DEVELOP AN OPEN MIND AND GATHER MARKET INFORMATION

At the International Institute of Trading Mastery, Inc., we conduct an advanced 3-day seminar twice each year on the topic of Developing a Winning System That Fits You. And we also have a tape series from a prior seminar conducted in February 1996. Most people learn a great deal from that seminar or set of tapes, but sometimes people don't learn enough until they've addressed some of their psychological issues first. For example, some people seem totally closed to what we are trying to teach. They have their own ideas about what they want and are just not open to a general model for improving their methodology—much less to specific suggestions on how they should change. And the interesting thing is that the people who are closed to the ideas presented are usually the people who need the material the most.

Thus, the first part of task 2 in system development modeling is to develop a completely open mind. Here are some suggestions for doing that.

First, you need to understand that just about everything you've ever been taught—including every sentence you've read so far in this book—consists of beliefs. "The world is flat" is a belief, just as is the statement "The world is round." You might say, "No, the second statement is a fact." Perhaps, but it is also a belief—with a lot of important meaning in individual words. For example, what does "round" mean? Or for that matter, what does "world" mean?

Anything that seems to be a fact is still relative and depends upon the semantics of the situation. It depends upon some assumptions you are making and the perspective you are bringing to the situation—all of which are also beliefs. You'll become a lot less rigid and much more flexible and open in your thinking if you just consider "facts" to be "useful beliefs" that you've made up.

The reality that we know consists solely of our beliefs. As soon as you change your beliefs, then your reality will change. Of course, what I've just said is also a belief. However, when you adopt this belief for yourself, you can begin to admit that you don't really know what is real. Instead, you just have a model of the world by which you live your life. As a result, you can evaluate each new belief in terms of its "utility." When something conflicts with what you know or believe, think to yourself, "Is there any chance that this is a more useful belief?" You'd be surprised at how open you'll suddenly become to new ideas and new input. One of my favorite quotes is the following from Einstein:

> The real nature of things, we shall never know, never.—Albert Einstein

Keep in mind the following:

You don't trade or invest in markets—you trade or invest according to your beliefs about the markets.

Thus, part of the necessity for having an open mind is the requirement to determine your beliefs about the market. When you are not open, they don't seem like "beliefs"—they just seem like "what is." Trading an illusion, which everyone does, is particularly dangerous when you don't know it. And you may be deluding yourself extensively with your beliefs.

Charles LeBeau, a veteran trader of 30 years, says that when he started to design trading systems for the computer, he had hundreds of beliefs about the market. Most of those beliefs did not stand up to the rigors of computerized testing.

When your mind is open, start reading about the markets. I strongly recommend almost any book written by Jack Schwager. It's probably best to start with *Market Wizards*[2] and *The New Market Wizards*. They are two of the best books available on trading and investing. Two new books by Schwager, *Fundamental Analysis* and *Technical Analysis,* are also excellent.

Computer Analysis of the Futures Market, by Charles LeBeau and David Lucas, is one of the best books available on the systematic process of developing a trading system. Indeed, I've learned a lot from reading that book and from conducting regular seminars with Chuck. I'd also recommend Perry Kaufman's book, *Smarter Trading;* Cynthia Kase's book, *Trading with the Odds;* and William O'Neil's book, *How to Make Money in Stocks.* Tuschar Chande's book, *Beyond Technical Analysis,*[3] is also good in that it gets the reader to think about concepts that are beyond the scope of this volume.

The psychological side of trading and investing is also critical. Here, I'd recommend my home-study course—*The Peak Performance Course for Traders and Investors.* Two other excellent books are by James Sloman—*Nothing* and *When You're Troubled.* The first book is about going with the flow—an extremely important concept when playing the markets. The second book is about getting rid of many personal issues that could prevent you from working at an optimal level. In addition, I also recommend *Mindtraps: Mastering the Inner World of Investing* by Roland Barach. It's all about how we're wired—both culturally and biologically—to lose a great deal of money in the market. The good news is that we can overcome those tendencies.

The suggested readings will give you the appropriate background required to develop useful beliefs about yourself and the markets that will support you in the game ahead of you. They will answer a lot of the pressing questions about trading that might be cluttering your mind. More detailed information about the readings is given in Appendix I at the end of this book.

Once you've completed your reading, write down your beliefs about the market. Every sentence in this book represents one or more of my beliefs. You might want to find the ones you agree with having to do with the market. They will be a good starting point for your task of finding your beliefs about the market. This step will prepare you for the tasks you will have to tackle in exploring the markets and developing your own system for making a lot of money.

3.   DETERMINE YOUR OBJECTIVES

You cannot develop an adequate system for making money in the market unless you totally understand what you are trying to accomplish in the markets. Thinking about your objectives and getting them clearly in mind should be a major task in system development. In fact, it probably should occupy 20 to 50 percent of your time in designing a system. Yet most people totally ignore this task or spend just a few minutes doing it. For example, how much time did you spend working on the exercise in Chapter 3?

Give Chapter 3 a lot of time and a lot of thought. If you took only 15 to 30 minutes to answer the same questions I asked Tom Basso, then you are not doing an adequate job. It's one of the tasks that most people want to avoid, but if you want to develop a great system for trading or investing, then you must give this task adequate attention. Remember how important it is to keep an open mind? Doing an adequate job with your objectives is part of being open.

4.   DETERMINE YOUR TIME FRAME
FOR TRADING

Your fourth task is to decide how active you want to be in the market. What is your time frame for trading? Do you want to have a very long-term outlook, probably only making a change in your portfolio once a quarter? Do you want to be a stock trader or a long-term futures trader where your positions last 1 to 6 months? Do you want to be a swing trader who might make several trades each day with none lasting more than a day or two? Or do you want the ultimate in action—being a day trader who makes three to ten trades each day and is always out by the close of the market?

Table 4–1 shows the advantages and disadvantages of long-term trading. Long-term trading or investing is simple. It requires little time each day and has minimal psychological pressures each

TABLE 4–1

The Advantages and Disadvantages of Long-Term Trading

Advantages	Disadvantages
No need to watch the market all day—you can use stops or options to protect yourself.	You can be whipsawed by intraday market moves each day.
Psychological pressure of the market is lowest in this type of system.	You can have large equity swings on a single position.
Transaction costs are low.	You must be patient.
It only takes one or two trades to make your whole year profitable.	It usually has a reliability (number of winning trades) of less than 50 percent.
You could have an expectancy (see Chapter 6) well over a dollar per dollar risked.	Trades tend to be infrequent, so you must capitalize by trading many markets.
You can use a simple methodology to make a lot of money.	It requires a lot of money to participate if you want to trade big liquid markets.
You theoretically have an infinite profit opportunity, it opportunity with each trade or investment.	If you miss one good trading opportunity, it can turn a winning year into a losing year.
Costs of data and equipment are minimal.	

day—especially if you take advantage of your free time to work or pursue your hobbies. You can typically use a fairly simple system and still make a lot of money if you adequately size your positions.

I think the primary advantage of long-term trading or investing is that you have an infinite profit opportunity (theoretically at least) on each position in the market. When you study many of the people who've gotten rich through investments, you'll find that in many instances wealth occurs because people have bought many stocks and just held onto them.[4] One of the stocks turns out to be a gold mine—turning an investment of a few thousand dollars into millions over a 10- to 20-year period.

The primary disadvantage of long-term trading or investing is that you must be patient. For example, you don't get a lot of opportunities, so you must wait for them to come along. In addition, once you're in a position, you must go through fairly extensive equity swings (although you can design something that minimizes them) and have the patience to wait them out. Another disadvantage of longer-term trading is that you generally need more money to participate. If you don't have enough money, then you cannot adequately size your positions in a portfolio. In fact, many people lose money in the markets simply because they don't have enough money to practice the type of trading or investing that they are doing.

Shorter-term trading (which might be anything from day trading to swing trading of 1 to 3 days) has different advantages and disadvantages. These are illustrated in Table 4–2. Read through the list and then compare it with the long-term table. Once you've done so, you can then decide for yourself what best fits your personality.

I once met a short-term foreign exchange trader who made

T A B L E 4–2

The Advantages and Disadvantages of Short-Term Trading

Advantages	Disadvantages
Most day traders get many opportunities each day.	Transaction costs are high and can add up.
This type of trading is very exciting and stimulating.	Excitement usually has nothing to do with making money—it's a psychological need!
If you have a methodology with an expectancy of 50 cents or more per dollar risked, you may never have a losing month—or even week.	Profits are limited by time, so you must have a reliability well over 50 percent to make money. However, I've seen some notable exceptions to this rule of thumb.
You don't have overnight risk in day trading, so there is little or no margin required even in big markets.	Data costs are very high because most short-term traders need live quotes.
High-probability entry systems, which most people want, work with short-term trading.	Many high-probability entries have losses that are bigger than the gains.
There's always another opportunity to make money.	Short-term systems are subject to the random noise of the markets.
	The short-term psychological pressures are intense.

about six trades a day. No trade would last more than a day or two. However, the fascinating thing about what he was doing was that his gains and losses were about equal and he made money on 75 percent of his trades. This is a fantastic trading methodology. He had $500,000 to trade with and a $10 million credit line with a bank. When you understand position sizing, as discussed in Chapter 12, you'll realize that this system is a potential Holy Grail system. He could easily have made a hundred million each year with that system and the capital he had.[5]

However, that's not the case with most short-term systems. Most of them seldom have a reliability much higher than 60 percent, and their gains are usually smaller than their losses—sometimes even leading to a negative expectancy.[6] Sometimes, one big loss can ruin the whole system and psychologically devastate the trader. In addition, the psychological pressures of short-term trading are intense. I've had people call me who will say something like:

> I make money almost every day, and I haven't had a losing week in almost 2 years. At least until now. Yesterday, I gave back all my profits of the last 2 years.

Keep that in mind before you decide that short-term trading is for you. Your profits are limited. Your transaction costs are high. Most importantly, the psychological pressures could destroy you.

5. DETERMINE THE BEST HISTORICAL MOVES IN THAT TIME FRAME AND NOTICE WHAT THOSE MOVES HAVE IN COMMON

Once you decide upon the time frame that you want to trade, determine what the best possible moves are within that time frame. Find many of them, in many markets, so that you have a large sample. Probably you want to collect a minimum of 50 to 100 sample market moves. Also be sure you include both up moves and down moves.

For example, if you subscribe to *Daily Graphs*, there is always an example of a stock in a pattern from which it moved more than 100 percent. You could collect many examples from past issues of *Daily Graphs*. However, William O'Neil has already done tasks 5 and 6 for you. You can read all about it in his book, *How to Make*

Money in Stocks. Unfortunately, most people will have trouble using O'Neil's CANSLIM system, in my opinion, to make money in bear markets. You will be much better off if you can make money from both good up moves and good down moves.

Once you have a collection of great moves, notice what they have in common. You might observe that all of them show a strong up move, establish a base, and then break out of that base. However, be willing to look at a lot more than just price conditions. For example, you might notice important volume conditions that occur with the moves. You might notice that the moves only occur under certain market conditions (e.g., most up moves in stocks may only occur when the stock market is in a major bull market). Are there fundamental conditions that seem to be necessary for such moves to occur? Are there certain timing relationships present? Many of these are setup conditions that are important for you to notice.

Also notice how these moves develop and how they tend to end. Do they end suddenly and sharply? Do they end gradually? How would you want to get out of those moves?

Chapter 5 includes a number of concepts that you might consider when you make your observations. However, if you can come up with something new, then so much the better.

6. WHAT'S THE CONCEPT BEHIND THOSE MOVES AND HOW CAN YOU OBJECTIVELY MEASURE YOUR CONCEPT?

What is the concept that you've observed? The first part of your concept should tell you the conditions under which the move occurs. How can you objectively measure that part of the concept? Typically, your answer to this question will give you two elements of your system—the setup conditions that you might want to use and the timing or entry signal. These topics are discussed extensively in Chapters 7 and 8, respectively.

Your setup and timing signal are important for the reliability of your system—how often will you make money when such a move occurs. The entry should be tested independently from all the other components of your system.

LeBeau and Lucas in their book, cited earlier, have an excellent method for testing such signals. What they do is determine the reliability (i.e., what percentage of time is it profitable) of the signal after various time periods. You might try an hour, the end of the day, and after 1, 2, 5, 10, and 20 days. A random entry should give you a reliability of about 50 percent (i.e., generally between 45 and 55 percent). If your concept is any better than random, then it should give you a reliability of 55 percent or better—especially in the 1- to 5-day time periods. If it doesn't do that, then it is no better than random, no matter how sound the concept seems to be.

When you do your entry testing, if entry reliability is your objective, then the only thing you are looking at is how often it is profitable after the selected time periods. You have no stops, so that is not a consideration. When you add stops, the reliability of your system will go down because some of your profitable trades will probably be stopped out at a loss. You also do not consider transaction costs (i.e., slippage and commissions) in determining its reliability. As soon as you add transaction costs, your reliability will go down. You want to know that the reliability of your entry is significantly better than chance before these elements are added.

Some concepts seem brilliant when you first observe them. You might find that you have a hundred examples of great moves. Your idea is common to all of them. As a result, you get very excited about it. However, you also must consider the false-positive rate. How often is your concept or idea present when there is not a good move? If the false-positive rate is very high, then you don't have a great concept and it might not be much better than chance.

One precaution you should keep in mind in using this kind of testing is that reliability is not the only consideration in your system. If your concept helps you capture giant moves, then it may be valuable. See step 9.

Some people would argue that I've neglected an important step in system development—optimization. However, optimization really amounts to fitting your concept to the past. The more you do this, the less likely your system is to work in the future. Instead, I believe that you should work toward *understanding* your concept as much as possible. *The more you understand the real nature of your concept, the less historical testing you will have to do.*

7. ADD YOUR STOPS AND TRANSACTION COSTS

An important part of your concept is to understand when it is not working. Thus, the next step is to understand the effect of adding a protective stop.[7] *Your protective stop is that part of your system that tells you when to get out of a trade in order to protect your capital.* It is a key portion of any system. It's that point at which you should get out in order to preserve capital, because your concept doesn't seem to be working. The way you'll know your concept is not working depends upon the nature of your concept.

For example, suppose you have some theory that says there is "perfect" order to the market. You can pinpoint market turning points to the day—sometimes to the hour. In this case, your concept would give you a setup which is the time at which the market is supposed to move. Your entry signal should be a price confirmation that the market is indeed moving, such as a volatility breakout (see Chapter 8). At this point, you need a stop to tell you that your concept isn't working. What might you select? If the market goes through the time window, when you expected a turn, without your making a significant profit, then you'd probably want to get out. Or you might consider the average daily price range (such as the average true range) of the last 10 days to be the amount of noise in the market. If the price moved against you by that amount (or some multiple of that amount), you might want to get out.

Examples of protective stops are discussed extensively in Chapter 9. Read that chapter in detail and pick one (or more) that best suits your concept. Or perhaps your concept leads to a logical stop point that isn't discussed in that chapter. If so, then use that logical stop point.

Think about what you are trying to accomplish with your entry. Is it fairly arbitrary—you simply think a major trend should be starting? If so, then you'll probably want to give the market lots of room so that the trend will develop. Thus, you'll want to use a very wide stop.

On the other hand, perhaps your concept is very precise. You expect to be wrong a lot, but when you are right, you don't expect to lose money on the trade. If that is the case, then you can have very close stops that don't lose much money when they are executed.

Once you've decided on the nature of your stop, add your stop plus transaction fees (i.e., slippage and commissions) to the calculations you did in the previous step and redo them. You'll probably find a significant drop in the reliability of your entry signal when you add in these values. For example, if your initial reliability was 60 percent, it will probably drop to 50 to 55 percent when you add on your stop and transaction costs to each trade.

8. ADD YOUR PROFIT-TAKING EXITS AND DETERMINE YOUR EXPECTANCY

The third part of your concept should tell you when the move is over. As a result, the next step is to determine how you will take your profits. Exits are discussed extensively in Chapter 10, where you'll learn about what exits are most effective. Read through that chapter and determine what exits best fit your concept. Think about your personal situation—what you're trying to accomplish, what your time frame is for trading, and what your concept is— before you select your exit.

Generally, if you're a long-term trader or investor who is trying to capture a major trend or enjoy the rewards of long-term fundamental values, then you want a fairly wide stop. You don't want to be in and out of the market all the time if you can help it. You'll only make money on 30 to 50 percent of your positions, so you want your gains to be really big—as much as 20 times your average risk. If this is the case, your exits should be designed to capture some big profits.

On the other hand, if you are a short-term trader who is in and out quickly, then you'll want fairly tight stops. You expect to be right on better than 50 percent of your positions—in fact, you must be because you are not in the market long enough for huge rewards. Instead, you're looking for small losses with a reward-to-risk ratio of about 1. However, it is possible to make money 50 to 60 percent of the time, have your losses at minimal levels, and still capture a few trades that will give you big profits.

Overall, what you are looking for when you determine your exits is to make the expectancy on your system as high as possible. *Expectancy is the average amount of money you'll make in your system—*

over many, many trades—per dollar risked. The exact formula for expectancy, plus the factors that go into it, is discussed extensively in Chapter 6. At this point in the model, however, your goal is simply to produce as high an expectancy as possible. You are also looking for as much opportunity as possible to trade (within a limited time frame) to realize that expectancy.

In my opinion, as discussed later in this book, expectancy is controlled by your exits. Thus, the best systems have three or four different exits. You'll need to test the exits you select one at a time. You'll probably want to select them logically, based upon your trading or investing concept. However, you'll want to test them with everything in place (up to this point) to determine what they do to your expectancy.

Once you determine your expectancy, look at your system results trade by trade. What is the makeup of the expectancy? Is it mostly made up of a lot of 1:1- or 2:1-reward-to-risk ratio trades? Or do you find that one or two really big trades make up most of the expectancy? If it's long term and you don't have enough contribution from big trades, then you probably need to modify your exits so that you can capture some of those big trades.[8]

9.   LOOK FOR HUGE REWARD TRADES

Step 9 is an alternative to steps 6 through 8, but it is a difficult step for most people. Step 9 is simply to look to capture huge rewards in comparison with the size of your losses. Another way of stating this is to look for huge R-multiple trades, where your payoff is many times the size of the potential loss you will suffer if you are stopped out at your initial risk (called R). The concept of R multiples is discussed much more extensively in Chapter 6.

Look at Figure 4–1. There is a long, narrow consolidation period (September–November) before the market starts to move. Let's say you entered the market three times during that consolidation period. Each time you are stopped out at a loss of about $0.75 per position. You now get into the market and make a $10 profit (a 12.5-$R$ multiple) per position. Would you like that kind of system?

Most people would hate it because they are "wrong" too

Figure 4–1 Breakouts in September and October 1992 in live cattle result in small losses, but eventually a large gain is possible

many times. In fact, in the example, we assume you are only "right" one out of four times, or 25 percent of the time. Yet look at your bottom line. You have a $10 profit from which you must subtract three $0.75 losses, or $2.25. The net result is a profit of $7.75—or over three times the size of your total losses. This kind of trading can be very profitable. It is not easy for most people, however, because they would typically give up after three or four losses.

If this type of trading appeals to you, then substitute this step for steps 6 through 8 of the model. Essentially, your job is to look for ways to capture huge R-multiple trades (10 R or bigger). Remember that one 10-R trade can be profitable with as many as 7 1-R losses—even when you take transaction costs into consideration.

If you decide to look for these trades, then your emphasis must be on (1) picking entry points from which the markets might make a huge surge, (2) choosing tight initial stops that make sense and that strictly limit your losses to a few dollars or even a few ticks, (3) being willing to leave your initial stop alone, even if it means letting a profit get away from you, and (4) being able to capture huge profits when they do come your way. When you elect to go this route, you are probably looking at a trading system with less than a 35 percent hit rate. However, it can still be very profitable despite the low percentage of winning trades.

10.   OPTIMIZE WITH POSITION SIZING

Your expectancy is a rough estimate of the true potential of your system. Once you develop a system with an adequate expectancy, then you need to determine what algorithm you will use to size your positions (i.e., determine how much). Position sizing is the most important part of any system, because if you have a good, positive expectancy system, then most of your profit or loss will come from position sizing. Position size can help you make a little profit, let you make a lot of profit, or cause you to go bankrupt—no matter how good your system is.

> Position sizing is the most important part of any system, because if you have a good, positive expectancy system, then most of your profit or loss will come from position sizing.

"How much" size will you put on in any one position? Can you afford to take even a single position (i.e., share of stock or futures contract)? These questions are keys to being able to achieve your objective—whether it is a triple-digit rate of return or whether it is an incredibly high reward-to-risk ratio. If your position-sizing algorithm is inappropriate, then you will go bust—no matter how you define going bust (whether it's losing 50 percent of your capital or all of it). But if your position-sizing techniques are well designed for your capital, your system, and your objectives, then you can generally meet your objectives.

We've developed a training program for professional money managers. At this time, we have three graduates of that program.

The first graduate, Webster Management, was ranked the number one fund above $10 million in September 1995 in terms of risk-to-reward ratio. One primary reason for Webster's ranking was its knowledge of position sizing and its ability to design a methodology, through position sizing, that would give it a huge reward-to-risk ratio.

The second graduate of our program, Maricopa Asset Management,[9] has achieved a 5-year average return of better than 40 percent per year with hardly a losing month. Part of the secret behind Maricopa's performance has been an understanding of position sizing plus regular private consulting.

The third graduate of our program is Ray Kelly. Ray achieved a track record of 8 years with a compounded annual return of 40 percent or better after working with me. In fact, during that 8-year period, he only had two losing months. Much of Ray's success could be attributed to special arbitrage situations (see Ray's section on arbitrage in the next chapter) and knowing when to really step on the gas.

Chapter 12 discusses a number of position-sizing models that you may want to consider in the design of your system. Once you have your objectives and a high-expectancy system, you can use these models to accomplish your objectives. However, you need to apply and test various position-sizing models until you find something that perfectly fits what you want to accomplish.

11.   DETERMINE HOW YOU CAN IMPROVE YOUR SYSTEM

The eleventh task in developing your system is to determine how you can improve it. Market research is an ongoing process. Markets tend to change, according to the character of the people who are playing them. For example, right now the stock market is dominated by professional mutual fund managers. However, of the 7,000-plus managers, fewer than 10 of them have been around long enough to have seen the prolonged bear markets that occurred in the 1970s. In addition, the futures market is dominated by professional CTAs—most of whom have trend-following strategies that they employ using very large amounts of money. In another 10 to

20 years, the markets might have quite different participants and thus take on a different character.

Any system with a good, positive expectancy generally will improve its performance if more trades are taken in a given period of time. Thus, you can usually improve performance by adding independent markets. In fact, a good system will perform well in many different markets, so adding many markets simply gives you more opportunity.

In addition, performance can usually be improved by adding noncorrelated systems—each with its own unique position-sizing model. For example, if you have a major trend-following system with a very short term system that takes advantage of consolidating markets, then you'll probably do very well when you combine them. The hope is that your short-term system will make money when there are no trending markets. This will lessen the impact of any drawdowns produced by the trending system during these periods, or perhaps you might even make money overall. In either case, your performance will be better because you will move into trends with a higher capital base.

12.   WORST-CASE SCENARIO— MENTAL PLANNING

It's important to think about what your system could do under a variety of circumstances. How will you expect your system to perform in all types of market conditions—highly volatile markets, consolidating markets, strong trending markets, very thin markets with no interest? You won't really know what to expect from your system unless you understand how it's likely to perform under each possible market condition.

Tom Basso was fond of telling students in our system seminar to:

> Imagine what it's like to take the other side of each trade. Pretend you just bought it (instead of sold it) or pretend that you just sold it (instead of bought it). How would you feel? What would your thinking be like?

This exercise is one of the most important exercises you can do. I strongly recommend that you take it seriously.

You also need to plan for any catastrophe that might come up. Brainstorm and determine every possible scenario you can think of that would be disastrous for your system. For example, how would your system perform should the market have a 1- or 2-day price shock (i.e., a very large move) against you? Think about how you could tolerate an unexpected, once-in-a-lifetime move in the market, such as a 500-point drop in the Dow (it has happened twice in 10 years!) or another crude oil disaster like the one we saw during the Gulf War in Kuwait. What would happen to your system if currencies were stabilized and you were a currency trader? What will happen when Europe develops a unified currency? Or what if a meteor lands in the middle of the Atlantic and wipes out half of the population of Europe and the United States? Or what about more mundane things like your communications being shut down or your computers being stolen?

When you have your list of disasters, develop several plans that you can implement for each one. Plan your responses in your mind and rehearse them. Once you've established your actions in the event of a calamity, your system is complete.

NOTES

1. There is a lot more to modeling excellence than just finding out what the key tasks are. You need to find the ingredients of each task, and you need to be able to install the model in other people. We've been able to accomplish this with the system development model. However, that topic would be an entire book by itself.
2. The references to all of these recommended books are given in the Recommended Readings in Appendix I.
3. Chande's book is very good, but I don't agree with all his conclusions, especially when he starts testing portfolios and developing conclusions about position sizing.
4. Such a person may have purchased a dozen low-capitalization stocks. Eleven may turn out to be worthless, while one turns into a new giant. Because the stocks were largely ignored, the owner neither gets rid of the losers before they become worthless nor finds out about the winner until it is worth a lot of money.
5. Somehow fate is often cruel to people with such a great system. In this person's case, he could not trade size. Nor was it possible to fix

his problem psychologically, because he did not believe that he had anything to do with the problem. In fact, at this point he cannot trade at all because he's nervous and he believes that his stomach is stopping him from trading. Thus, in my opinion, he doesn't understand the real meaning behind a Holy Grail system—finding yourself in the market.

6. One of my clients has developed a day-trading system based upon gains being significantly larger than losses. His system has a reliability rate of less than 50 percent, yet it nets him tremendous rates of return. This shows that there are other ways to conceive of short-term systems.

7. The word "stop" is used here because most people execute such stops by putting in a stop order in the market. This means "Execute my order as a market order once it reaches that price."

8. If you are looking at your expectancy based upon the results of real trading (i.e., what you have been doing in the market), then a low expectancy (15 cents per dollar risked or less) could be due to psychological problems such as not following your system or panicking and taking profits too early.

9. Headed by David Mobley, Sr., who wrote the Foreword to the book.

CHAPTER 5

Selecting a Concept That Works

The more you understand the concept you are trading, how it might behave under all sorts of market conditions, the less historical testing you need to do.

Tom Basso

My estimate is that fewer than 20 percent of the people trading the markets have a system to guide their trading or investing. Of those that do, most are just using predefined indicators. Very few people understand the concept behind their system. As a result, I asked a number of experts to write about the concepts that they trade. This is not an exhaustive discussion of the various concepts you might trade. It is just a sampling. Your goal in reading this chapter should be to think about each concept and determine if any of them fits your personality. The concept that "fits" will be the one you have the most success trading. But you must understand your concept thoroughly before you develop a system using it.

While I was first writing this book, I received a phone call from an expert on chaos theory. He said that he had been following my work for many years. He believed that I had a lot of integrity, but that I was very wrong about systems. He said that it was ridiculous to assume that any sort of system was possible—instead, it was all about luck and individual psychology. I said that I agreed with him if he were defining a system as just an entry technique. Instead, I said, one had to develop a methodology with a positive expectancy[1] through stops and exits in order to make psychology and position sizing meaningful.

Most people try to find a high-probability entry with no concept of an exit or of adequate position sizing. This usually leads to a trading methodology with a negative expectancy. On the other hand, if people understand the role that exits and position sizing play in systems, they could be quite satisfied with an entry system that only produced 40 percent winners. I think my caller was a little stunned, but he then went on to say that I was wrong: "People cannot develop any sort of expectancy based upon past data," he said.[2] Yet interestingly enough, this person has still written a book about how to make "big" money from the market through understanding chaos theory.

I found the conversation quite interesting. I thought that I was one of the most open people around because I come from the viewpoint that *you can trade ANY concept as long as you have a positive expectancy.* What I learned is that even this basic assumption about being able to trade any concept with a positive expectancy is still an assumption—an assumption that still forms the basis for my thinking about systems. Keeping that assumption in mind, let's look at a few trading concepts that are used by many traders and investors.

TREND FOLLOWING

I've contacted some great traders (and wonderful friends) to write about these various concepts. You've already met Tom Basso, since he was interviewed in Chapter 3. Tom and I have done about 20 seminars together, and I can testify from personal experience that he is the most balanced trader I have ever met. He's also the most mechanical trader I've ever met. Everything in his office is computerized. Even the trading orders go out to the broker by computer-generated fax. Tom trades two computerized trend following systems, so I thought he was the most logical choice to write on trend following.[3]

Tom Basso: The Philosophy of Trend Following

Many successful investors fall into a group called "trend followers." I will attempt to describe what trend following is all about and why investors should be interested in using these general principles in their investing endeavors.

Let's break down the term "trend following" into its components. The first part is "trend." Every trader needs a trend to make money. If you think about it, no matter what the technique, if there is not a trend after you buy, then you will not be able to sell at higher prices. You will take a loss on the trade. There must be a trend up after you buy in order to sell at higher prices. Conversely, if you sell first, then there must be a subsequent trend down for you to buy back at lower prices.

"Following" is the next part of the term. We use this word because trend followers always wait for the trend to shift first, then "follow" it. If the market is in a down direction and then indicates a shift to the upside, the trend follower immediately buys that market. In doing so, the trader follows the trend.

"Let your profits run. Cut your losses short." This old trader's axiom describes trend following perfectly. Trend-following indicators tell the investor when the direction of a market has shifted from up to down or from down to up. Various charts or mathematical representations of the market are used to measure the current direction and observe the shift. Once in a trend, the trader sits back and enjoys the ride, as long as the trend keeps going in the trader's direction. This is "letting profits run."

I once heard a new investor questioning a very successful trend follower. The trend follower had just bought some foreign currency contracts, and the novice asked, "Where's your objective on this trade?" The trend follower wisely answered, "To the moon. I've never had one get there yet, but maybe some day...." That tells a lot about the philosophy of trend following. If the market cooperates, the trend follower would get into the trade as soon as the market passed his or her criteria for "trending" and would stay in it for the rest of his or her life.

Unfortunately, the trend usually ends at some point. As a result, when the direction shifts, then the "cutting losses short" aspect of the axiom should come into play. The trader, sensing that the direction of the market has shifted against the position, immediately liquidates. If the position is ahead at that point, then the trader has made a profit. If, at the time, the position is behind, then the trader has aborted the trade, preventing a runaway loss. Either way, the trader is out of a position that is currently going against him or her.

The Advantage of Trend Following

The advantage of trend following is simple. You will never miss a major move of any market. If the market you are watching turns from a down to an up direction, any trend-following indicator must flash a "buy" signal. It's just a question of when. If it's a major move, you will get the signal. The longer term the trend-following indicators are, the lower the transaction costs—a definite advantage of trend following.

Strategically, the investor must realize that if he or she can get onboard a major move in almost any market, the profits from just one trade can be substantial. In essence, one trade can make your whole year. Thus, the reliability of one's strategy can be far below 50 percent and you'll still show a profit. This is because the average size of one's winning trades is so much greater than the size of one's losing trades.

The Disadvantage of Trend Following

The disadvantage of trend following is that your indicator cannot detect the difference between a major profitable move and a short-lived unprofitable move. As a result, trend followers often get whipsawed as trend-following signals immediately turn against them, causing small losses to occur. Multiple whipsaws can add up, creating concern for the trend follower and tempting him or her to abandon the strategy.

Most markets spend a large amount of time in nontrending conditions. Trending periods could be as little as 15 to 25 percent of the time. Yet the trend follower must be willing to trade in these unfavorable markets in order not to miss the big trend.

Does Trend Following Still Work?

Absolutely! First, if there were no trends, there would be no need for organized markets. Producers could sell to the marketplace without worrying about having to hedge to protect themselves. End users would know that they could obtain the products they need at a reasonable price. And people would buy shares of companies purely for the income from dividends. Thus, should trends stop occurring in the market for any length of time, those markets would probably cease to exist.

Second, if there were no trends, you could expect a fairly random distribution of price changes. Yet if you look at the distribution of price changes over time in almost any market, you'll see a very long tail in the direction of large price changes. This is because there are abnormally large price changes that you'd never expect to see by chance over a given period of time. For example, the S&P futures market opened in 1982 and within 5 years had a price move that you might expect to see once every hundred years. These abnormally large price changes over a short period of time are what make trend following work, and you see them all the time.

Is Trend Following for Everyone?

Trend following is probably one of the easiest techniques for the new trader or investor to understand and use. The longer term the indicators, the less that total transaction costs will affect profits. Short-term models tend to have a tough time overcoming the costs of doing more trades. Costs would include not only commissions, but also slippage on the trades. The fewer trades you make, provided you have the patience for it, the less you spend in transaction costs and the easier it is for you to make a profit.

However, there are numerous examples where trend following is not appropriate. Floor traders who are scalping ticks are not likely to want to use a trend-following concept. Hedging investors may find it more risky to hedge their risk by using trend-following indicators than by choosing some form of passive economic hedge approach. Day traders may find it difficult to use trend-following models. When day trading, you cannot let profits run due to the time limits of day trading. The day simply ends, forcing the trader to liquidate the position.

If trend following fits your personality and your needs, then give it a try. There are many examples of successful traders and investors who consistently use this time-tested approach to the markets. With the economic world as we know it becoming more unstable, there are constantly more new trends for the trend follower to exploit for profit.

Editor's Comments   Trend following is probably the most successful technique for trading or investing of all the concepts discussed. In fact, almost all the system models presented later in this book work because of trend following. As Basso points out, the biggest problem with it is that markets don't always trend. However, this is generally not a problem for people who play the stock market. There are thousands of stocks that you can trade—on either the long or the short side. If you are willing to go both long and short, then there are always good trending markets.

The difficulty people have with the stock market is that (1) there are times when very few stocks are trending up so that the best opportunities are only on the short side; (2) people don't understand shorting so they avoid it; and (3) the exchange regulators make it difficult to short (i.e., you have to be able to borrow the stock to short and you have to short on an uptick). Nevertheless, if you plan for short selling, then it can be very lucrative under the right market conditions.

FUNDAMENTAL ANALYSIS

I've asked another friend, Charles LeBeau, to write the section on fundamental analysis. LeBeau is well known as a former editor of a great newsletter entitled the *Technical Traders Bulletin*. He is also a coauthor of an excellent book, *Computer Analysis of the Futures Market*. Chuck is a talented speaker, and he frequently gives talks at Dow-Jones/Telerate Conferences and at AIQ meetings. And he has been a guest speaker at many of our How to Develop a Winning Trading System That Fits You seminars. He has his own trading firm, Island View Financial Group, with several million under management, and he's also starting a hedge fund.[4]

You might wonder why I asked Chuck, who has such an extensive technical background, to write about fundamental analysis. Chuck lectures about fundamental analysis for a major university, and he once ran a discretionary fundamentally based trading system for Island View Financial Group. In Chuck LeBeau's words, "I prefer to think of myself as a trader who is willing to use the best tools available to get the job done."

Charles LeBeau: Introduction to Fundamental Trading

Fundamental analysis, as it applies to futures trading, *is the use of actual and/or anticipated relationships of supply and demand to forecast the direction and magnitude of future price changes.* There may be more precise and detailed definitions, but this brief article is intended to be about the benefits and practical applications of fundamental analysis.

Almost all traders mistakenly assume that they must be either fundamentalists who rely solely on supply-demand analysis or technicians who ignore fundamentals entirely and make their decisions based solely on price action. Who forces us to make such unnecessary and illogical either-or decisions about how best to trade? If you ever have two (or more) good ideas, you will almost certainly be better off if you do them all rather than falling into the either-or trap.[5]

Fundamental analysis has a distinct advantage over technical analysis in the area of determining price objectives. Correctly interpreted technical indicators can give you direction and timing, but they will fall short in giving you any indication of the magnitude of the anticipated price movement. Some technicians claim that their methods give them price objectives, but after 30 years of trading I have yet to find any technical methods that were valid at forecasting price objectives. However, there is no question that good fundamental analysis can help you determine approximate profit objectives. By employing fundamental price targets you should have a general idea of whether you want to take a quick, small profit or hold for a major long-term price objective. As limited as the accuracy of fundamental price targeting might be, having even a general idea of the magnitude of the profit you are expecting is a big advantage in successful trading.

Fundamental analysis does have definite limitations. The results of the best possible fundamental analysis will be painfully imprecise. If you do everything right, or better yet, rely on the sophisticated analysis of a true fundamental expert, you might be able to conclude that a particular market will probably make a "big" move in an upward direction at some vague time in the future. At its best, fundamental analysis will tell you only the direction and general magnitude of future price movements. It will rarely tell you when the price movement will begin or exactly how far prices will travel. However, knowing the direction and general magnitude of future price changes is certainly critical information that can be invaluable to a trader. Our logical combination of fundamental and technical analysis will supply several important pieces of the trading puzzle—with position sizing (covered elsewhere in this book) being the missing piece.

How to Employ Fundamental Analysis

Let's deal with the practical aspect of successfully employing fundamental analysis. The suggestions that follow are based upon many years of actual trading with fundamentals and are not necessarily listed in order of importance.

Avoid doing your own fundamental analysis even if you have some highly specialized training. I've been trading futures for over 30 years and frequently lecture on fundamental analysis to graduate students at a major university, yet I wouldn't think of doing my own fundamental analysis. True fundamental experts, who are much better qualified than you or I, are devoting full time to this task, and their conclusions are readily available at no cost.

Start looking around to find qualified experts whose fundamental analysis is available to the public. Call the major brokerage firms and ask them to put you on their mailing lists. Get a trial subscription to *Consensus* and read all the analyses. Pick out the ones you like and weed out the weaker sources. Look for analysts who are willing to make helpful forecasts and don't beat around the bush all the time. Remember that you only need one good source of fundamental information for each market. If you get input from too many sources, you will receive conflicting input and become confused and indecisive.

News and fundamental analysis are not the same thing. Fundamental analysis *predicts* price direction, while news *follows* price direction. When I was a senior executive at a major commodity firm, the media would often phone me after the markets had closed and ask why a particular market had gone up or down that day. If the market went up, I would give them some bullish news that had come to my attention. If the market went down, I would give them some bearish news. There is always plenty of bullish and bearish news floating around the markets each day. *What gets reported in the papers is whatever "news" happens to correlate with the direction of the prices for that day.*

You will also observe that pending news will move a market longer and farther than actual reported news. The anticipation of bullish news can support a market for weeks or even months. When the bullish news is eventually reported, the market may well move in the opposite direction. That's why the old adage of "Buy the rumor, sell the fact" seems to work so well. (Of course, the same logic applies to bearish news as well.)

Be careful about reacting to fundamental reports. For example, let's assume that a crop report has just been released showing that the soybean crop is going to be 10 percent smaller than it was last year. At first glance this might seem to be very bullish because the supply of beans was being reduced substantially. But if the traders and analysts involved in this market had expected the report to show 15 percent fewer beans, the prices might decline severely on the "bullish" report. *Before you can analyze the bullishness or bearishness of a report, you have to be aware of what the expectations are and put the report into the context of the expectations.* Also, don't judge the bullishness or bearishness of a report by the initial reaction. Give the market some time to digest the news. You will often find that the first reaction to a report is either overdone or incorrect.

Look for markets that are encountering rising levels of demand. Demand is the motivator that makes for long sustained uptrends that are easy to trade for big profits. *Demand-driven markets are the markets where you can make long-term trades that produce unusually high levels of profitability.* Of course, markets will also rise because of supply shortages, but you will often find that price rallies motivated by supply concerns tend to be short-lived and the long-term price forecasts in these supply-shortage markets are generally overestimated. *Look for demand-driven markets to trade.*

Timing is important, so be patient with your fundamental scenario. The best fundamental analysts seem to be able to forecast price trends much more easily than most market participants. Of course, this is an advantage if you are careful about your timing. However, if you are impulsive and enter the market too soon, you can lose a great deal of money over the short run. Be patient and let your technical indicators tell you when the market is beginning to trend in the direction it should. Remember, the goal is not to be the first to have the correct forecast. The goal is to make money and keep your risk under control. *You may have to wait weeks or even months to take advantage of an accurate fundamental forecast.* Acting too soon could easily turn an accurate forecast into a losing trade.

Many forecasts of a major price change fail to materialize for one reason or another. If you have done a good job of finding accurate sources of fundamental information on a broad group of markets, you might expect to become informed of eight to ten forecasts of a major price change in a typical year. Of these forecasts, only six or seven are likely to occur. But if you can manage to get positioned in half of those in a timely fashion and then do a good job of letting the profits run, you should have an extremely profitable year.

Be decisive and willing to take your share of losses. Don't be afraid to chase after markets that are moving with big fundamental potential. Many traders, fundamental or technical, lack the nerve or discipline to get into a market once it has started running. It is human nature to want to get in at more favorable prices and to postpone your entry waiting for a pullback that may never come. You have to have confidence, and you have to have the courage to take action promptly. The best analysis, fundamental or technical, is worthless in the hands of a "trader" who lacks decisiveness and takes no action. If in doubt, start with a small position and then add to it later.

I hope this brief introduction to fundamental analysis has provoked an idea or two and perhaps convinced you that fundamental analysis might have a place in your trading plan. If so, I would strongly urge you to learn more about this topic. The best book, in my opinion, on the topic is entitled *Schwager on Futures: Fundamental Analysis,*[6] by Jack Schwager. Anyone interested in using fundamentals in trading should find this well-written book extremely helpful.

Editor's Comments   Chuck LeBeau's comments apply primarily to futures trading and could be used in the methodology developed by Gallacher that is presented later in this book. If you are a stock market trader or investor, two systems that involve fundamentals will be presented later for your consideration—William O'Neil's CANSLIM system and Warren Buffett's business model. Buffett's model is almost totally fundamental, while O'Neil's model relies on fundamentals for setups.

SEASONAL TENDENCIES

In my opinion, Moore Research Center, Inc., located in Eugene, Oregon, is the leading center for research on seasonal tendencies in the market. It specializes in computerized analysis of futures, cash, and stock prices. Since 1989 it has published a monthly report and studies on specific futures complexes that go all over the world. It also does great research on probabilistic tendencies in the market. As a result, I approached Steve Moore about doing this chapter. Steve said that the center had a specialist for communicating with the public—Jerry Toepke, the editor of Moore Research Center Publications. Jerry has authored many articles and has spoken at several conferences.[7]

Jerry Toepke: Why Seasonals Work

The seasonal approach to markets is designed to anticipate future price movement rather than constantly react to an endless stream of often contradictory news. Although numerous factors affect the markets, certain conditions and events recur at annual intervals. Perhaps the most obvious is the annual cycle of weather from warm to cold and back to warm. However, the calendar also marks the annual passing of important events, such as the due date for U.S. income taxes every April 15. Such annual events create yearly cycles in supply and demand. Enormous supplies of grain at harvest dwindle throughout the year. Demand for heating oil typically rises as cold weather approaches, but subsides as inventory is filled. Monetary liquidity may decline as taxes are paid but rise as the Federal Reserve recirculates funds.

    These annual cycles in supply and demand give rise to seasonal price phenomena—to a greater or lesser degree and in a more or less timely manner. An annual pattern of changing conditions, then, may cause a more or less well-defined annual pattern of price responses. Thus, seasonality may be defined as a market's natural rhythm, the established tendency for prices to move in the same direction at a similar time every year. As such, it becomes a valid principle subject to objective analysis in any market.

In a market strongly influenced by annual cycles, seasonal price movement may become more than just an effect of seasonal cause. It can become so ingrained as to be nearly a fundamental condition in its own right—almost as if the market had a memory of its own. Why? Once consumers and producers fall into a pattern, they tend to rely on it, almost to the point of becoming dependent upon it. Vested interests then maintain it.

Patterns imply a degree of predictability. Future prices move when anticipating change and adjust when that change is realized. When those changes are annual in nature, a recurring cycle of anticipation and realization evolves. This recurring phenomenon is intrinsic to the seasonal approach to trading, for it is designed to anticipate, enter, and capture recurrent trends as they emerge and to exit as they are realized.

The first step, of course, is to find a market's seasonal price pattern. In the past, weekly or monthly high and low prices were used to construct relatively crude studies. Such analysis might suggest, for instance, that cattle prices in April were higher than in March 67 percent of the time and higher than in May 80 percent of the time. Computers, however, can now derive a daily seasonal pattern of price behavior from a composite of daily price activity over several years. Properly constructed, such a pattern provides historical perspective on a market's annual price cycle.

The four primary components of any cycle are (1) its low point, (2) its rise, (3) its high point, and (4) its decline. When translated into a seasonal price pattern, those components become a seasonal low, a seasonal rise, a seasonal high, and a seasonal decline. A seasonal pattern, then, graphically illustrates an established tendency for market prices to anticipate recurring annual conditions of greatest supply–least demand, increasing demand–decreasing supply, greatest demand–least supply, and decreasing demand–increasing supply. From this pattern one may begin to better anticipate future price movement.

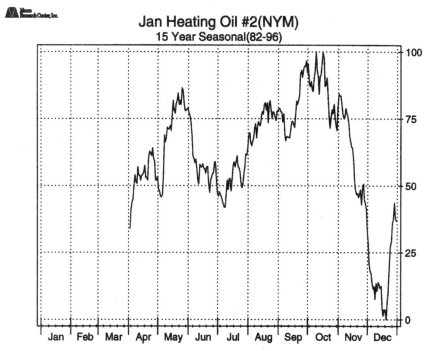

Figure 5–1 January heating oil

Consider the following seasonal pattern that has evolved (1982–1996) for heating oil deliverable in January (Figure 5-1). Demand, and therefore prices, is typically low during July—often the hottest month of the year. As the industry begins anticipating cooler weather, the market finds increasing demand for future inventory—exerting upward pressure on prices. Finally, the rise in prices tends to climax even before the onset of the coldest weather as anticipated demand is realized, refineries gear up to meet the demand, and the market focuses on future liquidation of inventory.

The other primary petroleum product encounters a different, albeit still weather-driven, cycle of demand as exhibited in the seasonal pattern (1986–1995) for August gasoline (Figure 5–2). Prices tend to be lower during the poorer driving conditions of winter. However, as the industry begins to anticipate the summer driving season, demand for future inventory increases and exerts upward

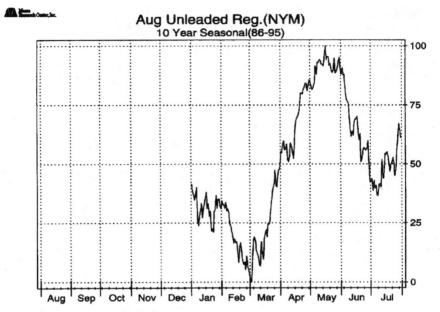

Figure 5–2 August unleaded gas

pressure on prices. By the official opening of the driving season (Memorial Day), refineries then have enough incentive to meet that demand.

Seasonal patterns derived from daily prices rarely appear as perfect cycles. Even in patterns with distinct seasonal highs and lows, seasonal trends in between are subject to various, sometimes conflicting, forces before they are fully realized. A seasonal decline may typically be punctuated by brief rallies. For example, even though cattle prices have usually declined from March–April into June–July, they have exhibited a strong tendency to rally in early May as retail grocery outlets inventory beef for Memorial Day barbecues. Soybean prices tend to decline from June–July into October's harvest, but by Labor Day the market has typically anticipated a frost scare.

Conversely, a seasonal rise may typically be punctuated by brief dips. For example, future uptrends are regularly interrupted by bouts of artificial selling pressure associated with first notice day for nearby contracts. Such liquidation to avoid delivery can offer opportunities both to take profits and then to enter or reestablish positions.

Therefore, a seasonal pattern constructed from daily prices can depict not only the four major components of seasonal price movement, but also especially reliable segments of larger seasonal trends. Recognizing fundamental events that tend to coincide with these punctuations can provide even greater confidence in the pattern.

Consider the seasonal price pattern that has evolved (1981–1995) for September Treasury bonds (Figure 5–3). The U.S. government's fiscal year begins October 1, increasing liquidity and easing borrowing demands somewhat. Is it merely coincidental that the tendency for bond prices to rise from then also tends to culminate with personal income tax liability for the calendar year?

Is the seasonal decline into May a reflection of the market anticipating tighter monetary liquidity as taxes are paid? Notice

Figure 5–3 30-year T-bonds

the final sharp decline beginning—surprise!—April 15, the final date for payment of U.S. income taxes. Does liquidity tend to increase sharply after June 1 because the Federal Reserve is finally able to recirculate funds?

Take a close look at the typical market activity surrounding December 1, March 1, June 1, and September 1—dates of first delivery against Chicago Board of Trade futures contracts on debt instruments. Finally, notice the distinct dips during the first or second week of the second month of each quarter—November, February, May, and August. Bond traders know that prices tend to decline into at least the second day of a quarterly Treasury refunding—at which time the market gains a better sense of the 3-day auction's coverage.

Consider also the pattern for November soybeans (Figure 5–4) as it has evolved in the 15 years (1981–1995) since Brazil

Figure 5–4 November soybeans

became a major producer with a crop cycle exactly opposite that in the Northern Hemisphere. Notice the tendency for prices to work sideways to lower in the "February break" as U.S. producers market their recent harvest and Brazil's crop develops rapidly. By the time initial notices of delivery against March contracts are posted, the fundamental dynamics for a spring rally are in place—the Brazilian crop is "made" (realized), the pressure of U.S. producer selling has climaxed, the market anticipates the return of demand as cheaper river transportation becomes more available, and the market begins focusing attention on providing both an incentive for U.S. acreage and a premium for weather risks.

By mid-May, however, the amount of prime U.S. acreage available in the Midwest for soybeans is mostly determined and planting gets under way. At the same time, Brazil begins marketing its recent harvest. The availability of these new supplies and the potential of the new U.S. crop typically combine to exert pressure on market prices. The minor peaks in late June and mid-July denote the tendencies for occasional crop scares.

By mid-August, the new U.S. crop is "made" (realized), and futures can sometimes establish an early seasonal low. However, prices more often decline further into October's harvest low—but only after rallying into September on commercial demand for the first new-crop soybeans and/or concerns over early crop-damaging frost. Notice also the minor punctuations (decline and rally) associated with the first notice day for July, August, September, and November contracts.

Such trading patterns do not repeat without fail, of course. The seasonal methodology, as does any other, has its own inherent limitations. Of immediate practical concern to traders may be issues of timing and contraseasonal price movement. Fundamentals, both daily and longer term, inevitably ebb and flow. For instance, some summers are hotter and dryer, and at more critical times, than others. Even trends of exceptional seasonal consistency are best traded with common sense, a simple technical indicator, and/or a basic familiarity with current fundamentals to enhance selectivity and timing.

How large must a valid statistical sample be? Generally, more is better. For some uses, however, "modern" history may be more practical. For example, Brazil's ascent as a major soybean producer in 1980 was a major factor in the nearly 180 degree reversal in that market's trading patterns from the 1970s. Conversely, relying solely on deflationary patterns prevalent in 1985–1991 could be detrimental in an inflationary environment.

In such historic transitions, a time lag in the relevancy of recent patterns may occur. Analyzing cash markets can help neutralize such effects, but certain patterns specific to futures (such as those that are delivery- or expiration-driven) can get lost in translation. Thus, both sample size and the sample itself must be appropriate for their intended use. These may be determined arbitrarily, but only by a user who is fully cognizant of the consequences of his or her choice.

Related issues involve projecting into the future with statistics, which confirm the past but do not predict in and of themselves. The Super Bowl–winner/stock market–direction "phenomenon" is an example of statistical coincidence because there exists no cause-and-effect relationship. However, it does raise a valid issue: When computers sift only raw data, what discoveries have meaning? Is a pattern that has repeated, for instance, in 14 of the last 15 years necessarily valid?

Certainly, patterns driven by fundamentals inspire more confidence, but to know all relevant fundamentals in every market is impractical. When one properly constructs seasonal patterns, one may typically find trends that have recurred in the same direction between specific dates with a great degree of past reliability. A "cluster" of such historically reliable trends, with similar entry and/or exit dates, not only reduces the odds of statistical aberration but also implies recurring fundamental conditions that, presumably, will exist again in the future and affect the market to one degree or another and in a more or less timely manner.

A seasonal pattern merely depicts the well-worn path a market itself has tended to follow. It is a market's own consistency that provides the foundation for why seasonals work.

Editor's Comments   Some people are promoting seasonal information that, in my opinion, has no meaning. This usually takes the form of information such as: The price of X has moved higher in 13 of the last 14 years on April 13. Computers will always find correlations of this nature, and some people will want to trade on the basis of them. However, trade a seasonal pattern without a logical cause-and-effect relationship behind it only at your own risk. The results of the January 1998 Super Bowl, for example, seem to predict a decline in the stock market for 1998.[8] Do you want to trade that?

SPREADING

Kevin Thomas is one of the more successful floor traders on the LIFFE exchange in London. He's also the first person to complete our 2-year supertrader program. Kevin trades mostly spreads on the floor. When I originally interviewed Kevin for one of my newsletters, he talked extensively about spreads. Consequently, I thought he was the logical person to write about the concept of spreading for this book.

Kevin Thomas: Introduction to Spreading

Spreads can be used in the futures market to create positions that behave like long and short positions. These types of synthetic positions are well worth considering. They have several advantages over outright trading—a lower risk profile and a much lower margin requirement. In addition, some spreads can be charted like any other market.

For instance, in Eurodollars one could be long the nearby contract and short a contract a year further out and this artificial position takes on the characteristics of a short position for only the spread margin rate. This type of spread is called an "intercontract spread," and it can be used in markets that have liquid forward contracts. However, the behavior of the spread varies from market to market.

In interest rate futures, trading calendar spreads (spreading a nearby contract versus a forward contract) is a common strategy depending upon your view of short-term interest rates. If you think rates are going to rise, then you would buy the nearby and sell the forward contracts. The more contract months you have between the two determines the responsiveness and the likely volatility of the

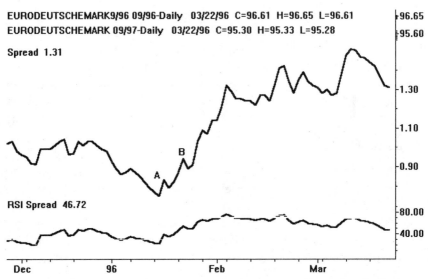

Figure 5–5 Nearby- (bottom) and distant-calendar spreads. (Graph done by Kevin Thomas with SuperCharts by Omega Research, Inc.)

spread. A spread between June and September of the same year is likely to be less volatile than a spread between September this year and September next year. The example in Figure 5–5 illustrates this.

Figure 5–5 shows the movement of the spread between September 1996 Euromarks and September 1997 Euromarks. I have drawn trendlines and included a 14-day RSI on the spread. Notice that there was a divergence at point *A* and a breakout at point *B*. This was a signal that short-term interest rates were about to rise. By being long the spread, you could have participated in the down move in the market that was coming. Notice that the spread then moved 76 ticks from the low to the high of the move.

The charts in Figure 5–6 show how the individual months moved over the same period. *Notice that the movement of the spread was in fact a good leading indicator of what was about to happen in the individual months.* In addition, the move in the spread was more than the down move in September 1996 and about 75 percent of the down move in September 1997. The margin for the spread is 600 deutschemarks per unit compared with 1,500 deutschemarks for a straight futures position.

Figure 5–6 Movement in individual months. (Graph done by Kevin Thomas with SuperCharts by Omega Research, Inc.)

Such spread trading is a concept that is popular among floor traders because they are able to participate in a position that has a lower risk profile than an outright futures position and has a good potential for profit. Once a spread position has been taken, then it can be treated like any other position you would have. Trend-following and position-sizing models can be applied.

By using spreads, you can create relationships that may not be available otherwise. Currency cross rates, for example, are spreads that can be created using IMM currencies such as the deutschemark versus the yen. This creates one of the most actively traded relationships in the world, but one you wouldn't think about if you just thought in terms of dollars or pounds. Another widely traded example would be trading cash bonds against bond futures, which is called "basis trading."

> By using spreads, you can create relationships that may not be available otherwise.

Another common strategy used in these markets is a butterfly spread, which is the difference between two spreads that share a common month (e.g., long 1 Sep 1996, short 2 Dec 1996, and long 1 Mar 1997). Butterfly spreads are very expensive to trade because of the commission costs for an off-floor trader. However, a floor trader in such a market as Eurodollars or Euromarks can utilize this strategy because of the lower commissions and his or her market-maker edge. The strategy usually has a very low risk with a very high expectation of making a profit. The floor trader, because he or she is trading two spreads, is often able to scratch one spread and make a tick on the other or, in the worst case, may scratch the whole butterfly spread.

Commodities also lend themselves to intercontract spreading. Let's assume that you predict that copper prices are going to rise because of a supply shortage. If that is the case, then you would buy the nearby contract and sell the forward. This occurs because in times of shortages nearby prices will rise above forward, creating a phenomenon called "backwardation."

Always bear in mind when trading commodities that physical delivery is part of the contract specifications. "Cash and carry" is a strategy that can be used in trading metals—both base and precious—when they are in good supply. The idea is to take delivery of the metal in a warehouse and redeliver at a future date if the return (the increase in price) will exceed the interest rate for that period of time. If the interest rate is more than the return or the return ends up being negative, then the strategy is not worth doing.

Intermarket spreading is another spread trading idea worth doing. Here you are simply trading different markets against each other, such as the S&P versus the T bonds, Eurodollars versus Euromarks, currency cross rates, gold versus silver, etc. John Murphy has devoted a whole book to the topic (*Intermarket Technical Analysis*),[9] but the basic idea behind such spreads would be because you believe that the relative move of the two markets is probably your best trading idea.

There are numerous forms of other spreads that you can look at, including (1) spreading option contracts and (2) arbitrage. Both of these are complete trading art forms by themselves. Spread trading can be as simple or as complex as you like, but it is definitely worth investigating.

Editor's Comments   All the previous concepts can be used with spreading. The advantage of spreading is simply that you can trade a relationship that was not tradable before. When you buy gold, for example, you are really buying the relationship between gold and the dollar. The relationship will go up if either the dollar goes down in value with respect to gold or gold goes up in value with respect to the dollar. A spread simply sets up another relationship that you can trade.

ARBITRAGE

Ray Kelly is a close personal friend and one of my earliest clients. He's also become a great teacher and one of the best traders I know. From the time I finished working with him in 1987 until early 1994, Ray averaged returns of 40 to 60 percent each year. He accomplished that partially by having only one losing month, a mere 2 percent loss, during that entire period. 1994 was not a great year for Ray, because he backed some futures traders who proceeded to lose money for him, but Ray still made money with his method of trading—arbitrage. Ray served as the model trader in our Peak Performance Trading Seminars for several years. He also is our third graduate. He currently trades for himself, has started a new arbitrage fund, and runs a retreat center for traders in Southern California.[10]

Ray Kelly: Arbitrage—What It Is and How It's Implemented

When people ask me what I do for a living and I say "arbitrage," I see the same blank stare that I often use myself when I lift the hood of my car engine or someone utters the word "calculus." Mothers gather their children to them and men eye me with suspicion.

If you can overcome your fear of the "A" word for about 10 minutes, I guarantee that you will understand not only the essence of arbitrage, but also the way it affects your everyday life. If you begin to "arb-think," you will see opportunities in every facet of your life that you previously had ignored. Your knowledge will secure you from having to excuse yourself for the punch bowl at the next cocktail party when someone says "those arb guys." You will be considered one of the intellectuals at the party and people will stare at you in admiration—all because you invested 10 minutes in reading this section of the book.

Arbitrage is done by entrepreneurs in almost every business. The dictionary defines "arbitrage" as "the buying of bills of exchange in one market and selling them in another." It also describes a woman as a "female human being." Both of these definitions are true, but they don't capture the essence of the word in total. Arbitrage is the magic of discovery. It is the art and science of delving into minute detail to the point of being obnoxious. It is the process of looking at every part of a situation as if it were a diamond slowly turning on a pedestal so you can observe all its facets and see them as unique rather than the same. It belongs to those of you who love to solve the impossible riddle.

> Arbitrage is the magic of discovery. It is the art and science of delving into minute detail to the point of being obnoxious. It is the process of looking at every part of a situation as if it were a diamond slowly turning on a pedestal so you can observe all its facets and see them as unique rather than the same. It belongs to those of you who love to solve the impossible riddle.

Edwin LeFerve, in the book *Reminiscence of a Stock Operator*,[11] describes what happened in the early twenties with the advent of the telephone. All stock quotes from the New York Stock Exchange were sent out by Teletyping houses that we now know as bucket shops. It was very similar to off-track betting. The shops allowed a person to know a quote and then place an order to buy or sell. The difference was that the shop owner was the bookie or regional specialist, and rather than call the exchange, he booked the trade himself. For example, the ticker would say Eastman Kodak trades for 66½. The customer would say "Buy 500 shares" and the shop owner would confirm the purchase and take the other side of this transaction.

A smart fellow with a phone finally figures out that the phone was faster than the Teletype operator on the floor of the New York Stock Exchange. He would transact some small trades to establish a presence with the shop but always keep in contact with a cohort by phone in times of volatility. If bad news came out, he may find that Eastman Kodak, while on the tape at 66½, was actually 65 at the post in New York. Consequently, he would sell to the shop owner as much as he could at 66½ and buy it back through his friend on the floor in New York at 65. Over time, this clever fellow hired others to trade at the bucket shops and put many of them out of business. Eventually, the remaining bucket shops got their own phones.

Is this action unscrupulous, or is it a way to more efficiently price a marketplace? Is it unscrupulous for the shop owner to book the trades? The important thing to remember is that economics per se does not have a moral code. It simply is. People ascribe "good" and "bad" or "right" and "wrong" to various practices. The shop owner feels that the actions of the arb player are wrong. The New York broker loves the increased commission business and loves the arb player.

Arb players themselves feel that since the phone is open to everyone, they are only implementing something that any clever person could figure out. They do not feel an obligation to negate their cleverness by spelling everything out to those who could eventually figure it out for themselves. Over time, there are always actions of others to stop the arbs or to join in and make the opportunity less profitable. Economics is neutral to the emotions of the players. It says, "If there is money on the table, it belongs to the person who picks it up."

> The important thing to remember is that economics per se does not have a moral code. It simply is....Economics is neutral to the emotions of the players. It says, "If there is money on the table, it belongs to the person who picks it up."

When I was a teenager, I did my first arb. I lived in a wealthy neighborhood, although I was broke. My dad kept getting "free" credit cards in the mail. One day in the 1960s we had a blizzard as we do now and then in the Midwest. I lived across from a hardware store, and I knew that it had a snow blower for sale for $265. It was a beast of a blower! I could see that even the snowplows couldn't get to the rich folks' houses.

I also noticed an unopened letter with a Towne and Country Credit Card on my father's desk. My name and my father's are the same, so I took it. (This is what is called risk arbitrage.) I bought the snowblower with the credit card when the store opened at 7 a.m. I did 11 long driveways by 8 p.m. that night and made $550. The next morning at 7 a.m. I sold the snowblower back to the guy in the store for $200. He gave me back the credit card slip and I gave him the slightly used snowblower, which was still in great demand. I netted $485 and felt like the cat that ate the canary!

A few years ago I was approached for advice by a man who had 3,000 shares of stock. He had an opportunity to buy more shares through the company at a discount. This was a chance to buy a $25 stock for $19. Even though the amount of stock he could buy was small, it still seemed like a good opportunity.

I had been on the Chicago Board of Options Exchange (CBOE) for 25 years and could not find any comparable investments. As a result, I told him it was a good deal and called the company to find out more about its dividend reinvestment plan. I also found out that other companies had similar plans and that the brokerage community was starting to participate in these plans.

I wondered, "How are they doing this? If they bought a million shares, they would only be able to reinvest the amount of the dividend, and the interest on the purchase would wipe out the profit." They also would have huge market risk. However, I saw others doing the trade and I became obsessed with how it was done. Some people were obviously making money. I dug through records, talked to margin clerks, and watched the trades that took place before the dividend payout dates. Slowly, the picture became clearer. I eventually solved the problem of what looked like a mathematical loser. However, I didn't have enough capital to do it myself, so I went through the painful and agonizing steps to find a company in the securities business that was not doing it and would not steal it from me once I explained it to the people there. That was a long process.

An arbitrager must find a company that is willing to look beyond the obvious—that's where the opportunity lies. Lawyers are usually a formidable wall of resistance. Lawyers for institutions are paid to investigate, and the status quo is normally hard to change. If something goes wrong, they are blamed. But if things drag out, the attorneys get paid anyway. If there is a little twist in the path, they are not paid to find another way, but just to tell you that the one you are on won't work. They do not like being pressed for specifics, nor do they like quick answers. That is their charm. On the other hand, once you get through the process, you become part of the status quo (at least, for a little while).

Arbitrage is usually time-sensitive. Once certain opportunities are discovered, competition usually lowers the profits, and regulators eventually plug the once overlooked loophole. This time frame is usually referred to as "the window." A company that has a dividend reinvestment plan, for example, may say, "We only meant this plan for small investors." The arbitrager may respond that the intentions of the company are not part of the legal text of its plan. The company, in turn, will usually seek remedy through legislation or by changing its plan. In either case, the arbitrage opportunity pointed to a flaw in the economics of the company's "intent." The arb player is paid by that flaw.

The institutions I have presented ideas to over the years have a problem called "infrastructure." Large companies are broken into divisions that manage specific parts of their business. In the securities area, one group may handle customer accounts, another will handle stock lending, another will handle proprietary trading, etc. Each division has its own profit goals and what is called a "hurdle rate." The hurdle rate is a computation of the minimum return the division head will accept to entertain a business proposal.

The CEO will usually turn management over to the division head. The problem here is that the economy (and the opportunity) doesn't care about the corporation's structure. What is perhaps efficient from a corporate viewpoint may leave inefficiencies that are accepted as a cost of doing business. Since it is anathema for one corporate division head to peek into another manager's area, these inefficiencies are rarely addressed quickly, if at all.

In a specific and actual situation, I presented one major brokerage firm with a strategy that returned 67 percent on capital net after my percentages were taken out. Unfortunately, I needed three divisions of the company to accomplish this. Each of these divisions had a 30 percent hurdle rate. None of them would take less because it weakened the individual division's overall picture even though it greatly enhanced the overall return to the company. During almost 2 years of negotiation the return went from 67 percent down to 35 percent. There were literally tens of millions of dollars of potential profit at stake. The company never did a trade, and to my knowledge all the same managers still work there.

Once you get through the infrastructure and gain credibility with a firm, there are other problems. The troops in the trenches get irritated because nothing you do is normal. They are always asked to do things somewhat differently for me than they do for their regular customers. We insist on minute-to-minute concentration on little, seemingly innocuous procedures.

For example, if a trade is executed on the New York Stock Exchange, I can negotiate a fixed ticket charge of say $150 regardless of the size of the trade. I cannot help my client negotiate with the Securities and Exchange Commission on its 0.003 percent charge on the sale of the stock. This seems to be a small amount of money. But on a $100 million trade, the amount is $3,333.33. To me, that is a lot of money.

A brokerage firm cannot change the U.S. government. It simply passes the charge on to the customer, and such charges go unchallenged. Yet if my client were to do 1,000 of these $100 million trades each year, the government charge would be over $3 million. Once again the economy of the opportunity does not concern itself with the intransigence of policy—even from the U.S. government. Yet if I suggest to my client that should she transact her trade in Toronto rather than the United States, she would save this fee, be reasonably free from questioning by governmental authorities, and not get any notoriety domestically, the client loves me. The clerk who has to process these trades, however, doesn't love me at all. I have upset his day with what he sees as trivia. If I were to cut him in on 10 percent of the saved fee, the light would dawn quickly. But the more I disclose information to people, the quicker the advantage goes away.

Eventually, others will figure out what I am doing and find a way to cut themselves in on the profit. This is called reverse engineering. Some firms have whole divisions that dedicate themselves to watching the street and uncovering strategies. It's my belief that this process is a critical part of price discovery in the economic system. The arbitrager points out in a way that can't be ignored or pushed back by bureaucracy some miscalculation or misperception. In many cases, it forces institutions to look at situations they would otherwise ignore.

I am still dumbfounded by all the precautions that securities firms and banks seem to take—yet they still come up with billion dollar snafus. The process of strategy approval is so rigorous that the arbitrage players who do the trading have no incentive to help their own corporations in risk evaluation. The arbitragers almost invariably wind up in an adversarial role by the nature of their business. The integrity of the trader should be heavily considered in all aspects of the trader's life. Integrity seems to be the last line of defense of most trading companies.

In conclusion, the case could be made that there is no stability to a career in arbitrage since everything always changes—the loopholes close and the profits become smaller. On the other hand, you can realize that everything in life changes constantly and accepting that change is to live a grand adventure. You can realize that errors and miscalculations are part of the human condition. They are how we learn and grow. Your mission, through arbitrage, is to correct inefficiencies whether people want you to or not. You get paid to correct errors. Your job is to pick apart the strategy or concept of someone else piece by piece. If you don't find anything, which is usually the case, you simply move on to another strategy or concept. The way you view things, your frame of reference, determines your view of arbitrage.

> Your mission, through arbitrage, is to correct inefficiencies whether people want you to or not. You get paid to correct errors. Your job is to pick apart the strategy or concept of someone else piece by piece. If you don't find anything, which is usually the case, you simply move on to another strategy or concept.

The arbitrager's success is determined by his or her commitment to go the extra distance. Arbitrage is the cleanser of inefficiency. It keeps me from being a spectator. After all, there are only two places you can be in life—on the playing field or in the stands. I prefer to be on the playing field.

Editor's Comments   In essence, most trading and investing is a form of arbitrage—looking for inefficiencies in the market. Ray Kelly's form of arbitrage, however, is the purest application of arbitrage. It's almost a license to print money, but for a limited period of time. If you are really serious about being a professional trader, then I strongly agree that you continually look for such opportunities.

NEURAL NETWORKS

I looked all over for an expert to write about neural networks for this book. One of the problems with neural networks is that they are complex, they tend to border on curve fitting, and you can spend a lot of effort simply trying to predict whether one market will be higher or lower tomorrow, with about 55 percent accuracy. It's quite frustrating, especially when my gut feeling was that more could be done with neural networks.

Finally, I happened upon Louis Mendelsohn through his web site and was quite impressed with what I saw there. Most of the articles he has written (over 50 of them) are presented in their entirety. Mendelsohn has gone way beyond predicting tomorrow's price and actually uses neural networks in some very useful ways. As a result, I was delighted when he agreed to write this section of the concepts chapter. He's an internationally acclaimed technical analyst, investment software developer, and financial author.[12]

Louis Mendelsohn: Introduction to Neural Networks

The integration of intermarket analysis with traditional single-market technical analysis is necessary for profitable trading in the 1990s and beyond. Today's limited single-market focus must yield to a broader analytic framework that addresses the nonlinear interdependence of today's financial markets. In 1991 I first wrote about this framework, referring to it as "synergistic market analysis." This approach allows traders to quantify complex intermarket relationships, assess the simultaneous impact of multiple related markets on a given market, and measure the leads and lags that exist within these relationships.

Neural networks are an excellent tool to implement synergistic analysis. They can be used to synthesize disparate data and find hidden patterns and complex relationships between markets. Neural networks are real, and they do work! In fact, they perform an outstanding job at processing extensive amounts of intermarket data. It is their ability to quantify subtle relationships and detect hidden patterns between numerous related markets that makes neural networks an important mathematical tool in the financial arena. How else could a trader examine the past 10 years of price data on 5, 10, or 15 related markets simultaneously to discern the effects that these markets have on a specific market?

Additionally, through the use of neural networks, financial forecasting becomes possible, so that traders can gain an *anticipatory*, not just a *retrospective*, vantage point on the financial markets. Anyone can tell you where a market has been in the past by simply looking at its price chart, but the real money is in correctly anticipating the future direction of that market! Through the use of neural networks applied to intermarket analysis, traders can actually forecast the financial markets, similar to the way meteorologists forecast the path that a hurricane is expected to take. Forecasting is never 100 percent accurate. It never will be. But from a decision-making standpoint under conditions of uncertainty, it's a major step in the right direction.

To incorporate intermarket analysis into your trading plan, it isn't necessary to change your trading style or stop using single-market indicators that work reasonably well. Intermarket analysis can be used to augment existing single-market approaches.

In order to appreciate the difference between single-market analysis and intermarket analysis, put one hand over one of your eyes. All of a sudden your peripheral vision is sharply restricted and your ability to grasp the entire environment is greatly reduced. That's what single-market analysis is like in today's financial environment. Now remove your hand and instantly your peripheral vision is restored. That's what intermarket analysis is all about— broadening your perspective.

Neural Networks Primer
I would like to present a cursory overview of what neural networks are and how they can be applied to the financial markets. Attention here will focus on neural network paradigms, architectures, and training and testing regimens for a financial forecasting application.

Neural networks "learn" to solve problems by transmitting information between neurons, which are the basic processing units of a neural network. A neural network typically includes several layers of neurons. Network architecture determines how many layers there are, how many neurons are in each layer, how they are connected, and what transfer function is to be used. There are numerous learning paradigms, including two that are popular in financial analysis. The first popular paradigm is a **recurrent back-propagation network** that learns temporal information through the order in which the facts are presented. The second paradigm is a **feed-forward back-propagation network** that trains through back propagation of error, in which temporal information is encoded into the input data by taking a preprocessed "snapshot" of the data. A typical back-prop network architecture is shown in Figure 5–7. This paradigm will be used here to illustrate network architecture.

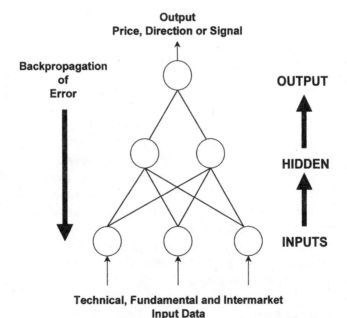

Figure 5–7 Simple feed-forward back-propagation network. A back-prop net using technical, fundamental, and intermarket data. The network trains by back propagation of error throughout the network.

The back-propagation network is composed of an input layer, one or more hidden layers, and an output layer. The input layer contains a neuron corresponding to each input (independent) variable. The output layer contains a neuron for each (dependent) variable to be predicted. The hidden layer contains neurons that are connected to both the input and output layers. The layers are typically fully connected, with every neuron in one layer connected to each neuron in an adjacent layer.

The values associated with each input neuron are fed forward into each neuron in the first hidden layer. They are then multiplied by an appropriate weight, summed, and passed through a transfer function to produce an output. The outputs from the first hidden layer are then fed forward either into the next hidden layer or directly into the output layer in networks that have only one hidden layer. The output layer's output is the prediction made by the network.

The number of neurons in the hidden layer is determined through experimentation. For any nonlinear problem such as prediction of stock or futures prices, the network needs at least one hidden layer. In addition, the transfer function should be a nonlinear, continuously differentiable function, such as the sigmoid, which allows the network to perform nonlinear statistical modeling. Figure 5-8 presents an example of a hidden neuron.

Input Data Selection and Preprocessing   Neural network modeling is based upon the developer's understanding of the underlying real-world relationship between the inputs and the output. Decisions must be made about what is to be predicted and what data will be used as inputs in the network. "Garbage-in, garbage-out" applies to neural networks. Knowledge of the financial markets, coupled with the use of various tools such as principal component analysis to find correlations between related markets, is necessary for appropriate input data selection.

Once input data have been selected, they must be preprocessed. By reducing the number of inputs to the network, preprocessing helps it learn more easily. Two widely used preprocessing methods are known as "transformation" and "normalization." Transformation manipulates raw data inputs to create a single

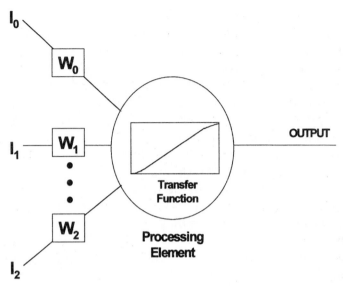

Figure 5–8 An example of a hidden neuron.
Neural networks are composed of individual, interconnected,
processing elements called "neurons."

input to a net. Normalization transforms a single data input to distribute the data evenly and scale the data to match the range of the input neurons.

In most neural network applications, transformation involves algebraic or statistical manipulation of the input data. In financial forecasting applications, a wide variety of technical indicators, commonly used by traders to interpret market behavior, can be used as transforms. Preprocessed inputs might include differences, ratios, and moving averages of the open, high, low, close, volume, and open interest raw data. Each neuron in the input layer represents one of the preprocessed inputs.

Various transformation and normalization methods can be explored, since some are more appropriate than others for specific applications. Once the network architecture has been selected and the inputs have been chosen and preprocessed, data facts must be selected.

Fact Selection   A fact is represented as a row of related numbers where the first i numbers correspond to the i network inputs and the last j numbers correspond to the j network outputs. A group of related facts is known as a "fact set." If two facts have exactly the same input and output values, only one of the facts should be included in the fact set. Once it has been defined, in most financial applications the fact set should be separated into mutually exclusive training and testing subsets.

Back-propagation networks operate in two modes: One is a learning mode in which the network uses facts from the training set to modify its internal representation through weight changes. The other is a recall mode in which the network processes inputs from the test set and utilizes its previously learned representation to generate associated outputs. The relative performance on the test set of various trained networks is used to determine which net should be incorporated into the final application.

Training and Testing   Once the facts have been selected, they are presented to the network serially during training. The weights, which allow the network to adapt its internal representation when modeling a problem, are typically initialized with small randomly assigned weights. If the weights are initially set to the same value, the network might never learn since error changes are proportional to the weight values. For each pass through the training set, the network computes a measure of the error between its generated output and the desired output for each output in the output layer. The errors are then propagated backward through the network, layer by layer, altering the connection weights between the neurons in order to minimize the total error associated with each output.

Each time the weights change, the network is taking a step on a multidimensional surface, representing the overall error space. During training the network is traveling along the surface, trying to find the lowest point or minimum error. The weight changes are proportional to a training parameter called the "learning rate." Other training parameters that can be adjusted during the training process include temperature, gain, and noise.

With various training parameters, preprocessing methods, and architectural configurations that can be explored, an automated training and testing regime that integrates testing with training is needed. Tools such as genetic algorithms and simulated annealing can be used to expedite searching these parameter spaces. Genetic algorithms are effective for many parameter optimization tasks. Simulated annealing automates learning rate adjustments during training by including a variable temperature term that affects the learning rate. When the temperature is high, learning is rapid. When the temperature drops, learning slows down as the network settles upon a solution.

Overtraining   Overtraining, analogous to curve fitting of rule-based trading systems, is one of the major pitfalls that must be avoided when developing neural networks. Overtraining occurs when a network memorizes the subtleties and idiosyncrasies specific to the training set, lessening its ability to generalize to new data. When overtraining occurs, a network performs well on the training set, but poorly on an out-of-sample test set and later during actual trading. To avoid overtraining, network training should be halted periodically at predetermined intervals and then run in recall mode on the test set to evaluate the network's performance on predetermined error criteria. Then the training resumes from the point at which it was halted. This automated process continues iteratively until the performance on the test set begins to degrade, suggesting that the network has begun to overtrain. All interim results that met the error criteria are evaluated further.

Error Statistics   Another important network design decision concerns which error statistics to use for training and testing. One measure might be the difference between the actual calculated statistic such as a moving-average value and the network's output. This difference would be calculated for each fact in the test set, summed, and divided by the number of facts in the test set. This is a standard error measure called "average error." Various error measures include average absolute error, sum-of-squares error, and root-mean-squared (RMS) error. After a neural network model has been selected, it will need to be retrained periodically. Ongoing research should be conducted to modify the inputs, outputs, architecture, and overall implementation of the testing and training process for the purpose of improving network performance and predictive accuracy.

You cannot expect to design an effective neural network financial forecasting application unless you have considerable trading experience, programming and mathematics expertise, and the time to devote to the task. Successful development of a neural network application is a combination of both "art" and "science." This endeavor can be extremely time consuming and labor intensive, even for a group of experts working collectively.

I speak from experience. In 1991 the Predictive Technologies Group, the research and development division of my firm, introduced VantagePoint Intermarket Analysis software, after experimenting with intermarket analysis since the mid-1980s. VantagePoint applies neural networks to intermarket analysis in order to predict market trends, moving averages, and next-day prices for various financial futures markets. Currently there are 21 custom-designed VantagePoint programs for currencies, interest rate markets, stock indices, and the energy complex which allow traders to benefit from intermarket analysis, without having to reinvent the wheel or become rocket scientists.

Practical Applications
While used extensively by traders to identify trends, simple moving averages, due to their mathematical construction, are considered a lagging indicator. This limitation has presented an enormous challenge to technical analysts for decades. Continuing research directed at reducing the lag has resulted in a steady stream of modifications to this relatively simple, yet effective, technical indicator. [These are discussed extensively in Chapter 8.]

Moving-Averages Primer   A moving average smoothes out fluctuations in prices to demonstrate an underlying directional trend. In a typical moving-average system, a crossover oscillator, involving either two moving averages or a price and a moving average, is developed. Entry and exit points are determined when one indicator crosses above or below the other indicator. For instance, a trader might rely upon Donchian's 5-day versus a 20-day moving-average method to determine entry and exit points.

Still, moving averages are slow to react at turning points. Traditional moving-average systems typically get in and out of trades *after* a change in market direction has occurred—often by several days—which gives back profits and can turn winning trades into losers. Additionally, crossover systems tend to generate false signals during sideways or nontrending markets, resulting in whipsaws when alternating buy and sell signals are triggered as the moving averages crisscross one another.

Through system testing, the size of the moving averages can be optimized in an effort to tailor them to each market's price behavior and to find the best crossovers that will capture the "turns" in that market and help reduce the lag. Additionally, other smoothing methods can be used in conjunction with moving averages to reduce the lag further, resulting in trading strategies that presumably will be more responsive to abrupt changes in the market. These include the use of price filters or sensitivity bands surrounding the moving averages and the addition of a third moving average, both of which were part of ProfitTaker's original system architecture. Other widely used methods include Bollinger bands and the popular 4-9-18-day moving-average combination.

Forecasting Moving Averages   Of all the variations on simple moving-average approaches that have been developed to date, displacing moving averages probably comes the closest to what is desired, since it is an attempt to convert them into an "anticipatory" technical indicator. Yet even a displaced moving average has one glaring weakness: the simplistic assumption that the moving-average value at a future time will be the same as its calculated value today. Basically, this is nothing other than a primitive prediction of the moving-average value for a time period in the future, in which that value is assumed to be identical to today's calculated moving-average value—a highly unrealistic assumption under real-world trading conditions. Why not take this concept one step further and actually predict moving averages? By doing so, their smoothing benefits are retained, while their *lag is totally eliminated* once and for all.

Related Intermarkets   Additionally, by incorporating intermarket inputs into the neural network design, the moving-average predictions are not limited to single-market inputs. In the case of the VantagePoint T-bond program, for instance, the inputs into the forecast of the moving averages take into consideration the open, high, low, close, volume, and open interest for the past 10 years from actual T-bond contracts during their most actively traded periods, plus nine related markets (T-bond cash, NY Light Crude Oil, CRB Index, deutschemark, US dollar index, Eurodollar, Comex gold, Japanese yen, and S&P 500 Index) that have been determined to have a significant effect on Treasury bonds.

Since correctly identifying trend direction is crucial to successful trading, *trend forecasting,* compared with *trend following,* offers a promising new way for traders to identify trends and changes in their direction as they are happening, not after the fact. Coupling neural networks with intermarket analysis, VantagePoint forecasts trends by predicting moving averages for up to 4 days in the future. To do this, VantagePoint is composed of five separate neural networks that are each responsible for predicting a particular output variable. One neural network predicts tomorrow's high, a second predicts tomorrow's low, and a third predicts a "neural index" which indicates when the market is about to make a *top* or a *bottom.* The fourth network predicts what a 5-day moving average of closes will be *2 days in the future,* while the fifth network predicts what a 10-day moving average of closes will be *4 days in the future.*

While the moving-average predictions are used to determine trend direction, the predicted highs and lows are used to set entry and exit points and stops. This predicted high-low range is analogous to support and resistance lines in traditional single-market technical analysis, except that VantagePoint's predicted daily range is based on the pattern recognition capabilities of the neural network coupled with the intermarket analysis of 10 related markets.

Position traders utilize the predicted highs and lows to help set entry points, and then use the predicted high-low range on subsequent days to tighten stops. For example, if you are long Treasury bonds and the market is expected to continue to move *up* tomorrow, you might set a trailing stop for tomorrow a few ticks below tomorrow's predicted low which acts as a support level. This would decrease the likelihood of being stopped out prematurely as the result of intraday volatility in the market, and yet protect profits in the event of an abrupt market downturn in which the predicted low is breached.

The predictions of the next day's high and low are useful for determining entry and exit points for day trading as well. If the forecasted indicators suggest that tomorrow will be an *up* day, day traders can wait for the market to trade down toward the predicted low and then enter a long position a few ticks above the predicted low, to be closed out intraday just below the predicted high. The reverse would involve entering a short position just below the predicted high on a day expected to be *down* and exiting the position a few ticks above the predicted low. This may be done several times daily.

Editor's Comments   Obviously, there are numerous procedures that you can do with neural networks. Mendelsohn is absolutely correct in saying that you must thoroughly understand what you are doing—both with respect to neural networks and with respect to financial modeling. When you read and thoroughly understand the subsequent chapters, you'll probably realize that there are vast untapped areas to apply neural networks to—such as exits and position sizing.

THERE'S AN ORDER TO THE UNIVERSE

The idea that there is an order to the universe is extremely popular. People want to understand how the markets work, so it is most appealing to them to be able to find some underlying structure. They believe, of course, that once you know the underlying structure, you can predict market movements. In many cases, such theories are even more exact because they attempt to predict market turning points. This naturally appeals to the psychological bias that most people have of wanting to be right and to have control over the markets. As a result, they want to catch market turning points. In addition, it's a highly marketable idea to sell to the public. There are a number of different types of theories involving market order, including Gann, Elliott Wave, astrological theories, etc.

I elected to write this part of this chapter myself because (1) someone who is an expert in one market-orderliness theory is not necessarily an expert in another, and (2) the experts seemed to be more concerned with proving (or disproving) their theories than with the issue of whether or not the concept is tradable. Since I believe that almost any concept is tradable, I thought it would be easier for me to discuss the concepts in general terms and then indicate how one might trade them.

Basically, *there are three types of concepts which presume there is some order to the markets.* All these concepts function to predict turning points in the market. I am making some gross oversimplifications in discussing them, so I ask the indulgence of any experts in the various concepts described.

Human Behavior Has a Cycle

The first concept says that the markets are a function of human behavior and that the motives of human beings can be characterized by a certain structure. The most well-known structure of this type is Elliott Wave theory. Here one assumes that the impulses of fear and greed follow a distinct wave pattern. Basically, the market is thought to consist of five up waves followed by three corrective waves. For example, the major upthrust of the market would consist of five waves up (with waves 2 and 4 being in the opposite direction) followed by three waves down (with the middle wave being in the opposite direction). Each wave has a distinct characteristic, with the third major wave in the series of five being the most tradable. However, the theory gets much more complex because there are waves within waves. In other words, there are Elliott Waves of different magnitudes. For example, the first wave of the major movement would consist of another whole sequence of five waves followed by three corrective waves. Elliott, in fact, decided that there were nine categories of magnitude of waves, ranging from the Grand Supercycle to the subminuette waves.

Certain rules aid the Elliott Wave theoretician in making decisions about the market. There are also variations to the rules in that waves may be stretched or compressed and there are some pattern variations. The nature of those rules and variations is beyond the scope of this discussion, *but the rules do allow you to arrive at market turning points that are tradable.* In other words, the task one has in "assigning" order to the market is one of determining which wave series was responsible for any given turning point.

Physical Systems Influence Human Behavior in Predictable Patterns

The second concept of order in the markets is based on the aspects of physical systems in the universe. The logic of looking at physical systems is based on the following assumptions: (1) Market movements are based upon the behavior of human beings; (2) human beings are influenced, both physically and emotionally, by the various physical systems and the energy they put out; therefore, (3) it seems logical that if there are patterns to those physical energies, then they should have strong predictable effects on markets.

For example, scientists have shown that there are regular cycles to sunspots. Sunspots are actually a release of electromagnetic energy from the sun and can have profound effects on the earth.

Large amounts of sunspot activity will cause huge amounts of charged particles to be trapped in the earth's magnetosphere. This seems to protect the earth from some of the harmful effects of the sun. In addition, the most intense periods of sunspot activity, as one might expect if this theory were true, seem to correlate with the high points in civilization. We're currently in one! In contrast, low periods of sunspot activity seem to correlate with what might be termed declines in civilization. Obviously, if such a theory is valid and if sunspot activity is predictable, then one would expect sunspot activity to have a strong effect on what happens in the market.

There are numerous attempts to correlate and predict markets based upon major physical systems such as the activity of the sun. It is very easy to put together enough best-case examples to prove to others—or yourself—that these theories are correct. I've seen it happen hundreds of times because there is a simple perceptual bias that will convince people of certain relationships from just a few well-chosen examples. Nevertheless, there is a big difference between theory and reality.

John Nelson—a radio propagation specialist—was able to predict 6-hour intervals of radio propagation quality at 88 percent accuracy. He did so by using planetary alignments. Several market researchers have taken the dates of the worst storms from 1940 through 1964 and run statistics on the percent change in the Dow Jones Industrial Average (DJIA) from −10 days to + 10 days from the onset of the storms. They find that the DJIA shows a statistically significant decline from 2 days before the storm until 3 days after the storm. And during a new moon or a full moon, the effect is amplified even more. However, during much of this time the stock market was in a bear market when there was already a downward bias.[13]

On March 5, 1989, a massive X-ray flare, lasting 137 minutes, erupted on the sun's surface. It overloaded the sensors on the equipment monitoring it; and in the region from which it occurred, a cluster of sunspots were clearly visible. On March 8 a solar proton flow began, and a large quantity of these ions began flowing toward the earth on a solar wind, lasting until March 13. Monitors of the earth's magnetism in the Shetland Islands registered a change in magnetism of as much as 8 degrees per hour (with the normal deviation being only 0.2 degree). There were huge surges in power lines, telephone lines, and cable networks. Radio and satellite communications were badly affected. Transformers overloaded in Canada, and over a million people were suddenly left without electricity. Yet this particular flare was by no means a spectacular event in solar terms.

The solar flare between March 5 and March 13, 1989, was small in terms of what the sun is capable of, but it was the largest recorded in this century—bigger than any of the storms reported by Nelson. So the question obviously is, what effect did it have on the markets? The answer, as best I can tell, was that it had no effect at all.

Nevertheless, despite some evidence to the contrary, let us assume that there is some rhythm to the activity of these physical entities and that it does have a slight effect on the markets. Perhaps, for example, it raises the odds of being "right" about a market change from 48 percent to 52 percent. That's about the same odds that a card counter at blackjack gets in Las Vegas, and the casinos kick out card counters. As a result, the physical system explanation of order in the markets is also a tradable one.

There's a Mysterious Mathematical Order to the Universe

The third concept relating to orderliness in the markets searches through mathematics in order to find the answers. It asserts that certain "magic" numbers, and the relationships among the numbers, influence the markets. For example, Pythagorus is rumored to have taught in an ancient "mystery school" that all the principles of the universe were based upon mathematics and geometry. Furthermore, certain "magical" societies and sects seem to carry this notion forward. The work of W. D. Gann, as currently promoted by many of his followers, is based upon mathematical orderliness.

Basically, mathematical orderliness theories are based on the following two assumptions: (1) that certain numbers are more important than others in predicting market turning points, and (2) that these numbers are important both in terms of price levels and in terms of time (i.e., when to expect a change in the market). For example, suppose you believed that 45, 50, 60, 66, 90, 100, 120, 135, 144, 618, etc., were magic numbers. What you'd do is find "significant" tops or bottoms and apply these numbers to them—looking at both time and price. You might expect, for example, a 0.50, a 0.618, or a 0.667 correction in the market. In addition, you might expect your target price to be reached in 45 days or 144 days or some other magic number.

If you have enough magic numbers, you can figure out and verify a lot of projections after the fact. You can then extend those projections into the future, and some of them might actually work out. This usually will happen if you have enough magic numbers to work with in your arsenal. For example, if you have at least 33 people in a room, your odds are quite good of finding two people with the same birthday. That doesn't necessarily mean, however, that the common date is a magic number, although some people might jump to that conclusion.

Let's make the assumption that such numbers do exist. Let's also assume that they are not perfect, but they do increase the reliability of your predictions beyond chance. For example, with magic numbers you might predict that the Dow Jones Industrial Average should make a major turn on July 23. You estimate that the reliability of your prediction is 55 percent. If you have that kind of edge, then you have a tradable event.

Conclusion

What do these three concepts about orderliness in the markets have in common? They all predict turning points. Turning points, in most cases, tend to give traders information about when to enter the market. In some cases, they also give profit objectives and a clue about when to get out of the market. You'll learn in Chapter 8 that it's possible to make money with a trading system in which the entry is totally random. As a result, if any prediction method gives you a better than chance expectation of predicting the market, you could have some advantage in trading it.

How should one trade such predictions? First, you could use the expected target date (with whatever time variance you are willing to give it) as a filter for entry. Thus, if your method predicts a market turn on July 23 with a possible variance of 1 day, then you should look for an entry signal between July 22 and July 24.

Second, you must look for the market to tell you that it is making the move before you enter. The move itself should be your trading signal. The simplest way of trading it would be to look for a volatility breakout signal during the window in which you expect a move. For example, suppose the average daily price range (e.g., the average true range) for the last 10 days has been 4 points. Your signal might be 1.5 times this range, or 6 points. As a result, you would enter on a 6-point move from yesterday's close. You would then use appropriate stops, exits, and sizing—to control the trade. These are discussed in subsequent chapters.

The keys to trading such concepts of orderliness profitably are the same as the keys to trading any concept properly. First, you need good exits to preserve your capital when your concept does not work and to create a high payoff when it does. Second, you need to size your positions appropriately to be able to meet your trading objectives. Thus, even if such concepts increase your accuracy by 1 percent, you can still trade them profitably. However, if you de-emphasize the prediction part of such systems (thus giving up your need to be in control and to be right), and concentrate on exits and position sizing, you should do quite well.

SUMMARY

The purpose of this chapter was to introduce you to a few of the many different concepts that you can use to trade or invest in the market, depending on your beliefs. I'm not saying that any of these concepts is more valid (or valuable) than any other. In addition, I'm not expressing any personal preferences for any of these concepts. My point in including this chapter is simply to show you how many different ideas there are.[14]

- Tom Basso started out with the discussions by talking about trend following, and he simply expressed the viewpoint that the markets occasionally move one direction for a long time or trend. These trends can be captured and form the basis for a type of trading. The basic philosophy is to find a criterion to determine when the market is trending, enter the market in the direction of the trend, and then exit when the trend is over or the signal proves to be false. It's an easy technique to follow, and it makes good money if you understand the concepts behind it and follow it consistently.

- Chuck LeBeau discussed the next concept, fundamental analysis. This is the actual analysis of supply and demand in the market, and many academics think it is the only way one can trade. The concept typically does give you a price objective, but your analysis (or some expert's analysis) may have no relationship to what prices actually do. Nevertheless, some people trade fundamental data quite well, and this is another option for you to consider. Chuck gives seven suggestions for you to follow if you wish to follow this concept. However, he only discusses fundamental analysis as it applies to the futures markets, not as it applies to equities. That is covered in future chapters.

- Next, Jerry Toepke discussed the concept of seasonal tendencies. Seasonal analysis is based upon the fundamental qualities of certain products to be higher priced at some times during the year and lower priced at other times. The result is a concept that combines both the supply and demand analysis of fundamental analysis and the timing value of trend following. It's another way to play the markets if you make sure that there is a valid reason for any seasonal tendencies that you find.

- Kevin Thomas, a floor trader on the LIFFE exchange, talked about spreading. The advantage of spreading is that you are trading relationships between products instead of the products themselves. As a result, new opportunities are available which could not come to you any other way. Kevin gives some wonderful examples of spreads in his discussion.

- Arbitrage, presented by Ray Kelly in a very humorous and artful way, is looking for opportunities that have a very narrow window of opportunity. While the window is open, the opportunity is like "free money." However, sooner or later the window shuts and then the arb player must find new opportunities. Ray gives many examples of such windows and gives some humorous stories of his frustrations in trying to capture some of them.

- Neural networks represent somewhat of a technology, rather than a concept. Computers can be trained to make predictions, as expert Louis Mendelsohn showed us. If that prediction is then combined with some other trading technique, as Mendelsohn suggests, you could have some interesting trading. However, the emphasis of the neural network, in my opinion, must be on the areas that make people money—such as exits and position sizing—not on the areas that excite people's biases.

- The final concept presented was a synopsis of many—there is an order to the markets. There are many theories that claim to understand some magic order to the markets. There are three types of order concepts: (1) based upon waves of human emotion, (2) based upon large physical events influencing human behavior, and (3) based upon mathematical order. Many of them may have little or no validity, and yet all of them can be traded profitably—just as random entry can be traded profitably. In this last discussion, you learned how to take one of the order concepts (if one of them appeals to you) and use it to your advantage. Such concepts are probably excellent for people who feel that they must know how markets work before they can commit themselves to trade.

NOTES

1. Expectancy will be discussed extensively in the next chapter. It is one of the most important topics that you need to understand as a trader or investor.

2. The CFTC requires that commodity trading advisors include a statement in their advertisements and disclosure documents that says that past results do not reflect upon future results.

3. Tom Basso can be reached by e-mail at tom@trendstat.com.

4. You can reach Chuck LeBeau at 310-791-2182.

5. I don't want to get off on a tangent discussing how to make life's decisions; that's a subject more suitable to one of Dr. Tharp's enjoyable seminars. The point is that you can easily and successfully combine fundamental and technical analysis in your trading.

6. See the Recommended Readings in Appendix I.

7. Moore Research Center, Inc., can be reached at 1-800-927-7257.

8. An old correlation that is right better than 80 percent of the time says that if an old AFL team (Denver being one) wins the Super Bowl, then the market will go down. If an old NFL team wins, then the market will go up. Obviously, an old AFL team won the 1998 Super Bowl and you also know how much the market has gone up as of May 1, 1998.

9. John Murphy, *Intermarket Technical Analysis* (New York: Wiley, 1986).

10. You can reach Ray Kelly at 1-909-698-4088 or at his web page at http://www.traderoasis.com.

11. See the Recommended Readings in Appendix I.

12. Mr. Mendelsohn is president and chief executive officer of Market Technologies Corporation (formerly Mendelsohn Enterprises, Inc.) in Wesley Chapel, Florida. He can be reached by e-mail at Predict@ProfitTaker.com or by phone at 800-732-5407.

13. This information came from an Internet posting by Greg Meadors and by Eric Gatey. The dates of the worst storms were March 23, 1940, August 4, 1941, September 18, 1941, October 2, 1942, February 7, 1944, March 27, 1945, September 23, 1957, April 24, 1960, July 15, 1960, August 30, 1960, November 12, 1960, April 14, 1961, and September 22, 1963. See http://www.mindspring.com/edge/home.html.

14. I haven't included a number of concepts, such as scalping, statistical trading, counter trend following, hedging, etc., simply because doing so would turn this chapter into a lot more than it was intended to be.

CHAPTER 6

Understanding Expectancy and Other Keys to Trading Success

He who thinks he knows, doesn't know. He who knows that he doesn't know, knows.

Lao Tse

When I told one of my clients that I was going to write a chapter in this book about expectancy, his response was, "Oh, no, knowing about that is one of our edges." However, I don't think expectancy is a trade secret. In fact, in my opinion, there are six key variables that must be included in a successful trading system. None of these variables are what most people would call "trade secrets." Before we go into the details of expectancy, let us explore these six variables that have such large effects on the profits and losses of a trader or investor.

THE SIX KEYS TO INVESTMENT SUCCESS

This chapter is probably the most difficult to understand in the book. The material is complex, but it is critically important if you want real success as a trader or investor! In order to simplify the material as much as possible, I have elected to repeat it through different metaphors many different times. You only have to "get it" once, however, to really understand the incredible benefits these variables can unleash for you.

Let's think about trading or investing in terms of the following variables:

1. Reliability, or what percentage of time you make money. For example, if you made 10 stock trades and made money on 6 of them, then your reliability is 60 percent. It's the number of winning trades you make divided by the total number of trades. Sometimes, reliability is called the "hit rate." Basically, it is the percentage of time you get to be "right" in your system.

2. The relative size of your profits compared with your losses when traded at the smallest possible level (i.e., one share of stock or one futures contract). For example, the relative size of your profits and your losses would be the same if you lost $1 per share on losing trades and made $1 per share on winning trades. However, the relative size would be quite different if you made $10 per share on winning trades and only lost $1 per share on losing trades. It would now be 10 to 1.

You can get a good idea of the relative size of your profits to your losses by taking the average size of your winning trades and comparing that with the average size of your losing trades. This will give you a rough idea of relative size. However, you might have one giant profit and many small losses, so this is not an exact measure.

A more exact measure would be to think of your gains as multiples of the initial risk (R) that you took in the trade. Thus, your gains might be a whole series of R multiples. For example, let's say you are willing to risk $500 on a trade (i.e., you'll get out immediately if you have a $500 loss so that it doesn't get any bigger). Your basic risk is $500. Thus, a $1,000 gain is a 2-$R$ multiple and a $5,000 gain is a 10-$R$ multiple. And if by some misfortune, you have a $1,000 loss, then you'll have a 2-R loss. You'll learn more about R multiples later in this chapter.

3. Your cost of making an investment or trade. This is the destructive force on your account size whenever you trade due to execution costs and brokerage commissions. Quite often, people simply include these costs when figuring the average gain or the average loss. However, it is also wise to be aware of just how big these costs are for you.

4. How often you get the opportunity to trade. Now imagine holding the first three variables constant. Their combined effect depends upon how often you trade. Let's say the combined effect of the first three variables is that you make 20 cents per dollar risked. That means that if you make 100 trades, each risking $100, you will end up with a total profit of $2,000.[1] However, now imagine that it takes one day to make 100 trades. You'd make $2,000 per day. Now compare that with a system that makes 100 trades each year—you'd only make $2,000 per year trading. The opportunity factor makes a big difference.

5. The size of your trading or investing capital. The effect of the first four variables upon your account depends significantly upon the size of your account. For example, even the cost of trading will have a significant effect on a $1,000 account. If it costs $100 to trade, then you would take a 10 percent hit on each trade before you'd make a profit. You'd have to average more than 10 percent profit per trade just to cover the cost of trading. However, the impact of the same $100 in costs becomes insignificant if you have a million dollar account.

6. Your position-sizing model or how many units you trade at one time (i.e., 1 share of stock versus 10,000 shares of stock). Obviously, the amount you win or lose per share is multiplied by the number of shares traded.

Different trades probably will have different risk levels, or different Rs. Thus, a 1-R loss probably will not be the same for trade X as for trade Y. Your reaction might be to say, "What good is the concept of R if it varies all over the place?" The value comes in through position sizing. For example, if you risk a constant percentage of your equity, like 1 percent, then you will be equating each 1-R risk. If you have $100,000, then you would only take a $1,000 risk (i.e., 1 percent) on each position. Thus, if 1 R is a single dollar on one trade, you would purchase 1,000 shares. If 1 R was $10 on another trade, then you would purchase 100 shares. In each case, your 1-R risk would be a constant, representing 1 percent of your equity. We'll be discussing position sizing in much more detail later in this book.

Would you want to focus on just one of those six variables? Or do you think that all six of them are equally important? When I ask the question in that manner, you probably agree that all six variables are important.

However, if you were to devote all your energy to focusing on just one of those variables, which one would it be? Perhaps you think this question is a little naïve since all of them are important. Nevertheless, there is a reason behind this question, so write your answer in the space provided.

ANSWER:

The reason I asked you to focus on one item is because most traders and investors often only focus on one of the six items in their day-to-day activity. Their focus tends to be on the need to be right. People are obsessed with it to the exclusion of all else. Yet if all six components are important to success, you can begin to understand how naïve it can be to just focus on being right.

The first four variables are part of the topic I call expectancy. They are the primary focus of this chapter. The last two variables are part of what I call money management or position sizing. We'll touch upon position sizing in this chapter, and we'll focus on it in detail in Chapter 12.

THE SNOW FIGHT METAPHOR[2]

To illustrate the importance of all six variables, let me guide you through a metaphor that might give you a different perspective from one of just thinking about money and systems. Imagine that you are hiding behind a large wall of snow. Someone is throwing snowballs at your wall, and your objective is to keep your wall as large as possible for maximum protection.

Thus, the metaphor immediately indicates that the size of the wall is a very significant variable. If the wall is too small, you couldn't avoid getting hit. But if the wall is massive, then you are probably not going to get hit. Variable 6, the size of your initial equity, is a little like the size of the wall. In fact, you might consider your starting capital to be a wall of money that protects you. The more money you have, assuming the other variables stay the same, the more protection you will have.

Now imagine that the person throwing snowballs at you has two different kinds of snowballs—white snowballs and black snowballs. White snowballs are a little like winning trades. They simply stick to the wall of snow and increase its size. Now imagine the impact of having a lot of white snowballs thrown at you. They would simply build up the wall. It would get bigger and bigger and you would have more protection.

Imagine that black snowballs dissolve snow and make a hole in the wall equivalent to their size. You might think of black snowballs as being "antisnow." Thus, if a lot of black snowballs were thrown at the wall, it would soon disappear or at least have a lot of holes in it. Black snowballs are a lot like losing trades—they chip away at your wall of security.

Variable 1, how often you are right, is a little like focusing on the percentage of white snowballs. You would naturally want all the snowballs coming to your wall to be white and add to your wall. It's probably easy for you to see how the people who don't focus on the big picture might devote all their attention to making as many snowballs as possible be white.

But let's consider the relative size of the two kinds of snowballs. How big are the white and black snowballs relative to each other? For example, imagine that the white snowballs are the size of golf balls, while the black snowballs are like 6-foot-diameter boulders. If that were the case, it would probably only take one black snowball to break down the wall—even if white snowballs were being thrown at the wall all day. On the other hand, if the white snowball was the size of a 6-foot boulder, then one snowball each day would probably build up the wall enough to protect you from a continual bombardment of black snowballs the size of golf balls. The relative size of the two kinds of snowballs is equivalent to variable 2 in our model—the relative size of profits and losses. I hope that by visualizing the snow fight metaphor you can understand the importance of variable 2.

Variable 3, the cost of trades, is a little like assuming that each snowball has a slight destructive effect on the wall—regardless of whether it is white or black. Each white snowball has a slight destructive effect on the wall, that is, less, one hopes, than its effect in building up the wall. Similarly each black snowball destroys a little of the wall just by hitting it, and this simply adds to the normal destructive effect of black snow upon the wall. Clearly, the size of this general destructive force could have an overall impact on the outcome of the snowball fight.

Let's assume that our snowballs only come at the wall one at a time. After 100 snowballs have hit the wall, the condition of your wall will depend upon the relative volume of white and black snow hitting the wall. In our model, you can measure the effectiveness of the snowball fight by the condition of the wall. If the wall is growing, it means that the total volume of white snow hitting the wall is greater than the total volume of black snow hitting the wall. And the growing wall is like growing profits. You'll feel more secure as it gets bigger. If the wall is shrinking, then it means that relatively more black, than white, snow is hitting the wall. Eventually, your wall will lose all its protection and you will no longer be able to play the game.

The relative volume of white versus black snow hitting the wall is essentially the snow fight equivalent of expectancy. If relatively more black snow arrives, then the wall will shrink. If relatively more white snow arrives and if the destructive factor of the snowballs is not too great, then the wall will grow. The relative volume of white versus black snow depends both upon the percentage of white and black snowballs and upon the relative size of the two kinds of snowballs. However, the bottom line is the net amount of white or black snow impacting upon the wall.

In the real world of investing or trading, expectancy tells you the net profit or loss that you can expect over a large number of single-unit[3] trades. If the total amount of losing trades is greater than the total amount of winning trades, then you are a net loser and have a negative expectancy. If the total amount of winning trades is greater than the total amount of losing trades, then you are a net winner and have a positive expectancy.

Notice that in the expectancy model you could have 99 losing trades, each costing you a dollar. Thus, you would be down $99. However, if you had one winning trade of $500, then you would have a net payoff of $401 ($500 less $99)—despite the fact that only one of your trades was a winner and 99 percent of your trades were losers. Let's also say that your cost of trading is $1 per trade, or $100 per 100 trades. Using this cost factor in the prior example, you would only have a net profit of $301. Are you beginning to understand why expectancy is made up of all of the first three variables? And just as the effect on the wall was the result of the net volume of black versus white snow, the effect on your equity is the result of the net profits minus the net losses.

Now let's continue our snow fight metaphor just a little further. Variable 4 is essentially the frequency at which snowballs are thrown. Let's say that the cumulative effect of 100 snowballs (white and black) is to add about 10 cubic inches of snow to the wall. Obviously, if a snowball is thrown once each minute, the impact will be 60 times greater than if a snowball is thrown once each hour. Thus, the rate at which snowballs are thrown will have a major impact on the status of the wall.[4]

The frequency of your trades will have a similar effect in the rate of change of your equity. If you make $500 net after 100 trades, then the amount of time it takes you to make those 100 trades will determine the growth of your account. If it takes you a year to make 100 trades, then your account will only grow by $500 per year. If you make 100 trades each day, then your account will grow by $10,000 per month (assuming 20 trading days per month), or $120,000 per year. Which method would you want to trade? One that makes $500 per year or one that makes $120,000 per year? The answer is obvious, but the methods could be exactly alike (i.e., in that both have the same expectancy). The only difference is the frequency of trading.

On the basis of our discussion of the snow fight metaphor, which of the six variables do you think are most important now? Why? What is the basis of your conclusion? I hope that at this time you can see how important variables 1 through 4 are. These are the basis for expectancy, and they determine the effectiveness of your trading system.

Variables 5 and 6—the size of the wall and the position-sizing variables—are the most important factors in your overall profitability. You should already understand how important the size of the wall (variable 5) is in playing the game. If the wall is too small, then a few black snowballs could destroy it. It must be big for protection.

Let's look at variable 6, the variable that tells you how much. Up to this point we've just assumed that our snowballs arrive at the wall one at a time. But imagine the impact of having snowballs arriving in large numbers at the same time. First, imagine the impact on the wall of one black snowball the size of a golf ball hitting the wall. It would make a single, golf-ball-sized dent in the wall. Now, imagine 10,000 of them hitting the wall simultaneously. It totally changes the impact of your thinking, doesn't it?

The metaphor of 10,000 snowballs simply illustrates the importance of position sizing—that part of your system that tells you how much. We've been talking about one unit of size up to now—one snowball or one share of stock. But 10,000 black snowballs the size of golf balls could totally demolish your wall unless the wall is massive.

Similarly, you might have a trading method that only loses a dollar per share of stock when it loses. However, when you purchase your stock in units of 10,000, your loss suddenly become enormous. It's now $10,000! Again, notice the importance of position sizing. If your equity is a million dollars, then a $10,000 loss is only 1 percent. But if your equity is just $20,000, then a $10,000 loss is 50 percent.

Now that you have the perspective of seeing all the key variables involved in the success of your system (or your snowball fight), we can focus in on the details of expectancy.

LOOKING AT EXPECTANCY UNDER A MAGNIFYING GLASS

Expectancy, as defined in this book, tells you how much you can expect to make on the average (over a number of trades) per dollar risked. So how do you find out the expectancy of a game or a system? Suppose that you are going to play a game drawing marbles. The bag from which you will draw your marbles contains 60 blue marbles and 40 black marbles. According to the rules of the game, when you draw a blue marble, you win the amount you risked, and when you draw a black marble, you lose the amount you risked. Each time a marble is drawn, it is replaced. Notice that you now have a definition for both variables 1 and 2 for this game. What is the expectancy of this game? How much can you expect to win, on the average, per dollar risked?

In this case, expectancy is defined by Formula 6–1:

Formula 6–1: Expectancy = (PW * AW) less (PL * AL)

where PW is the probability of a winning trade and PL is the probability of a losing trade. AW refers to the average gain (win) and AL refers to the average loss.

In the game, PW = 0.6 and PL = 0.4. The average amount won or lost in this game is $1—you win or lose exactly what you risk. So for each dollar risked, you either win a dollar or lose a dollar. Therefore, in our game:

Expectancy = (0.6 * 1) less (0.4 * 1) = 0.6 − 0.4 = 0.2

In this particular game, you could expect to make 20 cents for every dollar you risk on the average over many trials. This means that you'd get your dollar back plus make 20 cents on the average over many trials.

This certainly doesn't mean that you'll win every time. Indeed, in this particular example, you'll only win about 60 percent of the time. In fact, over 1,000 trials you could easily have 10 losses in a row. However, over that same 1,000 trials, you'll make on the average 20 cents per dollar risked. Thus, if you risked $2 on each one, you'd probably make $400 over the 1,000 trials.

What would happen if our bag of marbles were more complex, like the average system investing in the market? Let's say you have a number of different possibilities of winning and losing. For example, let's say you have a bag of 100 marbles of a number of different colors. And let's give each color a different payoff according to the matrix given in Table 6–1.

Once again, we'll assume that a marble is replaced in the bag once it is drawn out. Notice that the chances of winning are only 36 percent in this game. Would you want to play it? Why or why not? What's the expectancy of this game? How much will you make per dollar risked on the average playing this game? Is it better or worse than the first game?

Fortunately, the normal formula for expectancy is additive. Thus, Formula 6–1 can be transformed as follows into Formula 6–2:

Formula 6–2: Expectancy = $\Sigma_{(i\,=\,1\,to\,n)}$ (PW$_i$ * AW$_i$)

less $\Sigma_{(i\,=\,1\,to\,n)}$(PL$_i$ * AL$_i$)

T A B L E 6–1

Marble Payoff Matrix

Number and Color of Marbles	Win or Lose	Payoff
50 black marbles	Lose	1:1
10 blue marbles	Lose	2:1
4 red marbles	Lose	3:1
20 green marbles	Win	1:1
10 white marbles	Win	5:1
3 yellow marbles	Win	10:1
3 clear marbles	Win	20:1

The summation sign indicates that the formula is additive. In other words, you can add all the positive expectancies (i.e., the winning marbles) and then all the negative expectancies (i.e., the losing marbles). You can then subtract the total negative expectancy from the total positive expectancy to get the expectancy of the game.

Let's go through the process step by step. First, let's look at (PW*AW) for all the winning marbles and add them up.

1. For green, PW = 0.2 and AW = 1; therefore (PW * AW) = 0.2 * 1 = 0.2.
2. For white, PW = 0.1 and AW = 5; therefore (PW * AW) = 0.1 * 5 = 0.5.
3. For yellow, PW = 0.03 and AW = 10; therefore (PW * AW) = 0.03 * 10 = 0.3.
4. For clear, PW = 0.03 and AW = 20; therefore (PW * AW) = 0.03 * 20 = 0.6.

Now, let's add them all up: 0.2 + 0.5 + 0.3 + 0.6 = 1.6. This gives us the total positive expectancy in the game.

Second, let's look at (PL * AW)—the negative expectancy—for all the losing marbles and add them up.

1. For black, PL = 0.5 and AL = 1; therefore (PL * AL) = 0.5 * 1 = 0.5.

2. For blue, PL = 0.1 and AL = 2; therefore (PL * AL) = 0.1 *
   2 = 0.2.
3. For red, PL = 0.04 and AL = 3; therefore (PL * AL) = 0.04 *
   3 = 0.12.

Once again, let's add them all up: 0.5 + 0.2 + 0.12 = 0.82. This is
the total negative expectancy of the game.

Finally, the total expectancy of the game is the difference in the
two sums. We find the difference by subtracting the total negative
expectancy (0.82) from the total positive expectancy (1.6). The resulting answer is 0.78. Thus, over many marble draws in this game, you
could expect to make 78 cents per dollar risked. Notice that this
game is nearly four times more profitable than the first game.

Just with the two examples, you should have learned a very
important point. Most people look for trading games that have a
high probability of winning. Yet in the first game, you have a 60
percent chance of winning, but only a 20 cent expectancy. In the second game, you only have a 36 percent chance of winning, but your
expectancy is 78 cents. Thus, game 2 is almost four times as good as
game 1—assuming the same opportunity factor. Notice that the key
factor in your system is not the probability of winning. Instead, the
key factor in determining the value of your system is its expectancy
per dollar risked.

It's important to put in a word of caution here. Variables 5 and
6 are critically important to your profitability. *You can only realize
your expectancy over the long term if you size your positions
wisely according to how much equity you have.* Position sizing is
that part of your system that tells you how much to risk per position. It's a critical portion of your overall system, and we'll discuss
it extensively in Chapter 12.

But let's look at an example just to see how position sizing and
expectancy go together. Suppose you are playing game 1—the 60
percent marble game. You have a $100 total and you start playing
the game. Let's say you start the game by risking your entire $100
on the first draw. You have a 40 percent chance of losing and you
happen to draw a black marble. That can happen, and when it does,
you will have lost your entire stake. In other words, your position
size (i.e., bet size) was too large relative to your equity to be safe.
You cannot play any more because you don't have any more

money. Therefore, you cannot realize the 20-cent-per-dollar-risked expectancy over the long run playing the game.

Let's look at another example. Suppose you decide to risk 50 percent of your stake on each draw, not 100 percent. Thus, you start out with a $50 bet. You draw a black marble and you lose. Now your stake is down to $50. Your next bet is 50 percent of what's left, or $25. Again, you lose. You now have $25 left. Your next bet is $12.50 and you lose again. You are now down to $12.50. Three losses in a row are quite possible (i.e., about one chance in five with three consecutive events) in a system that only wins 60 percent of the time. You must now make $87.50 just to break even—that's an increase of 700 percent. You're not likely to make that much at all. Thus, because of improper position sizing, you've again failed to obtain your expectancy over the long run.

Remember that your position size on a given trade must be low enough so that you can realize the long-term expectancy of your system over many trades.

At this point, you might say that you control your risks by your exits, not your position size. However, remember the snow fight metaphor. Risk is essentially variable 2, the size of the wins compared with the size of the losses.

> ...your position size on a given trade must be low enough so that you can realize the long-term expectancy of your system over many trades.

That's what you control by your exits. Position size is essentially another variable (variable 6) on top of the relative size of the gains and losses. It tells you position size relative to your equity.

Opportunity Factor and Expectancy

There's one other variable involved in evaluating your system that's just as important as its expectancy. That factor is opportunity, our fourth variable. How often can you play the game? For example, suppose you could play either game 1 or 2.

However, you are only allowed to draw one marble every 5 minutes playing game 2, whereas you are allowed to draw one marble every minute playing game 1. Under those conditions, which game would you rather play?

Let's look at how the opportunity factor changes the value of the games. Suppose you could play the game for an hour. Since you could draw a marble every minute in game 1, you'd have an opportunity factor of 60, or 60 chances to play the game. Since you could draw a marble every 5 minutes in game 2, you'd have an opportunity factor of 12—or 12 chances to play the game.

Remember that your expectancy is the amount you would win per dollar risked over a large number of opportunities. Thus, the more times you can play a game, the more likely you are to realize the expectancy of the game.

In order to evaluate the relative merits of each game, you must multiply the number of times you can play the game by the expectancy. When comparing the two games over an hour, assuming that you only risk $1 each time, you'll get the following results:

Game 1: Expectancy of 20 cents times 60 opportunities = $12.00
Game 2: Expectancy of 78 cents times 12. opportunities = $9.36

Thus, given the opportunity restraints that we arbitrarily imposed, game 1 is actually better than game 2 assuming you only risked $1 each time. And when you evaluate expectancy in the market, you must give similar consideration to the amount of opportunity your system presents you. For example, a 50 cent expectancy system (after transaction costs) that gives you three trades per week is much better than a 50 cent expectancy system (again after transaction costs) that gives you one trade each month.

Prediction[5]

Let's pause for a moment to discuss a common trap for most traders and investors—the prediction trap. Thinking about the concept of expectation a bit will allow one to more clearly see why so many people have been tripped up over the years making *predictions* of what a market or stock will do in the future. They all base their prediction algorithms on history—sometimes even assuming that it will repeat exactly. However, an extremely successful prediction can even result in losing all of your capital. How? You can have a method that is 90 percent accurate and still lose all of your money trading it.

Consider the following *"system"* that has 90 percent winning trades, where the average winning trade is $275, and 10 percent losing trades, where the average losing trade is $2,700:

$$\text{Expectation} = (0.9 * 275) - (0.1 * 2,700) = -22.5$$

The expectation is negative. This is a system through which you get to be *right 90 percent of the time and you eventually lose all your money trading it.* There is a strong psychological bias to be *right* about what we do with our investments. In most people, this bias greatly overrides the desire to make a profit overall in our approach, or it inhibits us from reaching our true profit potential. Most people have overwhelming needs to control the market. As a result, they end up with the market controlling them.

It should be clear to you by now that it is the combination of the payoff and the probability that allows you to determine whether a method is viable or not. You also have to consider variable 4 (how often you get to play the game) to determine the relative worth of a system or method.

EXPECTANCY AND *R* MULTIPLES

So far we've been dealing with bags of marbles. In each bag of marbles, we know what the population of marbles is, what the probability of each marble being drawn is, and what its payoff is. None of those things are true when we deal with trades that our system generates in the market.

When you play the market, you don't know the exact probability of winning or losing. In addition, you don't know exactly how much you are going to win or lose. However, you can do historical testing and get some idea what to expect. You also can get large samples of data from real-time trading or investing. You can use either of those samples to get a general idea of the expectancy of your system. This effort entails investigating individual trades in an attempt to understand the **reward-to-risk** ratio of each trade and its frequency of occurrence. After thoroughly performing this exercise, you will have a far greater understanding of the true nature of your methodology.

If you are purely a discretionary, nonsystematic trader, you can review your past trading results to develop insight into how

you are either making or losing money. Following a similar procedure to what we will present here, you should look at each trade on
a *one-lot* or *one-share* basis. Knowing what your risk was going into
the trade (your initial exit point) and the closed profit and loss, you
can then calculate your **reward-to-risk** ratio for each trade.

R Multiples[6]

I refer to a trade's reward-to-risk ratio as an "*R* multiple"—*R* simply being a symbol for the initial risk. To calculate a trade's *R* multiple, simply take the number of points captured at the exit of the
position and divide by the initial risk. You can just as easily use dollar values per contract or per 100-share lot. For example, if you
risked $500 and made $1,500, you would have an *R* multiple of 3.
An example is shown in Figure 6–1.[7] The entry was on 8/4/97 at
2,511. The system uses a 3-times the average true range (ATR, see
definitions) stop which was 104 points. Thus, the initial exit is at

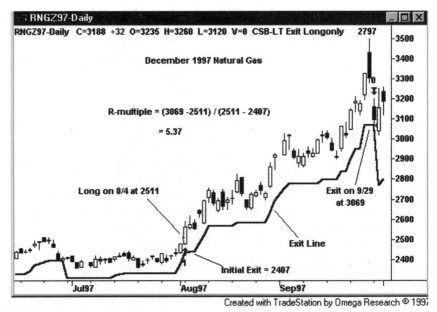

Created with TradeStation by Omega Research ® 1997

Figure 6–1 Multiples in a trade

2,511−104, or 2,407. The system eventually exits on 9/29/97 at 3,069 for a profit of 558 points. Since the initial risk (1 R) was 104 points and the final profit was 558 points, the profit was a 5.37 R multiple. Do this for all trades, winning and losing. The losing trades will simply be a negative R multiple.

The many individual R multiples that compose a historical simulation or previous trading results are the components of your expectation. The nature of these R multiples will totally determine your method's overall expectation. It will help you to define the appropriate money management algorithm to apply to the trading method to meet your overall objectives. By the *nature* of the R multiple I am referring to the size, frequency, and order of the individual R multiples.

For a moment, think of your system's trades solely as R multiples. Then pretend that each trade is simply a marble being drawn from a bag as in our previous examples. Once you draw the marble, you determine its R multiple and then replace it into the bag.

In playing this game you want to develop a position-sizing algorithm that is supportive in exploiting the expectation. In addition, you want it to be linked to the initial risk for each trade and the ongoing account equity. For starters, consider a percent risk algorithm where you decide to continuously risk a constant percentage of current account equity. This sort of position-sizing algorithm basically means that a 1-R risk becomes the same, no matter when it is taken or in what stock or market it is taken. This is because your position size is always a constant percentage (i.e., 1 percent) of your equity no matter how big the initial risk (R) is. See Chapter 12.

In addition, you want to consider the potential *distribution* (the order) of the marbles being drawn. The system's winning percentage is inversely proportional to the length of strings of losing trades. Therefore, you need a position-sizing algorithm that will allow you to withstand potential substantial strings of losing trades while being able to exploit the big winning trades.

Many traders have failed to trade a sound system because (1) they were not prepared for the distribution of trades that the markets presented to them through their method and/or (2) they were overleveraged or undercapitalized. You can estimate the maximum

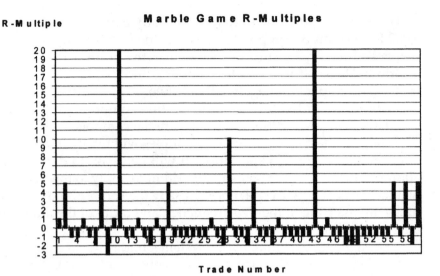

Figure 6–2 Multiples in a marble game

number of losing trades in a row for 1,000 trials given the winning percentage of the system, but you really never know the "true" value. Even flipping a fair coin can yield some lengthy streaks of heads in a row, for example.

Figure 6–2 shows the distribution of trades for one 60-trade sample of a marble game such as the one described in Table 6–1. Note the lengthy losing streak between trades 46 and 55. It's about this time that many people playing the game develop one of two opinions: (1) They decide it's *time* for a winning marble to be drawn or (2) they decide to bet against the expectation at some future point in the game so they profit from streaks like these. If the losing streak happens early in the game, opinion 2 is common. If the losing streak happens late in the game, then opinion 1 is common. The psychology of some participants forces them to bet bigger the deeper they go into a losing streak since they "know" a winner is just around the corner. I'm sure you can guess the typical results of such a game.

Figure 6–3 shows the equity curves for the above game betting a constant 1.0 percent, 1.5 percent, and 2.0 percent of current equity for each trade (and staying completely calm and detached the

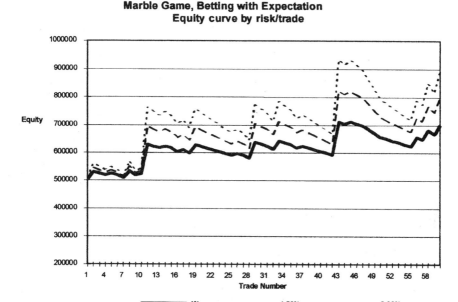

Figure 6–3 Equity curves on marble games according to bet size

whole time). The return for the 60 trials at 1.0 percent was 40.1 percent and the peak-to-trough drawdown was 12.3 percent. There
were three significant losing streaks of 5, 6, and 10 trades.

Figure 6–4 shows the equity curve betting a constant 1.0 percent of current equity **against** the expectation. Here you get to be
"right" 64 percent of the time and even enjoy a 10-trade winning
streak while you lose 37 percent of the starting equity.

If we were trying to better understand how this system works,
we would probably evaluate at least 10 times as many trades. At
that point we could make a better decision about the position-sizing (in this case, bet sizing) algorithm to use and the leverage level.
In addition, we would be able to train ourselves on what to expect
from this system in future trades.

We could develop mental rehearsals for many scenarios that
we could dream up that may occur in the future—rehearsing how
we will respond given each outcome. Keep in mind that even then
you don't know *for sure* what the marble bag (or the market) will

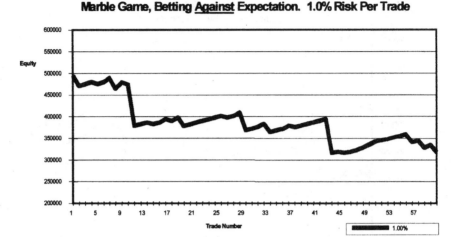

Figure 6–4 Equity curve betting with the probabilities and against the expectancy

reveal in the future. That's why part of your mental rehearsal should include rehearsing how you will respond to an event for which you are not prepared.

EXPECTANCY APPLIED TO THE MARKET

At a recent seminar, one of our attendees asked me why he should bother calculating expectancy when he could just look at his overall profits. The reason is simple. Expectancy is a way of comparing trading systems while factoring out the effects of time, position sizing, and the fact that one is trading various instruments that have different prices.

Let's look at a sample expectancy problem as it applies directly to investing in the market. Suppose you have a trading system that you've traded for 2 years. It has generated 103 trades, 60 of them winners (58.3 percent) and 43 of them losers (41.7 percent). The distribution of your trades is shown in Table 6–2 using only the effect of trading one unit per trade (i.e., minimal position sizing).

Total profit = $54,147; total loss = $43,304; net profit = $10,843

From the table we can calculate that expectancy = (0.417 *

T A B L E 6–2

Trades Produced by a Sample System over 2 Years

Winning Trades			Losing Trades		
$ 23	$ 17	$ 4	($ 31)	($ 18)	($ 16)
$ 12	$ 32	$ 8	($ 6)	($ 23)	($ 15)
$ 6	$ 489	$ 532	($ 427)	($ 491)	($ 532)
$ 611	$ 431	$ 563	($ 488)	($ 612)	($ 556)
$ 459	$ 531	$ 476	($ 511)	($ 483)	($ 477)
$ 561	$ 499	$ 521	($ 456)	($ 532)	($ 521)
$ 458	$ 479	$ 532	($ 460)	($ 530)	($ 477)
$ 618	$1,141	$ 995	($ 607)	($ 478)	($ 517)
$1,217	$1,014	$ 832	($ 429)	($ 489)	($ 512)
$ 984	$ 956	$1,131	($ 521)	($ 499)	($ 527)
$1,217	$ 897	$1,517	($ 501)	($ 506)	($ 665)
$1,684	$1,501	$1,654	($ 612)	($ 432)	($ 564)
$1,464	$1,701	$2,551	($ 479)	($ 519)	($ 671)
$2,545	$2,366	$4,652	($1,218)	($ 871)	($1,132)
$14,256			($ 988)	($1,015)	($ 978)
			($1,123)	($1,311)	($ 976)
			($1,213)	($1,011)	($ 993)
			($ 876)	($1,245)	($1,043)
			($1,412)	($1,611)	($3,221)
			($1,211)	($ 945)	($1,721)
Average gain = $1,353.68			Average Loss = ($721.73)		

$1,353.68) less (0.583 * $721.73) = ($564.48) less ($420.77) = $143.71. Obviously, when you have samples of data, you can also take the net profit and divide that by the number of trades and get the expectancy.

Notice that this figure is quite different from the expectancies we got from the marble bags. The reason is that it is not stated as "an expectancy per dollar risked." Thus, it's important to reduce your expectancy down to expectancy per dollar risked. In addition,

TABLE 6-3

Groupings of Gains and Losses

	Gains			Losses	
Range	Number	Total Gain	Range	Number	Total Loss
Scratch	7	$ 112	Scratch	6	($ 109)
$ 500	15	$ 7,760	$500	33	($17,081)
$ 1,000	10	$10,384	$1,000	17	($18,149)
$ 1,500	6	$ 9,521	$1,500	3	($ 4,744)
$ 2,500	3	$ 7,462	$3,000	1	($ 3,221)
$ 4,500	1	$ 4,652			
$14,000	1	$14,256			
Total		**$54,147**			**($43,304)**

it's important to determine just what sort of "marbles" make up your expectancy. Table 6–3 shows such distribution of gains and losses from this sample of trades. The trades are grouped into ranges of $500, simply because it was convenient and because $500 seemed to best describe the minimum loss.

When you look at a distribution of profit-and-loss groupings, you might notice that the minimum loss[8] has a particular value. In this particular distribution, that minimum loss is about $500. We can now look at the table somewhat like a bag of marbles and notice what to expect. Here we calculate the payoffs by dividing the approximate gain or loss by the approximate minimum loss of $500. Table 6–4 is the result of performing this action.

This system essentially made money on 40 percent of its trades (i.e., 36/90)—not counting the scratch trades. Since the total profitability of the system is about $10,000, you'll also notice that the entire profit is due to one trade—the one that gave you a $14,256 profit. Also notice that by just eliminating one loss—the $3,221 loss—you would increase your profits by 40 percent.

You need to look at these trades in detail. What produced the large gain? Can you expect to have more of them in the future? Is the real probability of such a gain about 0.011 percent, or can you figure out a way to produce more of them?

TABLE 6–4

Groupings of Gains and Losses as a Function of the Minimum Amount Risked (Assumed to Be $500)

	Gains			Losses	
Payoff	Probability	Positive Expectancy	Payoff	Number	Negative Expectancy
1 to 1	15/90 = 0.167	$7,760	1 to 1	33/90 = 0.367	($17,091)
2 to 1	10/90 = 0.111	$10,384	2 to 1	17/90 = 0.189	($18,149)
3 to 1	6/90 = 0.067	$9,521	3 to 1	3/90 = 0.033	($4,744)
5 to 1	3/90 = 0.033	$7,462	6 to 1	1/90 = 0.011	($3,221)
9 to 1	1/90 = 0.011	$4,652			
28 to 1	1/90 = 0.011	$14,256			

How about the losses? What produced the $3,221 loss? Is the true expectancy of that loss about 1.1 percent, or can you expect to have a lot more of them (or a lot less)? Was the loss due to psychological mistakes? If so, how can you avoid it in the future?

When you look at your system in terms of a payoff matrix as in Table 6–4, you can begin to answer a lot of questions. We can apply expectancy Formula 6–2 to determine the expectancy per dollar risked. Here we get the following positive expectancy by adding the positive expectancy from the set of winning trades:

Positive side of expectancy Equation = $(0.167 * 1) + (0.111 * 2)$
$+ (0.067 * 3) + (0.033 * 5) + (0.011 * 9) + (0.011 * 25)$

When we complete the multiplication, we get the following: 0.167 + 0.222 + 0.199 + 0.165 + 0.099 + 0.275 = 1.127. Thus, our total positive expectancy from the winning trades is $1.127.

Now we need to find the negative expectancy of the losing trades by determining the contribution of each group of losing trades as follows:

Negative side of expectancy equation = $(0.367 * 1) + (0.189 * 2)$
$+ (0.033 * 3) + (0.011 * 6) = 0.367 + 0.378 + 0.099 + 0.066 = 0.91$

Thus, our total negative expectancy from the losing trades is 91 cents.

Once again, to get the total expectancy per dollar risked we need simply to subtract the total negative expectancy from the total positive expectancy—$1.127 less $0.91 = $0.217. Thus, the expectancy of this system, per dollar risked, is 21.7 cents. This gives us a better basis for comparing this system with another. A $10,000 profit might make a system seem great, but knowing that the system produces a return of 21.7 cents per dollar risked puts it in a different perspective.

USING EXPECTANCY TO EVALUATE DIFFERENT SYSTEMS

Let's look at two different trading systems to determine how expectancy might be used.

Fred's System

The first system comes from an option trader named Fred. From May 1 through August 31, he's completed 21 trades, as shown in Table 6–5.

The system made $1,890.43 over 21 trades during the 4-month period. This amounts to an average gain of $90.02 per trade. But what is the expectancy of the system per dollar risked? We can break the table down into arbitrary dollar groupings, as shown in Table 6–6.

Since the minimum loss seems to be about $150 for Fred's trading, we'll convert Table 6–6 into a probability matrix (Table 6–7) with $150 being the minimum amount risked. We'll also delete the scratch trades, leaving a total of 18 trades.

Let's apply Formula 6–2 to this matrix to determine an approximate expectancy per dollar risked. First let's calculate the positive expectancy of the winning trades. The positive expectancy is equal to $(0.056 * 1) + (0.056 * 2) + (0.056 * 3) + (0.056 * 8) + (0.111 * 13) + (0.056 * 25)$. If we perform the multiplication, we end up with

$$0.112 + 0.168 + 0.448 + 1.443 + 1.4 = \$3.627$$

Next, we must calculate the negative expectancy created by the losing trades. The negative expectancy is equal to $(0.111 * 1) +$

TABLE 6–5

Fred's Option Trading Summary

	Gains	Losses
	$2,206.86	($143.14)
	$1,881.86	($68.14)
	$3,863.72	($543.14)
	$181.86	($1,218.14)
	$1,119.36	($143.14)
	$477.79	($3,866.57)
	$48.43	($340.64)
	$327.36	($368.14)
	$21.80	($368.14)
		($358.14)
		($493.14)
		($328.14)
Total	$10,129.04	($8,238.61)
N	9	11
Average	**$1,125.45**	**($748.96)**

TABLE 6–6

Dollar Grouping of Fred's Trades

Gains		*Losses*	
Range	Number	Range	Number
Scratch under $75	2	Scratch under $75	1
$100–$150	1	$150–$200	2
$325–$375	1	$325–$375	5
$475–$550	1	$475–$550	2
$1,200	1	$1,200	1
$2,000	2	$2,000	0
$3,800	1	$3,800	1

T A B L E 6–7

Fred's Trades as a Probability Matrix

Gains		Losses	
Payoff	**Probability**	**Payoff**	**Probability**
1 to 1	1/18 = 0.056	1 to 1	2/18 = 0.111
2 to 1	1/18 = 0.056	2 to 1	5/18 = 0.278
3 to 1	1/18 = 0.056	3 to 1	2/18 = 0.111
8 to 1	1/18 = 0.056	8 to 1	1/18 = 0.056
13 to 1	2/18 = 0.111	13 to 1	0
25 to 1	1/18 = 0.056	25 to 1	1/18 = 0.056

$(0.278 * 2) + (0.111 * 3) + (0.056 * 8) + (0.056 * 25)$. If we perform the multiplication, we end up with

$$0.111 + 0.556 + 0.333 + 0.448 + 1.4 = \$2.848$$

When we subtract the negative expectancy from the positive expectancy to obtain the total, we get the following: $3.627 less $2.848 = $0.779. Thus, Fred's system produces an expectancy of about 78 cents per dollar risked over the 4-month period of trading. Remember that a lot of rounding went into these calculations.

The biggest fault with Fred's system is that it has a giant 25-to-1 loss that offsets the one 25-to-1 gain. Without that one loss, Fred would have an outstanding system. As a result, Fred needs to study that loss and see if similar losses can be prevented in the future.

Ethel's System

Next, let's look at another group of trades—which we'll call Ethel's system. Ethel made these stock trades over a 1-year period. Ethel had one gain of $5,110 from the purchase of 1,000 shares of stock, another gain of $680 from the purchase of 200 shares of stock, and a loss of $6,375 from the sale of 300 shares of stock. All the rest were 100-share purchases. As a result, we will enter these gains and losses as if they were each a round lot of 100 shares to eliminate the

TABLE 6-8

Ethel's Stock Trading Summary

	Gains	Losses
	$511	$2,125
	$3,668	$1,989
	$555	$3,963
	$1,458	$589
	$548	$1,329
	$3,956	$477
	$340	$1,248
	$7,358	$501
	$499	$503
Total	$19,396	$12,221
N	10	8
Average	**$1,939.60**	**$1,527.63**

effect of position sizing. Table 6–8 shows a summary of Ethel's stock trading.

The system made $7,175 over 18 trades during the year. This amounts to an average gain of $398.61 per trade. Remember that Fred's system only made $90 per trade. In addition, Ethel's system makes money 55.6 percent of the time, while Fred's system only makes money 45 percent of the time. Ethel obviously has a better system. Or does she?

Let's look at the expectancy per dollar risked of Ethel's system and the opportunity factor. When these factors are considered, does Ethel have the better system? Table 6–9 shows the various dollar groupings of Ethel's system. Ethel had three minimum losses that were about $500 each—one of $477, one of $501, and one of $589. Thus, we'll assume that Ethel's minimum risk was about $500. We can develop a probability matrix for Ethel's trades as shown in Table 6–10.

Once again, let's apply Formula 6–2 to the matrix in Table 6–10 to determine an approximate expectancy per dollar risked. First, let's calculate the positive expectancy of the winning trades. The

T A B L E   6–9

Dollar Grouping of Ethel's Trades

Gains		Losses	
Range	**Number**	**Range**	**Number**
$300–$600	6	$300–$600	3
$1,200–$1,600	1	$1,200–$1,600	2
$1,750–$2,250	0	$1,750–$2,250	2
$3,500–$4,000	2	$3,500–$4,000	1
$7,300–$7,500	1		

T A B L E   6–10

Ethel's Trades as a Probability Matrix

Gains		Losses	
Payoff	**Probability**	**Payoff**	**Probability**
1 to 1	6/18 = 0.333	1 to 1	3/18 = 0.168
3 to 1	1/18 = 0.056	3 to 1	2/18 = 0.111
4 to 1	0	4 to 1	2/18 = 0.111
8 to 1	2/18 = 0.111	8 to 1	1/18 = 0.056
15 to 1	1/18 = 0.056		

positive expectancy is equal to $(0.333 * 1) + (0.056 * 3) + (0.111 * 8) + (0.056 * 15)$. If we perform the multiplication, we end up with a total positive expectancy of the following:

$$0.333 + 0.168 + 0.888 + 0.840 = \$2.229$$

Now we need to find the total negative expectancy of the losing trades. That negative expectancy is equal to $(0.168 * 1) + (0.111 * 3) + (0.111 * 4) + (0.056 * 8)$. If we perform the multiplication, we end up with a total negative expectancy of the following:

$$168 + 0.333 + 0.444 + 0.448 = \$1.393$$

When we subtract the total negative expectancy from the total positive expectancy, we end up with 2.229 less $1.393 = $0.836.

Ethel's expectancy of 84 cents per dollar risked is bigger than Fred's expectancy of 78 cents per dollar risked. In terms of expectancy, Ethel has a slightly better system.

Remember that Fred's profit was mostly a function of one good trade. Well, the same is also true of Ethel's profit. Her one profit of $7,358 was bigger than her entire 1-year net profit of $7,175. Thus, one trade made her entire profit over the 1-year period. This is quite often true of good long-term systems.

But what about the opportunity factor? Fred produced 18 trades in 4 months—actually more than 18, but some of them were excluded because they were scratch trades amounting to a gain or loss of less than $100. In 2 years, Fred might produce three times as many trades. Let's compare the expectancy times the number of opportunities for a 1-year period to really evaluate the systems.

Fred's System			Ethel's System		
Expectancy	Opportunities	Total	Expectancy	Opportunities	Total
78 cents	54	$42.12	84 cents	18	$15.12

When you look at the two systems in terms of expectancy times opportunities, then Fred has a much better system. However, this assumes that both investors made the maximum use of their opportunities.

The comparison of the two systems brings up an interesting variable with respect to opportunity. Ethel only made 18 trades in a 1-year period. But this did not necessarily mean that she only had 18 opportunities to trade. An investor only makes the maximum use of his or her opportunities under the following conditions: (1) He or she is fully invested (i.e., makes full use of the position-sizing algorithm) when there are opportunities to trade; (2) he or she has an exit strategy and exits the market when that strategy is triggered; and (3) he or she makes full use of other opportunities when cash is available to do so. If any of these three criteria is not met, then the comparison of systems by expectancy and opportunity is not necessarily a valid one.

A REVIEW OF HOW TO USE EXPECTANCY

Just as a review, once you have a system, or at least a rudimentary system, you need to calculate its expectancy and look at a number of issues involving expectancy. Here are the steps involved.

1. **Calculate the overall expectancy of your system.** If you already have a system that you have been using or have tested, you can calculate the expectancy of the system by simply dividing the total profit by the number of trades. Note that you do not yet have the expectancy per dollar risked at this point.

2. **Eliminate the effects of position sizing by only considering single units or 100-share blocks.**

3. **Divide your trades into groups of profits and losses, using $100 or $500 ranges depending upon the size of the typical smallest loss.** Your smallest loss relates to where you typically put your disaster stops. This is your system's 1-R level. In this step, you are simply assessing the expectancy of your system, not trying to improve it.

4. **Convert your groupings of trades into a probability matrix by using your "smallest loss" as a single unit.** This will help you find your expectancy per dollar risked.

5. **Calculate the expectancy of your system from the probability table using Formula 6–2.**

6. **If your system includes at least 100 trades and has an expectancy above 50 cents per dollar risked, then it is a good system.** These are just general guidelines for a good long-term system. You can be happier with a much lower expectancy if you get enough opportunity.

7. **Determine the opportunity you will have to obtain your expectancy.**

Look at the size of the "marbles" determined in your probability matrix. What do your marbles tell you about your system? How can you change your system to include more high-payoff winning trades? How can you change your system to include fewer high-cost losing trades?

Remember the following:

1. *Expectancy and probability of winning are not the same thing. People have a bias to want to be right on every trade or investment.* As a result, they tend to gravitate toward high-probability entry systems. Yet quite often these systems are also associated with large losses and lead to negative expectancy. As a result, always take your risk in the direction of the expectancy of the system.

2. *Even with a high positive expectancy system you can still lose money.* If you risk too much on a trade and you lose, you can (and probably will) have trouble recovering.

NOTES

1. $100 times 100 times 0.2 = $2,000. This assumes that your 100 trades actually net 20 cents per dollar risked.

2. Adapted from *Market Mastery*, January, 1998.

3. One share of stock or one futures contract would be a single unit.

4. This would seem to imply that if the cost of trading is factored in, it's better to trade more frequently than less frequently. While this assumption is true, it doesn't take into account the psychological wear and tear that comes from frequent trading.

5. This section was written by Chuck Branscomb and originally appeared in our *Market Mastery* newsletter (November 1996, pp. 3–5, and December 1996, pp. 2–6). It has been adapted for this chapter.

6. This section was written by Chuck Branscomb and originally appeared in our *Market Mastery* newsletter (November 1996, pp. 3–5, and December 1996, pp. 2–6). It has been adapted for this chapter.

7. Figure 6–1 was generated using TradeStation®. TradeStation is a registered trademark of Omega Research.

8. This value does not count scratch trades in which you either quickly get out for some reason or raise your stop to break even and then get out. What we are looking at is the typical minimum risk you have on a trade.

PART THREE

Understanding the Key Parts of Your System

This section is designed to help you construct your system. However, before you begin this section, you should thoroughly understand Parts I and II of the book. They form the necessary groundwork that you must have before you begin the actual construction.

Chapter 7 talks about setups. Setups are conditions that are necessary in order for something else to occur. I've put the setups chapter first, because most entry and exit systems usually consist of a setup plus a trigger for action. In Chapter 7, you'll learn about the most common entry setups—both for the stock market and for the futures market. These are all setups used by master traders and investors. Quite often they are promoted as systems all by themselves, and people tend to accept that because of the lotto bias. However, you'll be able to combine these setups with other critical parts of a system to create something that really is worthwhile.

Chapter 8 discusses entry techniques. Your entry technique essentially controls the reliability of your system—how often it makes money. However, you should know by now that reliability is not nearly as important as your expectancy in evaluating a system. In addition, reliability can be high, while expectancy can be negative—as illustrated in one of the problems in the last chapter. You'll also learn that entry becomes less and less significant to your trading as your time frame becomes longer. Chapter 8 will show that most entry techniques are not much better than random entry, but it will also give you the few entry systems that seem to produce system reliability that is higher than you might expect from just random entry.

The topic of Chapter 9 is taking losses with your system. Every system should have a method of getting out of the market to preserve capital. This is the "disaster stop" part of your system. It's one of the most important criterion of any system. We'll be discussing the purpose behind such disaster stops and the advantages and disadvantages of wide stops and narrow stops.

One of the most important topics of this volume is how to take profits. Profit-taking exits are the topic of Chapter 10. We'll be discussing the purpose of various exits, the advantages of multiple exits, and the importance of simplicity in your exits. You'll learn how to develop exits to meet the objectives you developed earlier.

Chapter 11 is about opportunity and cost factors—topics that are seldom discussed elsewhere. You'll learn that you don't need to be anywhere near perfect if you have enough trading opportunities. However, cost becomes a very important factor as you trade more.

The discussion in Chapters 7 through 11 is not exhaustive. Our goal is simply to give you techniques that work and to avoid discussing, except in a general way, techniques that do not work. My intention is not to give you a complete system. If I did that, it wouldn't be right for you. My intention is to give you the tools and help you overcome your psychological biases so that you can develop a system that is right for you.

We'll also be illustrating the parts of a system by showing you what is commonly known about some well-known trading systems. You can see what parts everyone focuses on and how you can improve them by emphasizing what everyone neglects. My goal is in no way to criticize these systems, since most of them are well known and they all have some excellent qualities. In fact, if you like one or more of them, I'd encourage you to go to the original source to learn more information. My goal in these chapters is to review them in enough detail so that you can find out what their strengths and weaknesses are and perhaps even improve upon them.

One of the more important topics of the whole book is discussed in Chapter 12—position sizing. Position sizing is the key topic behind any Holy Grail trading system. It's the difference between the ho-hum trading methodology and the world's best methodologies. It's a topic that few people think about, yet much more effort should be put into position-sizing strategies than into any other part of your system. Chapter 12 is designed to start you heading in the right direction.

Coverage of the topic of position sizing has been very inadequate in the past. In fact, most books on system development don't even cover it. You'll learn why in Chapter 12, and we'll give you a lot of ideas to get you started in the right direction. You'll also learn some ideas with respect to position sizing that are seldom, if ever, applied to the stock market, but that will give exceptional returns when they are used.

Finally, Chapter 13 concludes the book by addressing many of the issues that are important, such as data, software, testing procedures, portfolio design, and the management of other people's money.

CHAPTER 7

Using Setups

Speculation, in its truest sense, calls for anticipation.
Richard D. Wyckoff

Setups refer to conditions that must occur before other action is taken. They are an essential aspect of most entry and exit portions of any system. I've chosen to discuss them first, because they form a foundation for the subsequent discussions on entry and exit techniques.

Many of the ideas presented in the "concepts" chapter (Chapter 5), for example, simply have to do with setups for entry. For instance, the concept having to do with "there being an order to the market" in most cases simply gives you a window of opportunity during which you can expect a substantial move in the market—that window is nothing more than a time setup. It certainly is not an entry signal, nor a trading system.

For example, I recently consulted with an expert in Elliott Wave—one of the "there's-an-order-to-the-universe" concepts. He claimed that he was right on about 70 percent of his ideas, but only 30 percent of his trades made money. He typically had a very tight stop below his exit to preserve his capital. Quite frequently, the market would take him right out of a position. Thus, he would have to enter three or four times in order to capitalize on the idea. In addition, by the time the market went against him three or four times, he was often too nervous to reenter the market and would subsequently miss the move. Other times, he would be right about the idea, but the market would start to move so violently that he felt there was too much risk to take the move. Essentially, this trader's problem was confusing what is essentially a setup (i.e., the right conditions with respect to Elliott Wave analysis) with an entire trading system. He had no real entry criteria (as defined in the next chapter), and he had no way of capitalizing on the great reliability of his idea because he got stopped out too often.

We corrected both problems with ideas that you'll learn about in Chapters 8 and 9. However, the critical issue is a problem that most investors and traders have—they confuse their setups with a complete trading system. Most investors and traders buy books on their craft that consist of nothing but such setups. If the setups are accompanied by enough best-case examples, then the author can usually convince his or her readers that the book contains the Holy Grail.

If you learn one critical thing from this book, it should be that a setup is about 10 percent (or less) of your trading system. Most people will place 90 percent of their emphasis on finding the right setups, but setups are actually one of the least important parts of the system.

Let's look at another concept—fundamental analysis—to help you understand how setups come out of various concepts. Fundamental analysis simply gives you a number of conditions which, when favorable, suggest that the market is ripe for entry on the long or the short side.[1] Those conditions might mean that the market is overvalued or undervalued because of supply-and-demand conditions. However, fundamentals do not give you anything about timing—they simply indicate that conditions are ripe (i.e., set up) for an entry at some time in the future. The actual market move might not occur for months after the signal is "ripe" for a move.

To better understand what a setup condition means, let's talk about the four phases of entry into the market. Generally, every trader or investor should give some thought to each of these four phases.

THE FOUR PHASES OF ENTRY

Market Selection

The first consideration you should give to entering the market is your selection of what markets you will trade. What qualities must a market have before you want to be a part of it?

Give some thought to using one or more of the following criteria:

1. *Liquidity.* How active is the market (or security) you are planning on investing in the future? Basically, the issue is one of liquidity, which has to do with the ease of getting into or out of the market at the bid or ask price—or even in the spread between the bid and ask price. If the market is fairly illiquid, then that spread could be huge and you would have to pay a large price (beyond commissions) just to get in and out of that market.

Liquidity is a major factor in entry. Why? If you have substantial size, then the price might move a significant amount in an illiquid market simply because of your presence. On the other hand, if you are a small trader—who could enter into an illiquid market quite easily—you might want to avoid such markets because a "foolish" large trader might enter into those markets, causing a significant move just because of his or her presence.

Stock market traders, for example, might want to avoid stocks that trade less than 10,000 shares per day. This means that a simple round lot would be 1 percent of the daily activity. That could be a problem for you when you want to get into or out of that market.

2. *Newness of the market.* Generally it's best to avoid a new market—whether it's newly created futures contracts or stocks that have just been introduced onto the exchange. A lot of mistakes are made in such new issues because you have little idea of what the underlying product is going to be. On the other hand, if a market has been around at least a year, you'll have a much better idea of what to expect.

Some people specialize in new issues. Certainly, in strong bull markets, new stock issues often tend to go up rapidly. *They also collapse rapidly.* Perhaps your "edge" might be that you keep on top of enough information about new companies that you feel safe investing in new issues. However, just remember that this is a dangerous area for amateurs.

3. *Market makers and trading rules.* What exchange makes a market for the underlying investment, and do you know its rules of trading? In essence, who is behind the market you are trading? Who are the market makers? What is their reputation? What can you expect when you deal with these people? Who regulates these market makers? What's likely to happen if you put a stop order on at one of these exchanges? Is that order something that is executed easily for your benefit, or is it a license to steal?

For example, certain stock and commodity exchanges are much more difficult to trade than other exchanges. It's much more difficult to get good fills. If you have experience trading markets on these exchanges, and know what to expect, then it's probably okay to trade them. On the other hand, if you are new to the market, then it's probably best to trade only the most well-established exchanges—such as the New York Stock Exchange, the Chicago Board of Trade, or the Chicago Mercantile Exchange.

Overseas markets can also be great opportunities or disasters waiting for the uninitiated trader to step in. Find people who have traded the markets you want to trade. Ask them what to expect. What are worst case scenarios? Make sure that you can tolerate such worst-case scenarios before you trade in those types of markets.

4. *Volatility.* Volatility essentially means how much price movement has occurred within a specific time frame. Day traders, for example, need to trade highly volatile markets. Since they are typically out of a position at the end of the day, they need to trade markets that normally have enough volatility to allow for large profits even though they will still be out at the end of the day. Typically, only certain currency markets, the stock indexes, and the bond markets qualify as good markets for day traders.

If you happen to be trading a system that trades turning points in consolidating markets, then you probably need to select markets that have enough volatility to make that sort of trading worthwhile. Again, volatility of the markets would be an important consideration.

For both day trading and consolidation market trading, you need enough volatility to still make a profit that is two to three

times the size of your initial risk. This should be your most important criterion in selecting your markets.

5. *Capitalization.* Stock traders often select stocks on the basis
of capitalization. Some investors only want highly capitalized
stocks, while other investors only want low-capitalization stocks.
Let's look at the possible reasons for each criterion.

Typically, speculative investors who are looking for sharp
moves in the market want low-capitalization stocks (under $25 mil-
lion). Research has proved that low-cap stocks account for the
majority of stocks that go up by 10 times or more. Generally, as
demand for the stock goes up, the price will rise dramatically if
there is little supply, because there are only a few million shares
outstanding.

On the other hand, conservative investors don't want a lot of
price fluctuation. They don't want to see the price rising a point on
a 1,000-share order and then falling a point again on another 1,000-
share order. Instead, they want slow, smooth changes in price. You
are much more likely to see this kind of behavior in highly capitalized stocks with several hundred million shares or more outstanding.

6. *Markets and trading criteria.* How well does that market
follow your trading criteria—be it trendiness or seasonality?
Generally, no matter what your trading criteria are, you need to
find markets that fit those criteria well. And the less capital you
have, the more important this selection process is to you.

Thus, if you are a trend follower, you need to find markets that
trend well—be they stocks that show good relative strength or
futures markets that typically show good trends several times each
year. When the market typically has met your trading criteria in the
past, it probably will do so again.

The same goes for any other criteria you may be trading. If
you follow seasonal patterns, then you must trade markets that
show strong seasonal tendencies—agriculture products or energy
products. If you follow Elliott Wave, then you must follow those
markets for which Elliott Wave seems to work best. Whatever your
trading criteria seem to be, you must find the markets that best
meet those criteria.

7. *Selection of a portfolio of independent[2] markets.* This topic
is somewhat beyond the scope of this introductory book on devel-

oping a system. However, I would suggest that you look at the independence of the various markets you select. You will profit most by selecting markets that are relatively independent because you will be more likely to have at least one market that is in a legitimate profit-making trend than you will if all your markets are related or dependent.

Market Direction

Whether you are trading a market turning point or jumping on board a fast-moving trend, most people need to assess the predominant direction that the market has been moving in over the last 6 months. You need to understand what kind of "animal" you are dealing with in "today's" market. This is the long-term trend of the market.

Ed Seykota, who has made millions trading the markets, once told me that he would take a chart of the market, hang it on the wall, and walk to the other side of the room. If the trend of the market was obvious from the other side of the room, then it was a market that he would consider. Eds style had a lot of merit in the 1960s and 1970s when there were a lot of long-trending markets. Although the principle behind it is still valid, shorter criteria might be more appropriate now that market trends tend to be shorter.

Generally, people make money in up markets or down markets. However, there are really three directions in which the market can move—up, down, or sideways. Markets tend to trend—move up or down significantly—about 15 to 20 percent of the time. The rest of the time, they move sideways. You need to be able to assess when those conditions occur. For example, a lot of traders have systems that constantly keep them in the market. However, if you accept sideways as a condition of the market, then you probably want a system that will keep you out of the market the 70 percent of the time in which you are not likely to make money. You simply need some sort of signal to monitor when sideways is occurring. Perry Kaufman has developed an excellent vehicle for doing so. We will explore it later in this chapter.

The person who is always in the market is going to spend a lot of time in sideways markets, which could mean losses and high commissions. Thus, you might want to take a look at avoiding sideways markets as a part of your methodology.

Setup Conditions

Setup conditions, as mentioned earlier, are conditions that must occur, according to your concept, before you enter the market. When you have such setup conditions, they generally improve your chances of a significant move in your favor.

Most people make money in the markets because the market moves a significant amount from the entry point. The various concepts discussed in Chapter 5 are all designed to detail the conditions under which you can expect a significant market move. Generally, all these concepts consist of market setups.

Setups might consist of:

- A window of opportunity during which you might expect a turnaround
- Fundamental conditions that must exist before you enter the market
- Seasonal situations that might attract your attention
- Any of a number of other significant criteria that might be useful

Setups are not usually criteria for entering the market. Instead, they are necessary criteria that you should expect before you will even consider taking a position in the market.

Different kinds of setups that have proved themselves are the topic of this chapter. We'll be talking about setups that are useful for the stock market and setups that are useful for futures markets, forex[3] markets, option markets, or other speculative areas. In fact, you'll learn that many publicly offered systems, because of the lotto bias described in Chapter 2, consist of nothing but setups. But first let's discuss the last phase of entry—market timing.

> ...many publicly offered systems, because of the lotto bias described in Chapter 2, consist of nothing but setups.

Market Timing

Let's say you've selected the markets you want to trade. You understand your concept, and the current predominant direction of the market fits your concept for trading. You also have several market setups, and those conditions have also been met. However, one more key criterion should exist before you actually enter the market—the move you are expecting should start. In other words, if you are predicting a large up move in the market—because of fundamentals, a seasonal pattern, an expected turning point date, or any other reason—chances are that your move will not have begun at the time you first predict it. Profitable traders and investors usually wait for the move to begin before they enter the market.

As you'll see in the next chapter on entry, very few entry techniques beat a simply random entry—a coin flip at a random time to determine whether to go long or short in the market. Consequently, you need to do whatever you can to improve your odds. The best way of improving your odds is to make sure the market is moving in the direction you are expecting before you enter the market. This is basically your timing signal. We'll be discussing a number of significant timing signals in Chapter 10.

SETUPS FOR STALKING THE MARKET

Readers who are familiar with my home-study course on peak performance trading and investing know that one of the ten tasks of trading is called "stalking." It amounts to shortening your time frame to find entry conditions to make your risk even lower. Short-term setups constitute the best stalking tools.

There are many of these, so I will simply present three categories of short-term setups and give an example of each. My comments about these setups simply reflect my own opinion about them. Connors and Raschke have written a book, *Street Smarts*, covering many different short-term setups for those of you who would like a lot more detail. If you actually plan to trade these patterns, I'd suggest that you study their book.

"Failed-Test" Setups

Test setups are basically failed tests of a previous high or low. After that high or low occurs, many interesting patterns occur. The Ken Roberts method, given below, for example, is based upon a failed-test setup.

The reason such tests can work is because they are commonly used as entry signals. These entry signals might set up trades that return big profits, but they are not that reliable. The logic behind tests as an entry signal is to use false breakouts (moving to a new high or low) to set up the trade.

For example, Connors and Raschke have one pattern that they facetiously call Turtle Soup.[4] It's called Turtle Soup because a famous group of traders, called the Turtles, was known for entering the market on 20-day breakouts. In other words, if the market made a new 20-day high, they would enter a long position. Or, in contrast, if the market made a new 20-day low, they would enter into a short position. Today, most of these 20-day breakout signals are false breakouts—in other words, they don't work and the market falls back. Thus, Turtle Soup gets its primary setup from 20-day breakouts that are expected to fail. The Turtles have made a lot of money trading these breakouts (see "Channel Breakouts" in Chapter 8), so be careful here.

Figure 7–1 shows an example of a Turtle Soup pattern. The chart shows several 20-day breakout highs in mid-July. In each case the breakout high is followed by a substantial (albeit short-term) decline. You could make money with each of them as a short-term trader.

If I showed you enough examples of such patterns working, you'd probably get very excited about them. There are a lot of examples that work and many examples that fail. The pattern is only worthwhile, in my opinion, if you can combine it with the other parts of a trading system—such as exits and position sizing—that are really important to making money in the market.

Another high-probability setup is based on the observation that when a market closes in the top part of its trading range, it has a strong probability of opening higher. The converse is also true. This is an extremely high-probability setup with a 70 to 80 percent

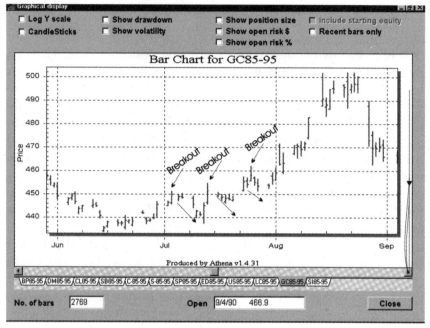

Figure 7–1 Turtle Soup setup

reliability for a more extreme opening in the same direction the next day. This could be used for an exit in a trading system, but it can also be used as a test setup.

Another observation is that even though there is a high probability of the market opening up in the same direction, the probability that it will close in that direction is much lower. In addition, when you have a trending day yesterday (i.e., the market opened up at one extreme and closed at the other), there is an even greater probability of a reversal. Thus, it might provide a basis for a "test-pattern" setup. What you need in this pattern is some sign of a reversal. Three setups are involved in this "test" pattern, as shown in Figure 7–2.

1. In Figure 7–2 look at the pattern beginning on the eighth of December. The market has a trending day—opening up at one extreme and closing at another. That is the first part of the setup.

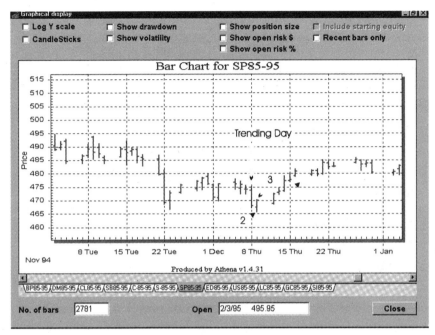

Figure 7–2 Trending day plus follow-through as a "test" pattern setup for entry

2. On December 9 the market continues its move by opening down more (i.e., that's the next part of the setup), shown at point 2 on the figure.

3. The market opens with another move in the same direction as the close (e.g., if it closed lower, then the market opens down even more; if it closed higher, then the market opens up even more). Notice that as the day continues on December 9, the market reverses and goes above yesterday's low close. This is the last part of the setup (and in this case it is actually the entry signal). It's shown at point 3 on Figure 7–2.

Notice in the figure that the market closes higher and then continues to go up for several more days. Remember that all I did was find a graph to illustrate the pattern. Don't get too excited about setups because they are only a small part of the equation for making money.

If your goal is to do short-term trading, or "swing" trading, then failed-test setups are probably what you want to use. Now that you understand the principle involved in failed-test setups—the market tests a new extreme principle and then falls back—you can design your own related setups without needing to rely on the ideas used by others. Experiment on your own!

Climax Reversals or Exhaustion Pattern Setups

These setups follow the same principle as the failed-test set-ups except that there is some additional evidence to suggest that the move is an extreme that will not follow through. These setups are typically designed to pick low-risk trades that signal a reversal of trend. They require, as part of the setup, each of the following:

- A signal that the market has already reached an extreme
- A highly volatile environment
- A move in the direction you want to trade as your entry point

These types of patterns can vary a lot, and many such "climax" moves are typically "chart" patterns that are difficult to objectively describe so that they can be computerized. I tend to dislike using chart patterns because there is strong evidence that many of them might not be "real" patterns that one can objectively trade. Thus, we'll just confine the discussion to a "gap" climax move.

Gap Climax Move

One sign of a climax move is that of the market gapping to a new extreme, but failing to show follow-through. The market then falls back and closes in the opposite direction of the climax move. Another possibility is that the market, on a subsequent day, shows signs of filling the gap. Such setups are based on two observations: (1) Gaps to an extreme tend to be filled, and (2) days that reverse from market extremes tend to have follow-through the next morning.

Here's how you might trade such a move:

1. The market gets to a new extreme (i.e., this is your climax setup).

2. You might want another setup indicating high volatility, such as the average true range of the last 5 days is 2 to 3 times the average true range of the last 50 days. However, this sort of criterion might not be necessary.
3. The market shows signs of weakness such as (a) closing at the opposite end of the range from the extreme or (b) starting to close the gap on a subsequent day.
4. You would then place an entry order, expecting a short-term move against the previous trend.

In my opinion, these patterns are dangerous. What you are attempting to do is stop a freight train that is going very fast. You are hoping it will reverse a little so that you can get something off it (i.e., some profits), knowing that it could take off again going just as fast as it did before.

Climax setups, in my opinion, are primarily for brave short-term traders. The primary use of these setups for long-term traders would be to become familiar enough with them to avoid entering the market around such moves, since they have a high probability for a short-term reversal. If you are interested in such trades, then by all means study the Connors and Raschke book, *Street Smarts.*

Retracement Setups

The next type of setup that you might want to consider in short-term trading (or stalking your long-term trades) is the retracement. Basically, this kind of setup involves (1) finding the longer-term trend of the market; (2) getting some sort of pullback from the trend; and then (3) entering in the direction of the trend based upon some third type of signal such as a resumption of the trend with a new high. These are very old trading techniques. For example, Wyckoff was fond of saying,

Don't buy on breakouts. Wait for the retracement test.

Trend-following signals, once triggered, will usually be followed by some sort of retracement—at least, intraday. That intraday retracement can be used as a low-risk setup for entry. Several such retracements, shown on a daily basis, are clearly visible in

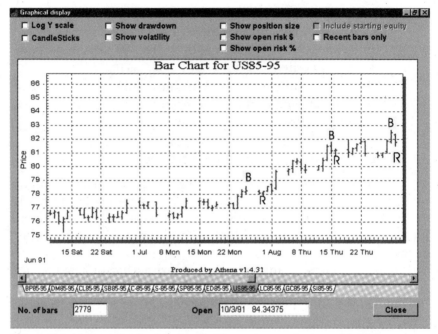

Figure 7–3 An example of a clear trend with numerous retracement setups

Figure 7–3. In each case, a breakout (labeled *B*) is followed by a retracement (labeled *R*).

Figure 7–3 shows a clear breakout signal in bonds from July 23 through July 25. This breakout is followed by a slight retracement on July 28 and 29 and then a very low-risk breakout to a new high on July 30. However, there may have been an even better intraday entry right after the first major breakout on July 23 or perhaps on July 24.

Retracement setups are an excellent consideration for trend followers. They have many advantages in that (1) they allow you to place tight stops and thus extract high reward-to-risk trades; (2) you can use them for short-term "swing" trading or for long-term "position" trading; (3) they give you a way to get into a market that you might have originally missed; and (4) they provide you with an excellent way to get back into a market once you have been stopped out. Consider developing your own retracement setup.

FILTERS VERSUS SETUPS

I used to say that filters were one of the ten critical components of a trading system. Chuck LeBeau, who often is a guest presenter at our system seminars, then usually said during his presentation that you should totally avoid filters. Filters might help you predict the market in hindsight, but they wouldn't help you trade the market in the present.

Let me explain Chuck's comment. Because of the lotto bias, people want to know the perfect entry signal to the market so that they can "control" the market prior to entry. When you are looking at past data, the more you can use indicators to fit the data, the more accurate those indicators will seem to perfectly predict every turn in the data.

> When you are looking at past data, the more you can use indicators to fit the data, the more accurate those indicators will seem to perfectly predict every turn in the data.

Most trading software will have several hundred indicators built into it. You can use those indicators, almost automatically, to totally curve-fit past markets. For example, you can use an oscillator, a moving average, and some cycles and almost perfectly predict what some historical market did at almost any time. The result is that you will probably feel extremely confident about trading, but find that your "highly optimized" indicators do not help you at all when trying to trade today's markets.

Some people try to get around this by optimizing over the short term (i.e., the last several months) in the hopes that indicators optimized for more recent historical data will accurately reflect today's market as well. The task is usually fruitless, however, if too many indicators are used.

Generally, the simpler your system is, the better it will work trading the markets. However, there is one general exception to this rule. Many different indicators will generally help you in trading the market if *each of those indicators is based upon a different type of data.*

This really provides us with a critical difference between filters and setups. Filters typically are based upon the same data and should be avoided in your system. Setups, which are based upon different data, are quite useful. As long as your setups are based upon different, but reliable, data, more is generally better.

Let's take a look at what I mean by different types of data by looking at some of the setups you can use. Here are some of the examples given previously.

> Filters typically are all based upon the same data and should be avoided in your system. Setups, which are based upon different data, are quite useful.

Time Filter

You have some idea when a move is supposed to occur because of your various models. Time is different from price data, so such a setup could be very useful. Time filters might include cycles, seasonal data, astrological influences, etc. Look at Chapter 5 for interesting time setups that might be useful in your trading.

Price Data in Sequence

You might require that your price data occur in a specific sequence. This kind of setup is usually more valuable than simple price data if it's based upon some high-probability relationship that you've observed in the market. Take retracement setups, for example: (1) The market establishes a trend; (2) the market makes a retracement; and (3) the market shows some sort of movement back in the direction of the original trend. These are all price data, but they occur in a specific, logical sequence that has some meaning.

Fundamental Data

You have some idea of what the "supply" and "demand" characteristics are for the market you are trading. For example, you might have statistics for the soybean crop and also some statistics about new foreign demand for this market. For an equity security, you have information on customer acceptance of a company's new product or the success of internal cost reductions. See the discussions of Gallacher and Buffett for some examples of fundamental setups.

Volume Data

The amount of activity in your particular market is quite different from the current price data and could be quite useful. There's a lot written about volume data, especially by stock market experts like Richard Arms. The Arms Index is now given regularly with market updates. It was originally known as the TRIN trading index. This is the ratio of advances to declines divided by the ratio of up volume to down volume.

Here's how you might use it as a setup. Use a moving average of Arms Index (typically use about five days). A reading above 1.2 indicates a potential bottom and a reading below 0.8 indicates a potential top. These are short-term trading opportunities of 1 to 3 days. However, these readings should be combined with an entry signal of price moving in the expected direction.

Composite Data

If your market consists of a number of items, then you might have some valuable information simply knowing what those various items are doing. For example, in the stock market knowing what the market as a whole is doing is quite different, but valuable, information from knowing what each component of the market is doing. How many stocks are advancing? How does the volume of rising stocks compare with the volume of declining stocks?

...People who try to trade a market index, such as the S&P, without looking at anything but the price data of the index could be at a severe disadvantage compared with all the experts who are looking at composite data.

If you are trading a market index, you can look at what all the individual stocks are doing. Generally, people who try to trade a market index, such as the S&P, without looking at anything but the price data of the index could be at a severe disadvantage compared with all the experts who are looking at composite data.

One example of a composite indicator, given with every market update, is the tick. The tick is the difference between all NYSE stocks on an uptick versus those on a downtick. Here's how you might use the tick as a setup. An extreme reading in the tick can often predict a market turn—at least in the short term. Thus, an extreme in the tick would be an example of a test setup. You would simply trade some sort of reversal signal that occurs once this extreme was reached.

Volatility

This refers to the amount of activity in the market and is generally defined by the range of prices. It's generally quite useful information that is very different from just price alone.

Several years ago I conducted a computer trading seminar in which the purpose was (1) to become familiar with some trading software and then (2) to develop some systems that, based upon historical testing, would return 100 percent per year or more without optimizing. I had assumed that most people would do this through developing a high-expectancy trading system using great exits and then combining it with a money management method that would stretch the system to its limits. Most people did it that way, except for one. The one exception found that a measure indicating that the market was in a very narrow range was a potential predictor of a movement of some force. When you combine a narrow-range setup with good entry, you have a great chance of a high reward-to-risk trade.

Here are a couple of ideas for narrow-range setups:

1. The market is in a trend as measured by any number of indicators such as being above or below a moving average, having a high ADX value, etc.
2. The market moves into a narrow range which might be shown by comparing the range of the last 5 days with the range of the last 50 days. The ratio would have to fall below some predetermined value such as the range of the last 5 days being less than or equal to 60 percent of the range of the last 50 days.

You would then need one of the entry signals given in the next chapter. This sort of setup can easily add 10 to 15 cents to your expectancy per dollar risked in a long-term trend-following system.

The second narrow-range setup might be something more like the following:

1. The market has an inside day (i.e., its price range is contained between the high and low of the previous day).
2. The market has the narrowest range of the previous X days.

When you have an inside day of this sort, a breakout in either direction is typically a good short-term trading pattern.

Business Fundamentals

Most of the setups used by Warren Buffett, as well as some of those used by William O'Neil, are business fundamentals. We'll be discussing those in the next section. These might include fundamentals such as: What are the earnings? What is the yield? What are sales? What are profit margins? What are the stock owner's earnings? How many shares are outstanding? What is the book value and what are the earnings per share? How has the business grown? All of this sort of information is quite different from price data.

Management Information

Who is running your potential investment and what is that person's track record? Warren Buffett has several tenets for management. And whether you buy a stock or a mutual fund, the track record of the person behind your investment is probably critical to the success of that investment.

There are probably other types of data that are also useful. For example, if you can find some data that are reliable and that few other people have access to, then you probably can create some very valuable setups for your trading.

Now that you understand that useful setups come from data other than price data, you have the basis to create your own setups. That might be one of the keys to your Holy Grail system.

Don't get caught up in the importance of setups. They will help you increase the reliability of your winners. However, you can still have a highly reliable system that will give you a negative expectancy because you have some very big losers. Spend at least as much time on your system stops and exits as you do on setups and entry. And spend more time on the money management portion of your system than on all the rest of your system put together. If you do that, you'll have a chance to find your Holy Grail.

SETUPS USED BY WELL-KNOWN SYSTEMS

Stock Market Setups

In this discussion of stock market setups, I have no intention of giving you an exhaustive collection of possible setups for use in the stock market. Instead, I think it's much more useful to examine three different approaches that make money in the market. Each method is quite different from the others. And by comparing the setups that are used in each, you'll get a much better understanding of them and be able to invent your own. If any of the systems interests you, I suggest that you study the original source material. All my comments simply reflect my opinions about the various models.

William O'Neil's CANSLIM Model

One of the most successful and widely followed models for trading has been promoted by William O'Neil and David Ryan—the CANSLIM model. O'Neil has presented the model in his book, *How to Invest in Stocks.*[5] The model is also promoted through his newspaper, *Investor's Business Daily,* and his chart service, *Daily Graphs.* Many people have also attended seminars that O'Neil and Ryan have given all over the United States. My purpose here is not to present their model or even evaluate their model. Instead, I'll refer you to one of O'Neil's own fine sources for those purposes. My purpose here is to use the CANSLIM model to illustrate the setups involved in a commonly followed model.

CANSLIM is an acronym—with **all the letters standing for setups.**

C stands for current earnings per share, with O'Neil's criterion being an increase of 70 percent over the same quarter a year ago. Therefore, current earnings per share is the first setup criterion for O'Neil.

A is for annual earnings per share. O'Neil believes that the annual earnings per share over the last 5 years should show at least a compounded 5-year rate of about 24 percent. Again, this is another setup.

N stands for something new about the company. This new factor could be a new product or service, a change in management, or even a change in the industry. It also means that the stock has reached a new high price. Thus, "N" would really be two setups for entry. However, the new high price might actually be the entry trigger signal as discussed in Chapter 8.

S refers to shares outstanding. O'Neil did a study of the best-performing stocks and found that their average capitalization was under 12 million shares, with a median capitalization of only 4.8 million shares. Thus, another setup criterion for O'Neil is a small number of outstanding shares—less than 25 million.

L means leader. O'Neil believes in a relative strength model of the market. People who use relative strength typically rank the change in the price of all stocks over the last 12 months. A stock in the top 75 to 80 percent would probably be one to consider. Some people also give more weight to the amount of change that has occurred in the last 30 days. O'Neil's ranking is probably something of that nature. He says to only pick stocks that he rates above 80 percent—so that's another setup.

I represents institutional sponsorship. It usually takes some institutional sponsorship to produce a leading stock. But a lot of sponsorship is not desirable, since there would be a lot of selling if anything went wrong. In addition, by the time all the institutions have found it, it's probably too late to expect a good move. However, some institutional sponsorship is another setup for O'Neil.

M in the formula stands for what the overall market is doing. Most stocks—75 percent or more—tend to move in the direction of the market averages. As a result, you want to have positive signs for the overall market as a setup, before you buy your stocks.

I've just given you the entire O'Neil Acronym, and **it consists entirely of setup criteria.** You know very little about the actual entry into the market except that the "N" criterion also includes the stock making a new high. In addition, you know nothing about the protective stops, nothing about how to get out of the market, and nothing about the most critical part of a system—position sizing. What most people think of as O'Neil's trading system just consists of his setups. Isn't that interesting? We'll talk more about O'Neil's criteria for other parts of the system when we get to them.

> What most people think of as O'Neil's trading system just consists of his setups.

The Warren Buffett "Value" Model

Warren Buffett has been one of the most successful investors in the world over the last several decades. Buffett has never really written about his approach to the market, but many books have been written about Warren Buffett and his approach to the market. Some of the better ones include *Of Permanent Value*, by Andrew Kilpatrick, *Warren Buffett* by Andrew Kilpatrick, *Buffett: The Making of an American Capitalist* by Roger Lowenstein, and *The Warren Buffett Way* by Robert Hagstrom, Jr. This last book includes a detailed explanation of the author's understanding of Buffett's philosophy of investing. All these books are listed in the Recommended Reading list in Appendix I.

Once again, this is not meant to be a detailed discussion of Buffett's strategy, but simply an overview of the setups that Buffett appears to use. I'd suggest that you go to Hagstrom's book if you are interested in a detailed account of Buffett's strategy. Buffett was selected simply because he has been one of America's most successful investors and his methodology is somewhat unique.

Buffett's real strategy is to buy a business—he does not consider that he is buying stock. Most times, when you buy a business, you have no intention of selling it—and Buffett likes to keep the rumor going, in my opinion, that he doesn't sell most of his holdings. Buffett would advise anyone who wants to learn about investing to learn about every company in the United States that has publicly traded securities and store that knowledge in your head in a way so that it is always available. If you are overwhelmed because there are over 25,000 publicly traded companies, Buffett's advice would be to "start with the A's."

Few people would be willing to do the kind of preparation that Buffett suggests. In fact, most people don't do anything like the research Buffett recommends, even with the few companies they select to actually buy, so you can understand what an advantage Buffett has in finding undervalued companies.

Buffett, according to researcher Robert Hagstrom, has 12 criteria that he looks for before buying any company. Nine of the criteria amount to setups, and the remaining three might be considered entry criteria. Indeed, the entry criteria might also be considered setups. Buffett really isn't concerned about timing since most of his investments are lifetime investments. However, we will discuss his entry criteria briefly in Chapter 8. In this chapter, we look at the nine setups used by Buffett.

The first three setups have to do with the nature of the business. Basically, (1) Buffett needs to be able to understand any business he might own and it must be simple. He's not willing to invest in great high-technology stocks, because he does not understand that sort of business or the risks involved. In addition, (2) the company needs to have a consistent operating history. He wants a long-term track record and tends to avoid companies that are going through any sort of severe change. Buffett believes that severe change and exceptional returns don't mix.

The last business setup that Buffett looks for is that (3) the company can raise prices regularly without any fear of losing business. The only companies that can do this are those that have a product or service that is needed and desired, that has no close substitute, and that has no problems with regulations.

The next three setups that Buffett uses have to do with the management of the company. Running a business, Buffett understands, is a psychological enterprise and depends entirely upon the strength of the management. As a result, Buffett demands that (4) management must be honest with the public. Buffett deplores managers who hide weaknesses in their business behind generally accepted accounting principles. In addition, he believes that managers who are not frank with the public are not likely to be honest with themselves. And self-deception definitely leads to sabotage of their leadership and their company.

The most important task that management does, according to Buffett, is to allocate capital. Buffett's next criterion is to look for (5) managers who are rational in their allocation of capital. If the company reinvests its capital in the company for a return that is less than the average cost of that capital, a very common practice among business managers, then it is being completely irrational. Buffett avoids those companies completely.

Buffett's last management criterion is (6) to avoid managers who tend to be conformists and constantly compare themselves with other managers. These people tend to resist change, develop projects just to use up available funds, imitate peer companies' behavior, and have yes-men working for them who will find reasons to justify whatever their leader wants. Obviously, this type of setup involves intensive study and research into the workings of the company.

Buffett's setups for buying a company also include four financial setups. The first financial setup is that (7) the business must achieve good returns on equity while employing little debt. Return on equity is basically the ratio of operating earnings (earnings less unusual items such as capital gains or losses, etc.) to shareholder equity, where shareholder equity is valued at cost rather than at market value.

Next, Buffett is very concerned about (8) owner earnings. Owner earnings consist of net income plus depreciation, depletion, and amortization less capital expenditures and the working capital necessary to run the company. Buffett says that about 95 percent of American companies require capital expenditures that are equal to their depreciation rates, so that should be considered when estimating owner earnings.

Buffett is very concerned with (9) profit margins. Consequently, he's looking for managers who are in tune with the idea of systematic cost cutting to increase margins. Buffett's market entry is based upon the belief that if you purchase something that's undervalued then the market price will eventually catch up to it so your returns will be superior. We'll be discussing Buffett's market entry in Chapter 8.

Once again, notice that Buffett is like William O'Neil. Most of his thought process goes into the decision to enter the market. However, since Buffett seldom sells a company, once he buys it, his criteria are justified—and his track record adds credence to that justification.

The Motley Fool "Foolish-Four" Approach[6]

I've selected the Motley Fool "Foolish Four" approach as the last stock market model, because it is a very simple approach that *anyone* can follow. Yet it is a good model. Most people can make money using it, and the amount of time required to do so is negligible. It still involves some setup conditions. The setup conditions are in sharp contrast to those of the other two models, so it is again a good illustration of what we are discussing.

The foolish-four approach is derived from some studies popularized by Michael O'Higgins and John Downes in their book, *Beating the Dow*.[7] It requires little work. The trading involves few commissions, and the method has very low risk. O'Higgins found that when one invests in the ten Dow Jones Industrials[8] stocks with the highest yield (or five with the highest yield and lowest price), one can almost double the rate of return of investing simply in the index. That's all there is to it.

The foolish-four approach is based on more research by O'Higgins that suggests that the highest-yielding Dow stock is often a dog, but the second best-yielding stock often yields as much as 30 percent per year. As a result, the foolish-four approach allocates 40 percent of your capital to the second best-yielding stock, and 20 percent of your capital to the third, fourth, and fifth highest-yielding Dow stocks, respectively. That's the whole approach.

Let's look at the setups on this approach, because there are two important ones. First, you have an index criterion. A stock has to be among the Dow Jones 30 Industrials stocks to qualify. Second, you have a setup that consists of uncovering the second through fifth highest dividend yields. That's all there is to the method.

In this case, I'll give you the entry trigger as well, since I won't be discussing a trigger like this one in Chapter 8. The entry is simply to buy the stocks on the first trading day in January—or you could also decide to buy on the day that you decide to implement the technique, such as today. O'Higgins does suggest that you might consider buying stock on November 1 and selling it on the first of May, since those are the best months for the stock market.

In this case, the technique has no stop-loss procedure. It has a profit-taking procedure, which I'll discuss in Chapter 10. And it also has a money management procedure (to allocate 40 percent, 20 percent, 20 percent, and 20 percent of your capital to the second through fifth highest-yielding stocks, respectively). I'll discuss this style of money management in Chapter 11.

The technique is obviously very simple—as are most techniques that work. And it consists mostly of setups, so you can definitely improve upon it by adding other, more critical components.

Futures Market Setups

Now, let's look at some models that have been used for futures trading. Once again, I have no intention of giving you an exhaustive collection of possible setups for use in the futures market. Instead, we'll examine several different approaches that make money in the market and look at the setups involved in those approaches. Once again, I've selected methods that I believe to be sound, and my comments simply reflect my opinions about these methods.

Perry Kaufman's Market Efficiency Model

Perry Kaufman, in his book, *Smarter Trading*,[9] gives some interesting adaptations of trend-following methods. He says that trading in the direction of the trend is a safe, conservative approach to the markets. But trend following must be able to separate the trend from the random noise of the market—the random activity of the market at any given time.

Kaufman argues that longer trends are the most dependable, but they respond very slowly to changing market conditions. For example, long-term moving averages barely reflect a large, short-term price move. Furthermore, when they do provide some sort of signal for action, the price move usually has finished. Thus, Kaufman argues that an adaptive method is necessary for trend following. You need a methodology that speeds up entry when the markets are moving and does nothing when the markets are going sideways. Kaufman's solution to this is to develop an adaptive moving average. I'll refer the interested reader to Perry Kaufman's book (and the brief discussion in Chapter 8) to learn more about this average. Here, we'll just present his "market efficiency" filter, which probably can be adapted to work with almost any type of entry.

Basically, the fastest "trend" that one can use is limited by the amount of noise that is present in the market. As the market gets more volatile (noisy), one must use a slower trend to avoid getting whipsawed in and out of the market. For example, if the average daily volatility is about 3 points, then a 4-point move is not that significant. It could easily "retrace" back into the noise. In contrast, a 30-point move, which might occur over a month or so, is very tradable within a daily background noise of 3 points.

However, at the same time, the faster prices are moving, the less significant the factor of noise becomes. If the market moves 20 points in a single day, then a background noise of 3 points per day is not that significant. Thus, you need some measure of market efficiency that includes both noise and the speed of movement in the direction of the trend. A price move that is either "cleaner" or "faster" can take advantage of a short time frame for entry, whereas a price move that is "noisy" or "slow" must use a longer time frame for entry.

Kaufman's efficiency ratio combines noise and speed. It essentially divides the net price movement between two time periods by the sum of the individual price movements (with each movement assumed to be a positive number). This is essentially a ratio of the speed of the movement to the noise of the market. Kaufman only uses 10 days in which to constantly update the ratio, but the reader could select a larger number.

Here are the formulas for the efficiency ratio:

Movement speed = close yesterday minus close 10 days ago
Volatility   = Σ absolute value [close today minus close yesterday] over the 10 days
Efficiency ratio = movement speed/volatility

The efficiency ratio essentially is a number that ranges from 1 (no noise in the movement) to 0 (noise predominates throughout the movement). This efficiency ratio is an excellent filter that can be mapped onto a range of speeds for a number of different entry signals. Doing so is slightly tricky. Kaufman gives a great example of how to do so with different moving averages. However, you could simply require that this number be above some particular value (i.e., 0.6) as a required setup prior to taking an entry signal.

More details of how Kaufman might trade the markets will follow in subsequent chapters as we explore the effect of other components of a system when added to this method of trading. However, I strongly recommend that you read Kaufman's book if the method interests you.

William Gallacher's Fundamental Trading Method

Gallacher, in his book, *Winner Take All,* provides a scathing critique of system trading[10] and then goes on to show how someone with a fundamental approach can make a lot of money. In this section, I'll show the setups in Gallacher's fundamental trading methodology.

First, Gallacher says that you must select markets according to value—meaning that they are historically "cheap" or "expensive." He says that this can be done for certain markets (i.e., a pound of bacon is cheap at $0.75 and expensive at $3.49), but not for other markets (e.g., gold has gone from $35 an ounce to $850 an ounce to $280 an ounce—so what is expensive and what is cheap?). Thus, the market selection phase of entry is an important part of Gallacher's methodology.

Second, Gallacher says that the trader must develop a critical eye for what is "important" fundamental information to a particular market. He says that what's important is constantly changing, but presents his current opinion about important fundamentals for various futures markets.

For example, he says that annual variations in supply are the big movers in corn. Generally, the corn produced in the United States is the main grain for hog production. Most of it is consumed domestically, with only about 25 percent being exported. The demand is fairly constant. Thus, variations in supply are the major determinants of value for corn. Gallacher says that previous bad markets were sheltered by large carryover stocks from previous harvests. However, he says that when such carryover is historically low, then a bad crop could push prices to very high levels. Thus, for corn the critical fundamental setups would be "carryover" and the amount of supply in the "new crop."

Gallacher goes on in this manner, covering soybeans, wheat, cocoa, sugar, cattle, pork bellies, precious metals, interest rate futures, stock index futures, and currencies. If you are interested in this type of fundamental information, take a look at Gallacher's book. My overall conclusion from this was that it is very difficult to get any precise setups from fundamentals. The only thing you really get is a bias that says (1) neutral, (2) bullish, or (3) bearish—based upon a lot of information which is different for each market. One's real setup, therefore, is simply the opinion you develop after looking at the data.

Once you develop an opinion, Gallacher still believes in using a price entry signal, limiting losses, taking profits systematically, and practicing sound position sizing—all techniques described in later chapters of this book.

Ken Roberts' Method[11]

Ken Roberts has been marketing commodity trading courses to thousands of beginners all over the world. The primary method taught, although several systems are given in his course, is quite simple and involves what I consider to be rather subjective setups. Essentially, the setups require that the market make a major high or low and then show a reversal hook pattern. You open a position when it's "clear" that the major trend is reversing.

> **The market makes a major high or low.** Essentially, in this method, the first setup is for the market to make a 9-month to 1-year high (or low.) Thus, if the market produces the highest high of the last 9 months or the lowest low of the last 9 months, you have the first setup.
>
> **The market makes a 1-2-3 reversal.** Point 1 is the high or low determined in the first setup. The next important setup is for the market to move away from the high or low to what's called point 2. The market then moves back toward the high or low and forms point 3. Point 3 cannot be a new all-time high or low. The market then goes back past point 2 and you

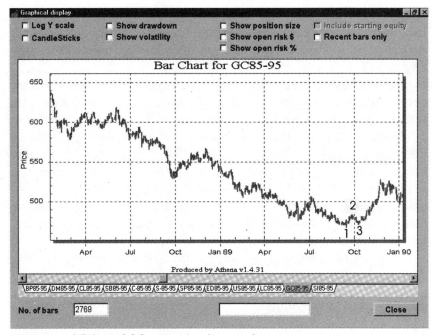

Figure 7–4 A Roberts 1-2-3 pattern in a bear market

have an entry point. Figure 7–4 shows an example of a 1-2-3 pattern.

Both setups in the Roberts' method seem subjective to me. The major high or low is fairly objective, but the exact time parameters under which it occurs are not. In addition, the exact conditions that define the 1-2-3 pattern are quite subjective. Such patterns occur in the market after almost every high that occurs—at least in a short time frame—and Roberts does not define the exact time conditions under which such a pattern must occur. Thus, there is a lot of room for subjective error and for false positives.

Figure 7–4 shows a typical long-term high plus a 1-2-3 bottom. The low comes in mid-September 1990. The market makes a 2 "high" in October and then falls back to a 3 low (that's not quite as low). Notice that the market then goes on to make new highs about a month later.

The problem with illustrating such setups is that your mind looks at them and gets excited about what might be possible. You do not realize how many false positives can occur with any pattern, much less a subjective one. However, this doesn't not mean that you cannot trade such a pattern if you develop proper stops, profit-taking exits, and position-sizing algorithms to go along with it.

Now look at Figure 7–5. It is the same as Figure 7–4, except that I've pointed out three other 1-2-3 patterns on the graph. All of them would have resulted in losses.

Although the methodology is somewhat subjective, it is still sound and is worthy of some consideration. We will be discussing other components of this Ken Roberts' system in subsequent chapters.

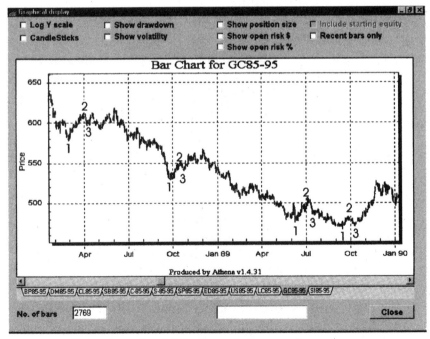

Figure 7–5 Notice three other 1-2-3 patterns in the same figure

SUMMARY OF SETUPS

- Most people give overwhelming importance to the setups in their system. In reality, about 10 percent of your efforts should be devoted to selecting and testing setups.
- There are four components to entering the market: market selection, market direction, setups, and timing.
- Three varieties of short-term trading setups are considered for use in short-term trading or as "stalking tools": tests in which the market hits a new extreme and then reverses, climax or exhaustion patterns as signals to reverse, and retracements that are used as setups for entering with the trend.
- Setups can be very useful as long as they come from a data set other than price. Such data sets might include time, the sequencing of events, fundamental data, volume data, composite data, volatility, business information, and management data. Each of these data sets could be the basis for some useful setups for traders or investors.
- Trying to trade stock market indexes on price data alone is very difficult because your competition is using much more information from other data sets.
- Filters are not very useful additions to trading systems because they just amount to multiple ways of looking at the same data. Such filters will allow you to perfectly predict price changes with historical data, but will not be very useful with today's market data.
- Three stock market systems were reviewed: William O'Neil's CANSLIM system, Warren Buffett's business purchase model, and the Motley Fool-Foolish-Four approach. These systems, as most people know them, are mostly setups.
- Three futures trading systems were reviewed in terms of setups: Perry Kaufman's idea of market efficiency, William Gallacher's fundamental model, and Ken Roberts' model that is so widely promoted around the world.

N O T E S

1. Fundamental analysis for stocks is somewhat different. Here you are looking at the earnings, the book value, the management, and other conditions that tell you about the internal structure of a company.

2. I originally used the word "noncorrelated" here. However, Tom Basso was quick to point out that under extreme conditions all markets tend to become correlated. Thus, "independent" is actually a better word.

3. "Forex" stands for foreign exchange. This is the big market in currencies that is set up by the large banks all over the world. It's a 24-hour market, and it's the largest market in the world.

4. Turtle Soup is a trademark of Connors, Basset, & Associates.

5. See the Recommended Readings in Appendix I.

6. See the Recommended Readings in Appendix I.

7. See the Recommended Readings in Appendix I.

8. Dow Jones Industrials stocks are chosen because the dividend yield approach to investing only works on large-capitalization companies. Small companies with a high yield are probably a sign of trouble.

9. Once again, all references to all the books discussed in this section can be found in the Recommended Readings in Appendix I.

10. To be fair to system trading, Gallacher only presents a simple reversal method—which despite its shortcomings appears to make a return of 350 percent. However, reversal systems keep you in the market all the time and do not have sophisticated exit techniques. Thus, in my opinion considerable improvement could be made to his "best-efforts" system trading method. Nevertheless, his book is excellent and presents some great ideas that most traders will enjoy.

11. Ken Roberts, *The World's Most Powerful Money Manual and Course.* See Recommended Readings in Appendix I for more detail. This method was developed and published by William Dunnigan in the 1950s. That book was reprinted in 1997. See William Dunnigan, *One Way Formula for Trading Stocks and Commodities* (London: Pitman, 1997).

CHAPTER 8

Entry or Market Timing

> Avoiding mistakes makes people stupid and having to be right
> makes you obsolete.
>
> *Robert Kiyosaki*[1]

The basic purpose of entry signals, most people assume, is to improve your timing in the market and thus increase the reliability of your system. I would estimate that 95 percent or more of the people who attempt to design trading systems are simply trying to find a "great" entry signal. In fact, traders are always telling me about their short-term systems that have reliability rates of 60 percent or better. Yet in many cases they are wondering why they are not making money. Unless you started with this chapter, you should know that a system with a high percentage of wins can still have a negative expectancy. The key to money making is having a system with a high positive expectancy and using a position sizing model that will take advantage of that expectancy while still allowing you to stay in the game. Entry only plays a small part of the game of making money in the market. Nevertheless, some energy should be devoted to finding entries that fit your objectives. There are two approaches to doing so.

The first approach is to assume that reliability has some importance and to look for signals that are better than random. In fact, a number of books are on the bookshelves that make the assumption that picking good stocks is all there is to making a fortune in the stock market. They have titles like *How to Buy Stocks the Smart Way, Stock Picking: The Best Tactics for Beating the Market, How to Buy Stocks, How to Pick Stocks Like a Pro,* and *How to Buy Technology Stocks.*[2] We will also make the assumption that reliability can be an important criterion for entry signals in this chapter and talk about some potentially good signals.

The second approach is to focus, not on reliability, but on finding entry signals that will give you high-*R*-multiple trades. This approach is totally different from the first approach, because it makes a totally different assumption about what is important to making big profits. While both approaches are valid, the second approach has the potential to totally change the way people think about trading.

Readers who have studied my *Peak Performance Course for Traders and Investors* know the importance of "stalking" the market. Stalking amounts to waiting for exactly the right moment to enter the trade so that the risk is minimized. The cheetah, for example, is the fastest animal in the world. Although it can run extremely fast, it doesn't necessarily need to do so. Instead, the cheetah will wait until a weak, lame, young, or old animal gets close. When it does, it requires much less energy to make an almost certain kill. That's what you want to do in your entry techniques. For many of you, stalking simply amounts to shifting down to a smaller time frame to determine the most opportune time to "jump on your prey."

I've divided this chapter into four sections. The first section has to do with random entry and with the research designed to increase one's reliability over random entry into the market. The second section discusses some common techniques that meet one of the two assumptions listed above. The third section has to do with designing your own entry signal. Finally, the fourth section continues our discussion of systems and gives you some entry techniques that have been used in well-known systems—both for the stock market and for more leveraged markets.

I've deliberately abstained from showing you many "best-case" illustrations to convince you of the validity of certain methods. This strategy would appeal to some of your natural biases and psychological weaknesses. However, I consider doing so to be hitting below the belt at best. Consequently, if you use any of the recommendations given in this chapter, I'd suggest that you test them out for yourself.

TRYING TO BEAT RANDOM ENTRY

I was doing a seminar with Tom Basso (see his sections in Chapters 3 and 5) in 1991. Tom was explaining that the most important part of his system was his exits and his position-sizing algorithms. As a result, one member of the audience remarked, "From what you are saying it sounds like you could make money consistently with a random entry as long as you have good exits and size your positions intelligently."

Tom responded that he probably could. He promptly returned to his office and tested his own system of exits and position sizing with a "coin flip"-type entry. In other words, his system simulated trading four different markets and he was always in the market, either long or short, based upon a random signal. As soon as he got an exit signal, he'd reenter the market again based upon the random signal. Tom's results showed that he made money consistently, even using $100 per contract for slippage and commissions.

We subsequently duplicated those results with more markets. I published them in one of my newsletters and gave several talks on them. Our system was very simple. We determined the volatility of the market by a 10-day exponential moving average of the average true range. Our initial stop was three times that volatility reading. Once entry occurred by a coin flip, the same three-times-volatility stop was trailed from the close. However, the stop could only move in our favor. Thus, the stop moved closer whenever the markets moved in our favor or whenever volatility shrank. We also used a 1 percent risk model for our position-sizing system, as described in Chapter 12.

> Our random entry system—consisting of random entry, a three-times-volatility trailing stop, and a simple money management system involving 1 percent risk—made money on 100 percent of the runs.

That's it! That's all there was to the system—a random entry, plus a trailing stop that was three times the volatility, plus a 1 percent risk algorithm to size positions. We ran it on 10 markets. And it was always in each market, either long or short, depending upon a coin flip. It's a good illustration of how simplicity works in system development.

Whenever you run a random entry system, you get different results. This system made money on 80 percent of the runs when it only traded one contract per futures market. It made money 100 percent of the time when a simple 1 percent risk money management system was added. That's pretty impressive. The system had a reliability level of 38 percent, which is about average for a trend-following system.

The LeBeau and Lucas Studies

Chuck LeBeau and David Lucas, in their book, *Technical Traders' Bulletin Guide to Computer Analysis of the Futures Market*,[3] did some marvelous studies with entry. They used various types of entry signals to enter the market when doing historical testing. The only exit they used was at the close of business 5, 10, 15, and 20 days later. Their primary interest in using this approach was to determine what percentage of their trades made money and if the percentage exceeded what one would expect from entering the market at random. Most of the indicators failed to perform any better than random—including all the oscillators and various moving-average crossover combinations that are so popular.[4]

If you have a market entry that has a reliability of 60 percent or more at the end of 20 days, it would seem to be very promising. However, when your only exit is at the close after so many days, you are wide open to catastrophic losses. You must protect yourself from those losses with a protective stop. Yet when you do, you reduce the reliability of your entry signal—some of those signals go below your stop (whatever it is) and then come back and become profitable—except that you're no longer in the market. In addition, whenever you add any sort of trailing stop (to reduce your initial risk and take profits), you are going to further reduce the reliability of your entry. Why? The reason is because some of the stops designed to reduce your initial risk will be hit and take you out at a loss. This is why a good trend-following system usually has a reliability below 50 percent.

Since most trend-following systems make money from a few good trades each year, another reason for their low reliability might be that the good systems concentrate on getting high-*R*-multiple trades. Let's look at some common entry techniques that might help you with one or both of these approaches.

COMMON ENTRY TECHNIQUES

Most people trade or invest using only a few categories of entries. In the following section, we discuss some of the most common entry techniques and their usefulness.

Channel Breakouts

Suppose you have a goal, as a trend follower, of never missing a major trend in the market. What kind of entry signal could you use? The classic answer to this question is an entry signal known as the "channel breakout." Basically, you enter the market on either the highest high of the last X days on the long side or the lowest low of the last X days on the short side. If the market is going to trend up, then it must make new highs. If you enter on one of those new highs, then you will not miss an uptrend. Similarly, if you enter on a new low, then you will not miss a downtrend. Figure 8–1 shows an example of a 40-day channel breakout working in an uptrending market. There are a number of breakouts in this chart, but the clearest one occurs on August 2.

In regard to Figure 8–1, the word "channel" is rather misleading. A channel assumes that the market has been moving along in a narrow range for a number of days and then suddenly "breaks out" on either the upside or the downside. Obviously, this entry technique would capture that type of move quite well. However, you would need to know (1) what is the length of the channel and (2) when the channel started.

This leads to the most important question having to do with channel breakouts—"How big a trend must be signaled before I get on board?" The answer to that question determines the number of days needed to produce the high or low at which you'll enter.

The channel breakout technique was originally described by Donchian in the 1960s. It was then popularized by a group of

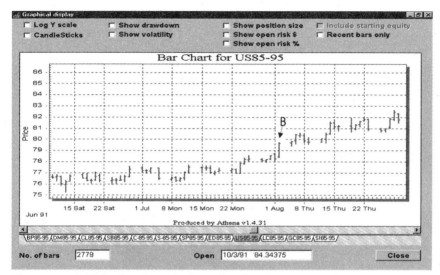

Figure 8–1 A 40-day breakout (indicated with a B) occurs August 2

traders known as the "Turtles," who have made billions[5] of dollars trading commodities using this entry technique. They originally entered on 20-day breakouts and were quite successful with it. But as they continued to use the method, eventually 20-day breakouts stopped working as effectively. As a result, they simply moved up to 40-day breakouts.

Today, research seems to indicate that breakouts between 40 and 100+ days still work fairly well. Breakouts involving fewer days are not that good, except to go short. Since bear markets tend to have swift, sharp moves, they may need a much quicker entry signal.

This technique is very simple to apply. You can plot the daily highs or lows. When the market makes a higher high than anytime in the last 20 days, you enter a long position. When the market makes the lowest low of the last 20 days, you enter a short position. Table 8–1 shows how this might work. It gives you 60 days of corn prices during early 1995. New 20-day-high prices are shown in bold-face. Each boldfaced price is an entry target or an actual entry signal.

Notice that the first 20 days are used for establishing a base-line which ends on January 30, 1995. That row is in bold in the

T A B L E 8–1

Early 1995 Corn Prices

Date	Open	High	Low	Close
1/3/95	164.5	164.5	161.5	162
1/4/95	162	163	**161.25**	162.25
1/5/95	163.5	164.5	163	164.25
1/6/95	165.25	165.5	163.75	165.25
1/9/95	165.25	166.75	164.25	166.25
1/10/95	165.25	166	165	165.75
1/11/95	166.25	166.25	165.5	166
1/12/95	168.5	**170.25**	167.75	167.75
1/13/95	168	168.5	166.5	167.5
1/16/95	167	168.5	166	168
1/17/95	168.5	170	168	169
1/18/95	169	169	167.75	168.25
1/19/95	167.75	168.25	167	167.75
1/20/95	167.75	168.5	166.25	167
1/23/95	166.25	166.5	165	166.5
1/24/95	166.75	167.25	166	166.75
1/25/95	167	167	166.25	166.75
1/26/95	166.5	167.5	166	166.5
1/27/95	166	166.5	165.5	165.75
1/30/95	**165**	**165**	**162.25**	**163**
1/31/95	162.75	164	162.5	163
2/1/95	163	165	162.75	164.5
2/2/95	164	165.75	164	165.25
2/3/95	165.5	166.5	165.5	166
2/6/95	166.25	170	165.75	169.25
2/7/95	168.25	169	167	167.25
2/8/95	167	167.5	166.5	167.25
2/9/95	166	167.5	165	167.25

TABLE 8–1

Early 1995 Corn Prices (*Continued*)

Date	Open	High	Low	Close
2/10/95	168	169	167	168
2/13/95	167.75	168	167	167.5
2/14/95	167.25	168.5	167	168.25
2/15/95	168	168.25	166.75	167.75
2/16/95	167.25	167.25	166.5	166.75
2/17/95	166.25	166.75	165.75	166.25
2/21/95	165.75	166	164.75	165.75
2/22/95	165.5	167	165.25	166
2/23/95	167	167.75	166.25	167.25
2/24/95	167	167.75	166.75	167.25
2/27/95	167.5	167.5	166.5	167.25
2/28/95	167	168	166.75	167.5
3/1/95	167	168.5	167	168
3/2/95	167.5	168.25	167	167.75
3/3/95	167.5	167.5	165.75	166
3/6/95	165.75	**171.5**	165.75	169.25
3/7/95	169	**171.5**	168.5	170.5
3/8/95	169.75	170.5	169	170
3/9/95	169.75	170.75	169.5	170.25
3/10/95	170.5	**171.75**	169.75	170.75
3/13/95	171.25	**173.25**	171.25	173
3/14/95	172.75	**173.5**	172.25	172.75
3/15/95	173.25	**174.5**	172.25	174
3/16/95	173.25	174.25	172	172.5
3/17/95	172.5	174	172	172.75
3/20/95	172.25	173.5	171.75	172

table. During the initial 20-day period the market high occurs on January 12 at 170.25. It almost reaches it on February 6 when it hits 170 and that soon becomes the 20-day high. No other prices come that close until March 6 when the market gives a clear entry signal by hitting 171.5. Notice that the market also gives entry signals on March 10, March 13, March 14, and March 15, which are all in bold. These would have set you up for one of the all-time best moves in corn.

In the case of the data given, we would have gotten the same signal if we had been looking for a 40-day channel breakout. The March 6 signal was also a 40-day high.

Now, let's look for downside signals. During the initial 20 days, the lowest price is 161.25 which occurs on January 4. That is not surpassed, and soon the 20-day low becomes the price on January 30 of 162.25. This again is not surpassed. By the end of February, the 20-day low becomes the price 20 days ago which continues to rise, practically each day. During this entire period, a new 20-day low was not set.

The channel breakout can be used with any number of setups, such as those given in Chapter 7 for both stocks and futures. For example, you might decide not to trade it unless you also have strong fundamentals in the item under question. You might require high earnings per share in a stock or a strong sign of demand in the commodity you are considering.

The channel breakout could also be used as a setup. You might look for a breakout and then enter on a retracement, followed by another breakout on a shorter time frame.

There are thousands of possibilities for using channel breakouts. If you use them as an entry signal, you'll never miss a big move because (1) you'll never get a big trend without a channel breakout, and (2) if you happen to miss a signal, then there will continually be new signals to enter if the trend is a valid one.

There are two major drawbacks with the channel breakout systems. First, they tend to produce large drawdowns. This, of course, is a function of the size of the stops used. For example, if you use another channel breakout as the exit—even if it's a smaller one—you still could give back lots of profits. However, that's more of an exit problem than a problem with the entry.

The second major problem with the channel breakout is that a lot of money is usually required to trade it successfully. We did extensive testing with entering on a 55-day breakout and exiting on a 13-day breakout with various position sizing algorithms starting with a million dollar portfolio. The results suggested that a million dollars was probably an optimal account size for this sort of system. A $100,000 account, in contrast, could only trade a few markets—as opposed to the 15 to 20 markets that are normally traded with such a system.

In summary, the channel breakout entry is a good entry system that ensures that you will never miss a trending signal. However, it does get whipsawed a lot. As a result, its reliability is not much better than random entry. In addition, it requires a large account size to trade it optimally, because it needs to trade at least 15 markets simultaneously.

If you plan to trade a channel breakout, I would make the following recommendations. First, use a setup with the entry that involves a sequential condition with price (i.e., something that happens to the price before you are willing to take a breakout signal). For example, you might require (1) a narrow band of volatility before the breakout occurs, (2) an "efficient market" before you take a breakout signal, (3) a clear sign of a trend signaled by a high relative strength in the stock you are considering. Generally, the setups that will help you are those that involve a sequence of price changes prior to the entry or involve some element other than price as discussed in Chapter 7.

Second, most of the problems that are associated with drawdowns or require large accounts in breakout systems can be solved by market selection and a careful selection of your stops and exits. However, those are both topics of other chapters.

Visual Entry Based upon Charts

Many experts don't have an exact entry signal into the market. Instead, they visually inspect the charts and act on their gut feelings about what they see.

For example, Ed Seykota, a market wizard, said that his entry technique was to look at a long-term chart of the market he was

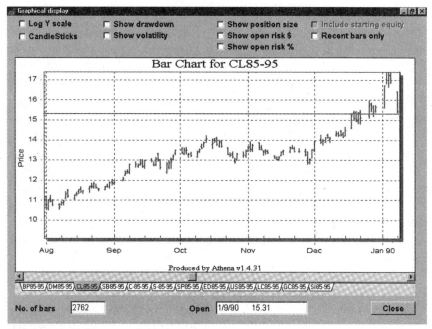

Figure 8–2 A clear visual trend—crude oil in 1989

considering. He'd put the chart, such as the one in Figure 8–2, on the wall and go to the other end of the room and look at it. He said that if the market's trend was obvious from the other side of the room, then he would have no trouble entering that particular market in the direction of the trend.

One of my clients regularly makes a million dollars in profits each year trading stocks for his own account. He only uses visual patterns for entry, although he claims that his visual entries are somewhat intuitive.

This particular type of entry has some real advantages for people with the discipline to follow it. For example, price information is much purer that any summary information you might get from some indicator. If price information indicates a clear trend, then the chances are pretty good—probably as high as 60 percent—that the trend will continue for some time. Thus, entry in the direction of the trend is probably much better than a random entry.

Patterns

Many people take the visual interpretation of charts much further. For example, the art of technical analysis focuses on the many types of chart patterns that markets tend to form. Some patterns are described as bullish and other as bearish. Thus, those patterns could give you your entry signals. Types of chart patterns include daily patterns such as gaps, spikes, key reversal days, thrust days, run days, inside days, and wide-ranging days. These patterns are typically used as short-term trading signals.

Other patterns are better described as continuation patterns. These include triangles, flags, and pennants. These have little meaning unless you wish to enter in the direction of the major trend after a breakout from these patterns.

Finally, there are top and bottom patterns. These include double bottoms and tops, head and shoulders patterns, rounded tops and bottoms, triangles, wedges, and island reversals. Obviously, these would tend to be entry signals for top and bottom pickers.

Other charts are composed of candlesticks, where the difference between the open and the close is either "clear" or "filled in" depending upon whether the price is up or down, respectively. Books have been devoted to describing the various patterns that can be made with these candlesticks. The patterns have such obscure names as "doji," the "hammer," the "hanging man," etc.

If you are interested in a pattern approach to trading, then read the appropriate chapters of Jack Schwager's book, *Schwager on Futures: Technical Analysis*.[6] It has excellent descriptions of all these patterns as well as numerous chart examples. However, such patterns are very difficult to computerize and thus test. In addition, when people do test these various patterns, they do not find any evidence that they increase the reliability of entry signals beyond the 50 percent level. That being the case, I have elected not to spend a lot of effort describing patterns in this chapter. Most people are much better off just entering in the direction of a major trend than they are looking for a particular pattern in the trend.[7]

Pure Prediction

A number of prediction techniques were discussed in the concepts chapter—Chapter 5. Prediction techniques include Elliott Wave, Gann, and various forms of countertrend trading that predict tops and bottoms. My belief is that prediction has nothing to do with good trading. Many good forecasters, despite being excellent at their craft, have a great deal of trouble making money in the markets.

I once met a man who described himself as the Michael Jordan of the markets—meaning that he believed that no one was better than he was at trading the markets. He claimed that the markets were perfectly orderly and that he had worked out some "patented secrets" that he wouldn't sell for a million dollars. He showed me some old accounts that he had taken from $5,000 to $40,000 in less than 6 months to prove his knowledge and skill.

I wasn't particularly interested in his secrets, but I was interested in how he traded. As a result, I watched him trade for about 6 months. During that time, the account he was trading dropped in value by 97 percent. *Just over 22 percent of his trades made money, and the account was never profitable throughout the entire 6 months.*

Be wary of people who claim extensive trading skill. Watch their trading, and in particular, how they size their positions. If they don't practice low-risk position sizing, then don't walk away—run!

> One of the reasons his trading accuracy was so dismal, and this is true for most market predictors, was that he always anticipated turning points in the market.

One of the reasons his trading accuracy was so dismal, and this is true for most market predictors, was that he always anticipated turning points in the market. For example, in November he anticipated an early freeze in the Midwest that would destroy next year's soybean crop. It didn't happen. Several times he said the market was due for cycle turns. He said they would be dramatic so he wanted to get into the market early. The turns never happened or were insignificant.

Prediction is fine if it is accompanied by market confirmation. In other words, **if you think you can predict a market bottom or**

top, fine. But don't trade it until the market shows you some sort of confirmation that it is turning. A good example of such a confirmation is a volatility breakout, as discussed below.

Volatility Breakouts

The next two techniques, volatility breakouts and directional movement, were first described by J. Wells Wilder, Jr., in *New Concepts in Technical Trading Systems.*[8] The techniques are simple and have withstood the test of time.

Volatility breakouts are essentially sudden dramatic price movements in a particular direction. Suppose the average true range is about 3 points. We might define a volatility breakout to be a move of 0.8 times the average true range (from the prior close) in a single day, or 2.4 points. Let's say today's price closed at 35. A volatility breakout would be a move of 2.4 points from the close, either up or down. If the price moved to 37.4, then you'd have an upside volatility breakout and you'd want to buy. If the price moved to 32.6, then you'd have a downside breakout and you'd want to short the market. *This is the general type of entry signal that I would recommend for those of you who have setups that involve market prediction.*

Wilder's system is somewhat different from what is described above. He recommends that the average true range be multiplied by a constant of 3.0 (called the ARC). This essentially is used as a trailing stop from the close, and it becomes both an exit point for a current position and an entry point for a new position. In essence, the exit is almost exactly the same as the exit that we use on the random entry system (i.e., three times the average true range).

Generally, when the market makes a strong move in some direction, it's a good sign that you may want to be in the market on the side of that move. For example, you may have a strong uptrend, but a solid volatility breakout to the downside would be a good indication that the trend was over and that you need to go with the market in its new direction. **At minimum, you probably don't want to go against a strong volatility breakout.**

Figure 8–3 shows an example of a volatility breakout in bonds. Depending upon how the volatility breakout is defined, a clear

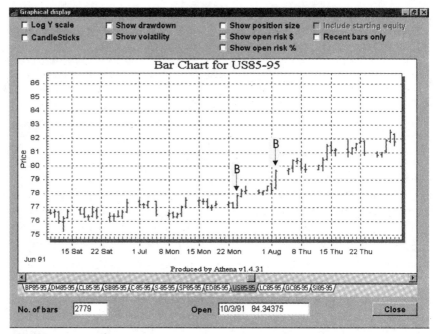

Figure 8–3 Sample volatility breakouts (Indicated with a B) in the same bond chart

breakout seems to occur on July 24 and an even stronger one occurs on August 2. Notice the large range of prices on the breakout day and notice how far from the old close the new prices break out.

When you use a volatility breakout, you have some interesting advantages. First, this type of price movement is quite different from the channel breakout—which requires a clear trend when you have a long (40 days plus) channel. However, the examples shown in Figure 8–3 were also both channel breakouts.

The volatility breakout could simply signal the end of a trend and the start of a new one. As a result, at least part of the movement in a volatility breakout would have little correlation with a channel breakout. In fact, if the exit is quick enough, there may be no correlation between the profits generated by these two diverse entry signals.

The second advantage, which I've already mentioned, is that volatility breakouts are ideal for people who use various models to predict price movement. Price prediction is very dangerous unless it is accompanied by a sound trading system. Volatility breakouts could help you achieve the entry part of that solid system to trade your "secret knowledge" about how the markets work.

Directional Movement and the Average Directional Movement

Market technicians for some time have struggled with the concept of "trendiness" in the market. How do you know when a market is really trending?

> Price prediction is very dangerous unless it is accompanied by a sound trading system. Volatility breakouts could help you achieve the entry part of that solid system to trade your "secret knowledge" about how the markets work.

J. Wells Wilder, Jr. (again from *New Concepts in Technical Trading Systems*), developed two concepts called directional movement and average directional movement, which for many people define trendiness. For example, Bruce Babcock has published for many years a book called *Trendiness in the Market.*[9] In that book, he ranks the various tradable markets according to their trendiness. The book is based on the idea that if you trade the markets with the most "history of trending," you're most likely to catch a future trend in those markets. Babcock's measure of trendiness was simply a measure of the profitability of using a 28-day directional movement index (see below) to trade each market. When the net directional movement is up, you go long. When the net directional movement is down, you go short. Profitable markets were deemed to be "trendy," and the most profitable market was deemed to be the most "trendy."

The basic assumptions behind directional movement are that:

1. When the trend is up, today's high price should be above yesterday's high price. Thus, the difference between the two prices is the "up" directional movement.

2. When the trend is down, today's low price should be below yesterday's low price. Thus, the difference between the two prices is the "down" directional movement.

3. Inside days, when the high and low of today do not fall outside of yesterday's range, are essentially ignored.

4. Outside days, when both the high and low are outside of yesterday's range, will add both an up and down directional movement. Only the larger value is used.

The directional movement indicator is calculated as follows:

1. Add the up days (ΣDI+) and the down days (ΣDI−) for a predetermined period of days (Wilder suggests 14).
2. Divide each sum by the average true range for the same number of days. The directional movement indicator is then calculated as follows:
3. Determine the difference between the ΣDI+ and the ΣDI− and find the absolute value, that is, DI difference = [(ΣDI+) − (ΣDI−)] treated as a positive number.
4. Determine the DI sum: DI sum = ΣDI+ plus ΣDI−.
5. The directional movement index is defined by (DI difference)/(DI sum) * 100. Multiplying by 100 normalizes the directional movement index so that it falls between zero and 100.
6. Although Wilder suggests 14 days for your calculations, LeBeau and Lucas report that 14 to 20 days are all good, with 18 days being optimal.

Perhaps the most important extension of the directional movement indicator is the average directional movement index, or ADX. The ADX is simply a moving average of the directional movement index. It's usually averaged over the same number of days that was used previously (e.g., 14).

LeBeau and Lucas claim that "the proper interpretation of the ADX allows traders to significantly improve their odds of finding good markets and avoiding bad ones." They believe that the ADX actually provides a means to quantify the strength of various trends and claim to have done more work in that area than anyone else. Since I've done many seminars with Chuck LeBeau, I'm also quite familiar with his love of, and use of, the ADX.

Generally, the higher the ADX, the more directional movement there has been in the market. You don't know, however, whether the movement has been up or down. The lower the ADX, the less directional movement there has been in the market. Thus, the size of the ADX tells you the strength of the trend, but it says nothing about the direction of the trend.

According to LeBeau and Lucas you cannot use the absolute value of the ADX to indicate whether a trend is strong or not. Instead, they make the following observations:

1. As long as the ADX is rising, any level of the ADX above 15 indicates a trend.
2. The greater the increase in the ADX, the stronger the trend. For example, a jump in the ADX from 15 to 20 is probably a better signal than a jump from 25 to 27.
3. Decreases in the ADX only mean that the trend is weakening or that the market is no longer trending.
4. When the ADX is rising, indicators such as overbought or oversold oscillators will not work. Such oscillators only work when the ADX is falling.

Before suggesting ways to use the ADX or directional movement as an entry signal, let's first discuss a few of the problems that tend to occur with the ADX. These include spikes and the lag factor.

When the market changes direction suddenly in the form of a spike, the ADX has a hard time adjusting. For example, when the market suddenly shifts direction, the longer-term ADX, as recommended by LeBeau and Lucas, may suddenly appear to go into a downtrend—indicating a trendless market. As a result, a substantial downtrend could be totally ignored by the ADX.

The long-term ADX also has a lag built into it. That is, you won't know that you are in a trending market until the trend is well under way. This is a real disadvantage if you are a short-term trader and you want to get into trends early. On the other hand, if your objective is to only get into strong trends with a clear signal, then the lag in the ADX is not a problem at all.

Now that you understand what directional movement and the ADX are, we can give you some useful entry signals. The following entry signals are only some suggestions for you to ponder:

1. Enter after crosses of the DI+ and the DI−. Long trades would occur after the DI+ goes above the DI− and the high of the previous day is penetrated. Short trades would

occur after the DI− goes above the DI+ and the low of the previous day is penetrated. This is Wilder's original use of the indicator, and he believes that the price penetration is an important part of the signal.

2. Enter in the direction of the market movement when the ADX rises more than 4 points[10] in 2 days. Of course, you'll need a setup (such as a visual inspection of the chart) to tell you whether to go long or short since an ADX rise only indicates a strong trend.

3. Enter when the ADX reaches the highest value of the last 10 days. Once again, you'll need another signal (also a setup) to tell you which direction to go.

Moving Averages and Adaptive Moving Averages

Moving averages are very popular trading indicators because they are simple and easy to calculate. As far as I can tell, they have been used since trading markets were first invented by human beings.

The concept behind such an average is simple. You represent the price over the last X days by a single number, an average. It's the sum of the prices over the X days, divided by the number of days. That number moves with time. When you get tomorrow's price, you simply drop the price X days ago (i.e., the number of days in the moving average), add in the new price, and once again divide by the number of days.

One bar is simpler for most people to grasp than, for example, 30 bars might be, even though the 30 bars might give you a lot more information about what the market was really doing. But people feel more control over the market when they transform data in some way. As a result, a lot of traders and investors use moving averages.

If you have a lot of days in your average, then you will have a slow moving average. If your moving average only includes a few days, then it will move quickly. For example, many stock market followers use 1-year moving averages to indicate the overall trend of the market. When the price has been going up consistently, it should be well above the 1-year average. When the price drops below the 1-year moving average, some people make the assumption that the direction of prices has changed. Colby and Meyers, in their *Encyclopedia of Technical Market Indicators*,[11] found that the strategy of buying stock when the price crossed above the 1-year average and selling it when it crossed below that average outperformed a buy-and-hold strategy by a large margin.

Short moving averages, in contrast, are quick moving. A market does not have to go up too many days for the price to be above its 5-day moving average. Similarly, prices could quickly drop below that average.

> ...the strategy of buying stock when the price crossed above the 1-year average and selling it when it crossed below that average outperformed a buy-and-hold strategy by a large margin.

Donchian was one of the first people to write about a system using moving averages. He used both the 5-day and the 20-day moving averages. When the 5-day average crossed above the 20-day average, you went long. When the 5-day average went down and crossed below the 20-day average, you reversed and went short.

This kind of system works well in pure trending markets. However, it assumes that the market only has two directions, up and down. Unfortunately, markets tend to trend about 15 percent of the time and spend 85 percent of the time consolidating. As a result, during the consolidation periods such a system gets whipsawed continually.

To overcome this problem, traders have decided to use three moving averages. R. C. Allen[12] popularized a method in the early 1970s involving the 4-, 9-, and 18-day moving averages. When the 4-day and 9-day averages have both crossed the 18-day average, you would enter the market—long if they are moving up and short if they are moving down. When the 4-day signal crosses back across the 9, you get an exit signal. However, you don't get a new entry signal until both the 4 and the 9 are on the same side of the 18-day average. Thus, this sort of system gives you a neutral zone.[13]

There are numerous types of moving averages and moving-average systems. For example, you have simple moving averages (as described), weighted moving averages, exponential moving averages, displaced moving averages, and adaptive moving averages. Each type is designed to overcome particular problems of the others, but they also each create their own problems.

Weighted Moving Average

The simple moving average gives as much weight to the day that drops off as it does to the most recent day. Some people argue that this is not the best way to trade, because the newest price is the most important. As a result, weighted moving averages give more weight to the most recent data and less weight to distant data.

Weighted moving averages can get very complex, because you can just give the most recent day extra weight or you can give a different weight for each day. For example, you could have a 10-day weighted average that multiplies the first day (most distant) by 1, the second day by 2, the third day by 3, etc. This is probably nonsense, but some people think that complex calculations make trading easier. The assumption is wrong, but people do it anyway.

Exponential Moving Average

The exponential moving average weights the most recent data most heavily, and it doesn't drop anything out. For example, a 0.1 exponential moving average (equivalent to about a 20-day average) would multiply the current day's price by 0.1 and add it to yesterday's average. Nothing would be subtracted. This procedure is quite handy for calculations, and it does give more weight to the most recent data.

Displaced Moving Average

Since a moving average tends to be very close to the prices, the signals can often be too quick. As a result, some people have elected to "displace" their moving averages by moving them into the future a number of days. This simply means that you are less likely to get whipsawed by a moving-average signal.

Adaptive Moving Averages

Adaptive moving averages have become quite popular in the mid-1990s. Both Kaufman[14] and Chande and Kroll[15] have various versions of adaptive moving averages. These particular systems change speed according to some combination of market direction and speed.

Think about the amount of noise in the market. The daily price fluctuation is a good measure of the market noise. When there is a lot of noise, the moving average must be very slow to avoid being whipsawed in and out of the market. However, when the market is quite smooth, then fast moving averages can be used because there is much less chance of a whipsaw. As a result, adaptive moving averages first measure the velocity of market movement against the amount of noise in the market. They then adjust the speed of the average according to the speed and noise factor.

Thus the adaptive moving average must (1) have at minimum some measure of the current efficiency of the market (i.e., how much noise exists) and (2) be able to map that scenario onto various moving averages. A specific example of using an adaptive moving average is given under the entry technique designed by Perry Kaufman that is discussed later in this chapter.

Oscillators and Stochastics

Oscillators such as RSI, stochastics, Williams %R, etc., are all designed to help people who are trying to pick tops and bottoms. In my opinion, this is a fool's game, and there is no evidence that entry signals based upon oscillators have a reliability much better than chance. In fact, in most cases there is no evidence that the market generally meets the assumptions that many oscillators are making. As a result, I've elected not to give a long discussion on something in which I have little faith.

However, there is a way that you can use an "overbought/oversold" oscillator—such as Wilder's RSI—to help you trade with narrow stops (see Chapter 9 on protective stops). Here's what you need to do this sort of trading:

1. Wait until the market gives a clear signal of being in a trend. This is a price-based setup.

2. Wait until the market reverses slightly and your oscillator gives a sign that the reaction has probably reached an extreme. This step also is a price-based setup, only it must occur after step 1.

3. Enter the market in the direction of the previous trend when the market gives a signal that it will again move in that direction. An example would be a return of price to the previous high (or low for a short signal) prior to the extreme oscillator signal.

This sort of trading sets up the possibility of a highly reliable trading signal with a very small stop (i.e., the extreme of the reaction). In addition, since the risk of such a trade is quite small, it means that the reward-to-risk ratio of the potential trade could be very high. This is actually an example of a retracement setup as discussed in the last chapter, and it is, in my opinion, the best way to use oscillators.

DESIGNING YOUR OWN ENTRY SIGNAL

The best entry signal for you is probably one that you design for yourself. The best way to design such a signal is to thoroughly reason out the concept upon which your signal should be based. I have designed the following example as an illustration of such thinking—just to give you an example. We'll start out with an idea that is widely used by traders and investors and then go on to something that is not. The ideas suggested are not tested, but feel free to use them if you want to work with them until you find something useful.

Let's design a system around basic ideas behind motion in physics. For example, think about predicting the movement of a car. You have no idea where the car is going (assume you are on a giant parking lot so that there are an infinite number of turns the car could make), but you know where the car has been. You also know its direction, speed (velocity), velocity changes (acceleration and deceleration), and momentum. If you know that information, then under certain conditions you'll have a good idea what the car will do in the near-term future. What you want to determine is when the car will move quickly in the same direction for as long a period as possible.

If the car is moving in a particular direction, it's more likely to continue in that direction than not. It could change directions, but chances are that it will continue in the same direction. Furthermore, if you know more about the car's velocity, velocity changes, and momentum, then there will be certain circumstances when it's even more likely that the car will continue in the same direction.

A car typically has to slow down in order to change directions. Thus, if a car is going fast (fast velocity), it is more likely to continue going fast in the same direction than it is to do something else.

The same is true of the market. If it is moving rapidly in one direction, then it is more likely to continue going fast in that direction than to do something else. Think about it. A quickly advancing market is much more likely to slow down first before there is a major change in direction. Market technicians call this "momentum," which is a really misleading name.[16] The technical indicator known as momentum simply measures the change in price (usually the closing price) from one time frame to another. However, we'll use the word "speed" or "velocity" because both are more accurate.

Speed is really stated in terms of distance per unit of time (such as 60 miles per hour). If you use a constant distance (such as 10 days) in your velocity calculations, then you can simply assume that speed is the distance traveled per X-day period, where X is the number of days you pick. *Interestingly enough, more professional traders probably use velocity (which they call momentum indicators) in their studies of the market than any other indicator.*

How would you use speed as an entry signal? Zero speed means no movement. The speed indicator tends to be a number that moves back and forth across the zero line from fast up movement to fast down movement or vice versa. When speed changes direction and begins to accelerate in the opposite direction, you have a potential entry signal.

> When speed changes direction and begins to accelerate in the opposite direction, you have a potential entry signal.

Acceleration and Deceleration

Acceleration and deceleration refer to changes in speed. If a car is increasing its speed, then it is even more likely to keep going in the same direction than a car that is simply moving fast. On the other hand, if a car is decreasing its speed, then the chances of it changing direction are much greater.

Although the change in velocity of market movement is not as significant to predicting its future movement as acceleration or deceleration is in predicting the movement of a car, it still is an important factor. However, I have never seen anything that directly looks at acceleration or deceleration in the market. The formula, if it existed, would look something like the following:

Velocity change = [(Velocity today) − (velocity on day X)]/time

Although we haven't done extensive research on acceleration or deceleration as an entry indicator, we have programmed some data to look at them. Table 8–2 shows the closing prices of the same corn data from 1995–1996 that we looked at earlier. Recall that both a 20-day channel breakout and a 40-day channel breakout occurred on the sixth of March. Table 8–2 also shows the average rate of change of prices (i.e., speed) over 20 days. Decreases in speed are shown in boldface, while increases in speed are in regular type.

Notice that a positive 20-day velocity period actually starts on February 24—7 trading days before the channel breakout. The last two columns in Table 8–2 show 3- and 5-day accelerations/decelerations (i.e., how much speed actually changes over a 3- to 5-day period). The longer-term acceleration (i.e., the 10-day) also starts a positive acceleration that only becomes negative briefly for 1 day.

Figure 8–4 shows the three variables on a time graph. Notice that the channel breakout, which actually begins on March 6, starts on day 46. Velocity and acceleration start to move much earlier. However, there is a dip in both velocity and acceleration that occurs just before the breakout, but the numbers still stay positive except for a slight dip of the 10-day acceleration into the negative.

What does this mean? I'm certainly not suggesting that you use a positive velocity or a sign of acceleration (as opposed to deceleration) as an entry system. Instead, I'm just pointing out relationships. Relationships, when you understand them, form the basis for concepts that you can use in your trading.

Remember that money is not necessarily made by being right about entry. Instead, if you can determine an entry that will give you a high probability (say, 25 percent) of a large-R-multiple trade,

T A B L E 8–2

Velocity and Acceleration Study

Date	Close	20-Day Velocity Periods	5-Day Accelerations	10-Day Accelerations
1/30/95	166.5	0.225		
1/31/95	165.75	0.175		
2/1/95	163	−0.0625		
2/2/95	163	−0.1125		
2/3/95	164.5	−0.0875	−0.3125	
2/6/95	165.25	−0.025	−0.2	
2/7/95	166	0	0.0625	
2/8/95	169.25	0.075	0.1875	
2/9/95	167.25	0.0625	0.15	
2/9/95	167.25	−0.025	0	−0.25
2/10/95	167.25	−0.0125	−0.0125	−0.1875
2/13/95	168	0	−0.075	0.0625
2/14/95	167.5	−0.075	−0.1375	0.0375
2/15/95	168.25	0	0.025	0.0875
2/16/95	167.75	0	0.0125	0.025
2/17/95	166.75	−0.0125	−0.0125	−0.0125
2/21/95	166.25	−0.0125	0.0625	−0.0875
2/22/95	165.75	−0.05	−0.05	−0.1125
2/23/95	166	−0.0375	−0.0375	−0.0125
2/24/95	167.25	0.0375	0.05	0.05
2/27/95	167.25	0.075	0.0875	0.075
2/28/95	167.25	0.2125	0.2625	0.2875
3/1/95	167.5	0.225	0.2625	0.225
3/2/95	168	0.175	0.1375	0.175
3/3/95	167.75	0.125	0.05	0.1375
3/6/95	166	0	−0.2125	0.0125
3/7/95	169.25	0	−0.225	0.05
3/8/95	170.5	0.1625	−0.0125	0.2
3/9/95	170	0.1375	0.0125	0.1
3/10/95	170.25	0.15	0.15	0.075
3/13/95	170.25	0.1125	0.1125	−0.1
3/14/95	173	0.275	0.1125	0.05
3/15/95	172.75	0.225	0.0875	0.05
3/16/95	174	0.3125	0.1625	0.1875
3/17/95	172.5	0.2875	0.175	0.2875
3/20/95	172.5	0.3125	0.0375	0.3125

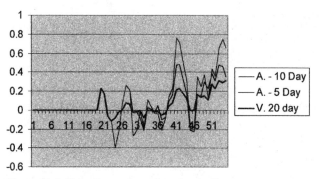

Figure 8–4 Velocity and acceleration in the corn move

you have a good chance of making large, consistent profits. The start of an acceleration might give you a low-risk point at which you can place a very narrow stop. This means that R is low, so you have the potential of a high-R-multiple profit. This, of course, would require extensive testing.

Acceleration might prove to be the perfect tool for a good retracement setup. For example, you might simply need to look for a deceleration right after the channel breakout. As soon as the deceleration turns to acceleration, you could have a perfect signal that would require only a tight stop and give you the potential for a very high R-multiple profit. In the example shown, deceleration had started just before the channel breakout.

AN EVALUATION OF ENTRY USED IN SOME COMMON SYSTEMS

Our last task with respect to entry is to review some of the typical entry signals used in some stock market systems and in some systems used in more speculative markets.

Some Stock Market Systems Reviewed

William O'Neil's Stock Market System

The William O'Neil stock market trading system is one that uses the CANSLIM setups as discussed in the previous chapter. Entry is the timing portion of the system which is based upon various chart patterns one might find in the stocks under consideration. The key portion of the entry is a price breakout from a consolidation period that has lasted anywhere from 7 weeks to 15 months. Typical patterns would include a cup and a handle, a breakout from a long base, a saucer and a handle, a double bottom, a double base, etc. However, the first two patterns are by far the most common. William O'Neil presents many examples of these patterns in his excellent book.

The other critical point about entry is that the breakout should be accompanied by a large increase in volume. O'Neil, for example, suggests that the breakout volume should be at least 50 percent above the daily average for that stock. This large increase in volume is the most important aspect of O'Neil's entry that fewer people follow. Most just look for the patterns such as a cup and handle or a simple breakout. Think about volume as the mass of a vehicle. If a heavy truck starts moving fast, it's much more likely to keep going than a tiny car that can turn or stop on a dime.

Warren Buffett's Business Evaluation Model

Buffett's business evaluation model, with all the filters given in the previous chapter, probably does not have an entry technique—although this assumption is somewhat speculation on my part. My guess is that as long as enough money is available, Buffett will buy a new company as soon as he discovers one that meets his criteria. Thus, the discovery of a company that meets all his criteria is probably his entry signal—although I'm not sure any companies would meet his criteria in an overvalued market. Buffett certainly cares little for what the market is doing, as evidence by the following quote:

> The market is there only as a reference point to see if anybody is offering to do anything foolish. When we invest in stocks, we invest in a business. You simply have to behave according to what is rational rather than according to what is fashionable.[17]

Motley Fool Foolish-Four Approach

Remember that the Motley Fool Foolish-Four approach is based upon finding the stocks in the Dow Jones Industrial Average with the second, third, fourth, and fifth highest yields. The highest-yielding stock is skipped. These foolish-four setups are described in Chapter 7. The entry task is typically performed on the first business day of the year. The entry signal would be to enter at the market on that day. However, a variation of this approach would be to simply enter the market on the day you determine the four stocks that meet your criteria. This could be on any business day of the year.

In addition, remember that Michael O'Higgins and John Downes in their book, *Beating the Dow*,[18] suggested that one might enter the market November 1 and exit on May 1. These dates seem to correspond with that part of the year when people are more likely to buy (as opposed to sell) stocks and could give you higher returns.

Obviously, this technique could be improved with a reasonable amount of timing such as adding a channel breakout. If you select your high-yielding Dow stocks at the beginning of the year, but only buy them when they move up (i.e., reach a 20-day breakout), then you'll probably improve your return greatly.

Some Futures Market Systems Reviewed

Perry Kaufman's Adaptive Trading

If you recall from our discussion of Kaufman's adaptive approach in Chapter 7, Kaufman designed an efficiency ratio that was based both on the speed and direction of the market's movement and on the amount of noise in the market. Several examples were given of possible efficiency ratios that one might use.

In the calculations below, we'll assume that you have an efficiency ratio that goes from zero to 1—zero meaning no market movement except for noise and 1 meaning that the market was all movement and no noise. In a very efficient market, the total price movement will be equal to the price movement between the two time periods. The ratio would be 1.0 because there is no noise. For example, if the price moved up 10 points in a 10-day period and the price moved up by 1 point each day, then you'd have a ratio of $10/(10 * 1) = 1.0$.

In a very inefficient market, there would be a very small total price movement and a lot of daily price movement. The resulting ratio would tend to go toward zero. For example, if the price only moved 1 point over a 10-day period, but the price moved up or down by 10 points each day, then you'd have a ratio of $1/(10^*10) = 0.01$. And, of course, if there is no price movement—no matter what the total price movement is—the ratio would be zero.

The next step in calculating the adaptive moving average is to map the efficiency ratio onto a range of moving-average speeds. We could call a 2-day average a fast speed and a 30-day average a slow speed. Kaufman converts the moving-average speed into a smoothing constant (SC) by using the formula

$$SC = 2/(N + 1)$$

The smoothing constant for the fast speed is $2/(2 + 1) = 2/3 = 0.66667$. The smoothing constant for the slow speed is $2/(30 + 1) = 2/31 = 0.06452$. The difference between these two values, which Kaufman uses in his formula, is 0.60215.

Finally, Kaufman recommends that the formula for mapping the smoothing constants onto the efficiency ratio be as follows:

Scaled smoothing constant = [efficiency ratio * (SC difference)]
+ slow SC

Plugging in our numbers, we get the following:

Scaled smoothing constant = [efficiency ratio * 0.60215] + 0.06452

Thus if the efficiency ratio were 1.0, our scaled smoothing constant would be 0.66667; and if the efficiency ratio were 0, then our scaled smoothing constant would be 0.06452. Notice how this corresponds to the numbers for 2 and 30 days, respectively.

Since the 30-day number can still produce an effect, Kaufman recommends that you square the final smoothing constant before you apply it. This basically means that you will eliminate trading when the efficiency ratio (ER) is too low.

The formula for the adaptive moving average (AMA) is as follows:

$$AMA = AMA \text{ (yesterday)} + SC^2 * [\text{today's price} - AMA \text{ (yesterday)}]$$

Let's say that yesterday's AMA is 40. Today's price is 47—a 7-

point difference. In an efficient market, this would produce a major change in the average—raise the AMA by nearly 3.1 points—almost half of 7. In an inefficient market, with an ER of about 0.3, the differential would hardly make a dent in the AMA, moving it up about 0.4 point. Thus, you'd be much more likely to get a trade from a movement in the AMA when the market is efficient.

According to Kaufman, the AMA is equivalent to an exponential smoothing and such averages should be traded as soon as they signal a directional change. In other words, you buy the market when the AMA turns up and you sell when the AMA turns down.

However, trading these signals will cause a lot of whipsaws. As a result, Kaufman adds the following filter:

$$\text{Filter} = \% * \text{standard deviation (1-day AMA change over last 20 days)}$$

Kaufman suggests using a small percentage filter for futures and forex trading (i.e., 10 percent) and a larger percentage filter (i.e., 100 percent) for equity and interest rate markets.

Determine the appropriate filter for the market you wish to trade. Add the filter to the lowest price in a downtrend for a buy signal and subtract the filter from the highest price in an uptrend for a sell signal. This is basically your adaptive entry.

You probably could map a market efficiency ratio onto many of the techniques we've discussed for entry. For example, you could have an adaptive channel breakout system where the length of the channel is adaptive, or an adaptive volatility breakout where the size of the breakout required depends upon market efficiency.

William Gallacher's Fundamentals

Recall from Chapter 7 that Gallacher believes in determining the fundamentals of the market as a setup. When the fundamentals are strong, then you can enter in the direction that those fundamentals suggest for the direction of the market. Recall that fundamental data could be different for each market. In addition, recall from LeBeau's discussion of fundamental trading in Chapter 5 that one should defer to experts to determine what the fundamentals are of any particular markets. LeBeau also cautions that you can be right about the fundamentals, but terribly wrong about the timing. Thus, you need a good timing system to trade fundamentals.

Gallacher, for the sake of illustration, gives a 10-day channel breakout reversal system to illustrate the folly of technical analysis. While no one that I know of would trade this kind of system, Gallacher suggests that once you know the fundamentals, taking 10-day breakouts in the direction of the market predicted by the fundamentals is a very sound strategy. I personally believe that such a system would lead to many whipsaws. However, a channel breakout of 50 days or more, combined with fundamental support, might be an excellent entry.

Ken Roberts' "1-2-3" Reversal Approach

Ken Roberts recommends the use of two setups before entering the market. The first is that the market must make a 9-month high or low. The second is that the market makes a 1-2-3 reversal. See Chapter 7 for exact details and several illustrations of the market making new 9-month extremes, followed by such 1-2-3 reversals. When you have such setups, what kind of entry should you use?

When these two setups are present, you enter the market when it again moves toward point 2 (as shown in Figure 8–5) and makes a new extreme price. This new extreme price is your entry signal. Figure 8–5 shows a new extreme price after an all-time high and then a 1-2-3 reversal. The line in Figure 8–5 is your entry signal. You could also enter as soon as the price at point 2 is passed in the direction you expect the market to move.

The whole assumption behind this particular method of trading is that after the market has completed a long-term trend and done a 1-2-3-4 pattern, with 4 being a new extreme in the opposite direction, the market will turn around. *Quite often the market doesn't turn around.* Instead, it goes into a long consolidation period that could create many whipsaws. Nevertheless, this method could be traded successfully with the right stops, exits, and position sizing, which will be discussed in subsequent chapters.

SUMMARY

- Entry receives more attention from most people than any other aspect of a trading system. This attention is largely misplaced and often at the expense of ignoring the most

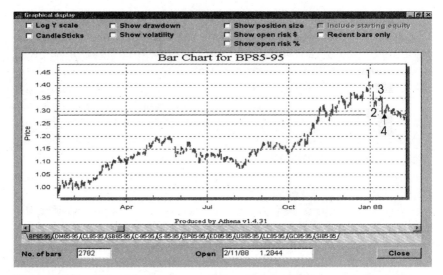

Figure 8–5 Ken Roberts' entry. A new all-time high (point 1) occurs in December 1987 in the British pound. This is followed by a sharp decline to point 2, a reversal to point 3, and then another sharp decline to a new low at point 4—the entry signal. This worked for a few months, and then the market recovered to new highs.

critical aspects of a system. Nevertheless, if good timing can increase the reliability of your trading without changing its reward-to-risk ratio, then entry certainly deserves some of your attention.

- You can make money with a random entry system. In fact, few entry techniques show a reliability that is much better than random—especially over 20 days or more.
- The best entry indicators would include:

A channel breakout of over 40 days.

A volatility breakout in a single day that's about 0.8 times the average true range. This is particularly good for market predictors.

A large ADX movement in a single day (or 2-day period) when combined with a clear indication of a trend.

Use of an indicator that shows that velocity is increasing in the direction of the trend.

An adaptive moving average changing direction and moving a predetermined distance based upon a predefined filter.

An oscillator that indicates an extreme move against the major trend followed by a clear resumption of the trend.

- Common entry techniques were discussed for various systems. In a few cases, improvements to the techniques were discussed.

N O T E S

1. Robert Kiyosaki. *If You Want to be Rich and Happy, Then Don't Go to School* (Lower Lake, CA: Asian Press, 1992).

2. My comment is in no way a reflection on the quality of any of these books. It simply is an observation that people write books to fulfill the needs of people who want to buy them. I suggest that you judge these books for yourself:

   Stephen Littauer, *How to Buy Stocks the Smart Way* (Chicago: Dearborn Trade, 1995).

   Richard J. Maturi, *Stock Picking: The Best Tactics for Beating the Market* (New York: McGraw-Hill, 1993).

   Louis Engel and Harry Hecht, *How to Buy Stocks*, 8th ed. (New York: Little, Brown, 1994).

   Michael Sivy, *How to Pick Stocks Like a Pro* (New York: Warner Books, 1996).

   Michael Gianturco, *How to Buy Technology Stocks* (New York: Little, Brown, 1996).

3. See the Recommended Readings in Appendix I.

4. It's much easier to find an entry system with a reliability above 50 percent if your time frame is 1 day or less (i.e., such as a planned exit on tomorrow's opening) than it is to find a long-term reliable exit.

5. The success of the Turtles' trading had much more to do with their position-sizing algorithm, as is usually the case, than it did the fact that they traded a channel breakout system.

6. See the Recommended Readings in Appendix I.

7. The focus of this research was not on finding a high-*R*-multiple trade or developing a high expectancy system, as we advocate in the book. The focus of the research was on finding highly reliable entries.

8. See the Recommended Readings in Appendix I.

9. Bruce Babcock, *Trendiness in the Market* (Sacramento, CA: CTCR Products, 1995). Call 916-677-7562 to order.

10. Or whatever number your testing suggests that you should use to meet your objectives.

11. See the Recommended Readings in Appendix I.

12. See LeBeau and Lucas (full citation given in the Recommended Readings in Appendix I) for a thorough discussion of this work.

13. Chuck LeBeau told me that they tested every possible combination of moving-average crossover that they could imagine. All of them worked fairly well in trending markets but failed in sideways markets. None of them were much better than random entry.

14. See the Recommended Readings in Appendix I for Kaufman's book, *Smarter Trading*.

15. Tushar Chande and Stanley Kroll, *The New Technical Trader: Boost Your Profit by Plugging into the Latest Indicators* (New York: Wiley, 1994).

16. Momentum in physics means mass times acceleration, which might be the market equivalent of acceleration on a large volume of shares of stock.

17. "The Big Bad Bear on Wall Street." *Fortune,* January 4, 1988, p. 8.

18. Michael O'Higgins and John Downes, *Beating the Dow: A High-Return, Low-Risk Method for Investing in the Dow Jones Industrial Stocks with as Little as $5,000* (New York: Harperperennial Library, 1992).

CHAPTER 9

Knowing When to Fold 'Em: How to Protect Your Capital

> Your protective stop is like a red light. You can go through it, but doing so is not very wise! If you go through town running every red light, you probably won't get to your destination quickly or safely.
>
> *Richard Harding*
> *Speaking at one of our system development seminars*

One of the attendees of a seminar I gave in the summer of 1996 was so depressed that he could hardly concentrate on the seminar. He was depressed over his recent stock market losses. During the first part of 1996, he'd grown his Keogh account from $400,000 to $1,300,000. He said that he had planned to attend the seminar, partly so he could tell me what a great investor he'd become. However, in the past 2 weeks, a number of stocks in his account had fallen dramatically and his account had dropped by 70 percent. He had one stock in his account that had fallen from just over $200 per share to about $50 per share—where he had sold at a loss. The stock was now $60 a share, and he was convinced that he'd gotten out at the bottom.

That story, I hope, is not a familiar one, but I suspect that it happens all too often. People get into the market on a tip or with some hot new entry technique. But once they have a position in the market, they have no idea when or how they will exit. Exits, whether aborting a losing position or taking profits, are the keys to making money in the market. In fact, the golden rule of trading says to:

Cut your losses short and let your profits run

That golden rule seems to me like a commentary on exits.

In his marvelous book *Campaign Trading*, John Sweeney makes the following observation:

> Just as it was tough when we were children to look under the bed or in a dark closet for night monsters, it's equally tough to look at a loss and acknowledge it. It was easier to hide under the covers back then and now it's easier to adopt some defense mechanism. (The one I hear most is "Oh, that trading rule doesn't work!" as if the entry strategy caused the loss.)*

The important point here is that getting out of a losing trade is critical if you want to be a successful trader. Most people think mostly about entry or setups, and that just doesn't help you become a success. You'll get rich trading through your exits and mastering the art of position sizing.

> In my opinion, you do not have a trading system unless you know exactly when you will get out of a market position at the time you enter it.

In my opinion, you do not have a trading system unless you know exactly when you will get out of a market position at the time you enter it. Your worst-case exit, which is designed to preserve your capital, should be determined ahead of time. In addition, you should also have some idea about how you plan to take profits and a strategy for letting your profits run. That aspect of exits is reserved for Chapter 10.

Here's what some other market legends have said about protective stops:

William O'Neil: "The whole secret to winning in the stock market is to lose the least amount possible when you're not right."

Jesse Livermore: "Investors are the big gamblers. They make a

---

*John Sweeney, *Campaign Trading*, copyright © 1996. John Wiley & Sons, p. 42. Reprinted by permission of John Wiley & Sons.

bet, stay with it, and if it goes the wrong way, they lose it all."

WHAT YOUR STOP DOES

When you set a stop loss in the market, you are doing two important things. First, you are setting a maximum loss (risk) that you are willing to take. Let's call this initial risk, R. *We'll call it* **R** because it is the basis for determining your R multiples as discussed in Chapter 6 on expectancy. Over many trades, you'll find that your average loss is about half of that, or 0.5-R, depending upon your strategy for raising stops. However, sometimes the market will also get away from you and your loss with be 2-R or perhaps even 3-R. I hope that such larger losses are very rare for you.

Let's say that you take a position in corn and you decide to use a stop loss that is three times the daily volatility. The daily volatility is about 3 cents, which when multiplied by 5,000 bushels per contract equals $150. Thus, your stop is three times that amount, or $450. If your average loss is only half of that, or 0.5 R, then you'll most likely lose about $225 if the trade doesn't work for you.

> R is the amount that you would expect to lose on a trade when you need to get out to preserve your capital. If you haven't predetermined R for every position that you take in the market, then you are just gambling your money away.

Let's look at an example in stocks. Suppose you buy 100 shares of ABCD Company. The stock is trading at $48. The daily volatility is about 50 cents, so you decide to use a stop loss of $1.50. Thus, you will sell the stock if it moved down to $46.50. That's not a big move, and it only represents a loss of $150 per 100 shares.[1]

The second important thing that you do when you enter a stop loss is to set a benchmark against which to measure subsequent gains. Your primary job as a trader should be to devise a plan that will earn profits that are large multiples of R. For example, it doesn't take many 10-R profits or 20-R profits to make a tremendous trading system. In the case of the corn trade, it would be nice to make a profit of $2,250 or even $4,500. You can tolerate a lot of $225 losses when you make a few profits like that.

Let's look at our stock market example again with this thought in mind. You purchase 100 shares of a $48 stock and you plan to get out at $46.50. Now, let's say you held on to the stock long enough for it to appreciate by 20 percent. This would amount to a gain of $9.60, or a price rise to 57.625. Basically, you have taken a risk of $150 per 100 shares for the opportunity of making $960—that's a little more than a 6-R gain, which is quite possible in today's stock market.

Realistically, commissions and slippage in the stock market, however, could easily represent another $150 in either the loss or the gain, especially if you don't trade through the Internet. If we include costs, we have a possible loss of $300 ($150 + $150 in costs) to produce a gain of $815 ($965 − $150 in costs). That means that your gain is a 2.6-R gain. Do you understand how this works? Thinking in terms of R is one of the most important concepts you need to understand. It will transform the way you approach the markets.

Most people[2] think that their entire $4,800 is at stake when they buy 100 shares at $48. That's not the case if you have a clear idea of when to exit the market and the capacity to do so.

Your stop loss predefines your initial risk, R. *But your primary job as a trader should be to devise a plan that will get you profits that are large multiples of R.*

Think about the implications of what I've just said: *One of your primary goals as a trader should be to get big-R-multiple trades.*

Remember that the first purpose of your stop loss is to set up the initial R value that you will tolerate. That R value, if small, will make it possible for you to have very large R-multiple wins. However, small stops also make your chances of losing on a given trade much higher and will cut down on the reliability of your entry technique. Remember that the reliability of our random entry system was about 38 percent. It should have been 50 percent, but the 12 percent increase in the rate of losses was due to transaction costs and the fact that we had a stop (albeit, a large one). A tighter stop would cut down your reliability even more. It could stop you out of a trade prior to a big move in your favor. You could get right back in on another entry signal, but many such trades would give you very large transaction costs.

As a result, it's important to look at some criteria that might be useful in a stop loss that you might use. These would include (1) assuming that your entry technique is not much better than chance and putting your stop beyond the noise of the market, (2) finding the maximum adverse excursion of all your winning trades and using a percentage of that as your stop, (3) having a tight stop that will give you high-R-multiple winners, and/or (4) using a stop that makes sense based upon your entry concept.

Going Beyond the Noise

The day-to-day activity of the market could be considered noise. For example, if the price moves a point or two, you never know whether it's because a few market makers were "fishing" for orders or whether there was a lot of activity. And even if there is a lot of activity, you have no idea whether it will continue or not. Thus, it's reasonable to assume that the daily activity in the market is mostly noise. It's probably better for you to place your stop outside of the likely range of any such noise.

But what is a reasonable estimate of the range of noise? A lot of people like to put their stops in the vicinity of recent support or resistance. However, one problem with this particular strategy is that everyone knows where those stops are. Quite often, markets tend to stampede in reverse and fill everyone's stop orders before they quietly return in the direction of the trend.

You might want to consider putting your protective stop at a level that isn't "logical" to the market and that is still beyond the noise. Let's assume that noise is represented by the activity of the day—i.e., the whole day's activity is mostly noise. The activity of the day could be represented by the average true range. If you take an average of this activity over that past 10 days (i.e., a 10-day moving average), you have a good approximation of the daily noise. Now, multiply the 10-day moving average of the average true range by some constant between 2.7 and 3.4 and you'll have a stop that's far enough away to be out of the noise.[3] This is probably a good stop for most long-term trend followers.

Your response to a stop that far away might be something like: "I'd never want to put that much risk in any one position." However, there's another way to look at it—which you'll understand better after going through the position-sizing chapter, Chapter 12. A wide stop is not a lot of risk if your position size is small or minimal. And if a minimal unit with that big of a risk seems like a lot of money to you, then you probably should not be trading that particular instrument—either it's not a good opportunity or you are undercapitalized.

Also remember that your initial stop is your worst-case risk, your R unit. Most of your losses will probably be about $0.5R$, because your exit will move up as the market moves and with the progression of time.

Maximum Adverse Excursion

John Sweeney, the former editor of *Technical Analysis of Stocks and Commodities,* has introduced the concept of campaign trading.[4] If you understand the concept of R, mentioned earlier, you will understand what Sweeney is trying to convey in writing about campaign trading. Campaign trading, in my opinion, is simply understanding that trading success is more a function of the price movement once you are in a trade than it is a function of your entry.

Let's think about the idea of *excursion*—what the price does from the point of entry. When you start thinking about price movement from your entry point, it introduces you to several more interesting concepts. The first of these is the *maximum adverse excursion* (MAE). This is the worst intraday price movement against your position that you are likely to encounter during the entire trade. The worst case is usually taken as being the high or low of that particular day depending upon whether you are short or long, respectively.

Figure 9–1 shows an example of adverse price excursion from an entry point on the long side. A bar chart is shown, and the dark line illustrates the MAE for the price data on a long signal. In this case the MAE is $812, yet the initial stop (i.e., a three-times-ATR stop that is not shown) is $3,582 away. Thus, the MAE is less than 25 percent of the stop value employed.

Figure 9–2 is the adverse price excursion on a losing trade. You enter the position long at 85.35 on September 23 with a stop $5,343 away. The MAE is at 80.9—a potential loss of $2,781.25. However, the stop is still several thousand dollars off that price. Eventually,

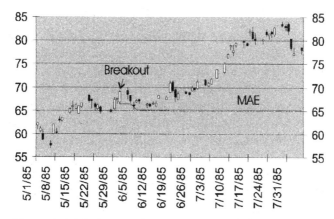

Figure 9–1 Maximum adverse excursion in a long winning trade

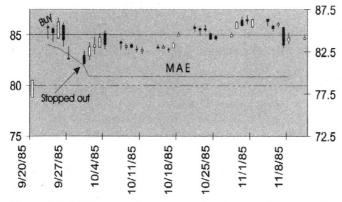

Figure 9–2 Maximum adverse excursion in a long losing trade

the price goes up, along with the stop, and you close out the position with a loss of $1,168.75—nowhere near the stop or the maximum adverse excursion of $2,781.25. In the case of the losing trade the MAE was twice the eventual loss, but only half of the stop value.

Let's create a table showing the MAE of winning and losing trades. In this case, we looked at British pounds from 1985 through

1992, using a channel breakout system and a three-times-ATR stop. Winning and losing trades were separated in the table. The MAE was entered for each winning and losing trade—both in terms of the dollar amount and in terms of its relationship to the average true range. Those data are shown in Table 9–1.

This is a small sample and not meant as anything more than an illustration of how to use the technique.[5] Notice the differences between the winning and the losing trades. You don't have any winning trades with MAE greater than 1.5 times the average true range, and only 3 of 24 winning trades (i.e., 12.5 percent) had a maximum adverse excursion above 1 average true range. In contrast, 66.7 percent of the losing trades had an MAE above 1 average true range, and almost half of them were above 1.5 average true ranges, with a mean for all losing trades of 1.44 average true ranges. Do you see a pattern here?

When you compile such data (and you give yourself a big enough stop), you will find that the MAE of winning trades will seldom go below a certain value. In other words, good trades seldom go too far against us.

| Good trades seldom go too far against us. |

If you constantly check for what this value is (i.e., in case markets change), you will find that you might be able to use much tighter stops than you originally anticipated. The advantages of tighter stops include smaller losses (although you may get a few more of them) and bigger R multiples on your winning trades.

Tight Stops

Tight stops can be used under certain conditions, such as when we're predicting a major change in the market and the market starts to confirm that prediction. Tight stops can also be used when we are looking at shorter-time-frame data. If your trading methodology will permit tighter stops, and remember that this is also a function of your personal tolerance, then you have some strong advantages going for you. First, you will lose much less money when you abort the trade. Second, because of your small loss, you can make multiple attempts to capture a big move. And, third, if

TABLE 9-1

Maximum Adverse Excursion for Winning and Losing BP Trades (1985–1992)

Winning Trades

Date	Profit	Maximum Adverse Excursion		
		In $	ATR	in ATR
3/25/85	4,350	0	2,063	0
5/31/85	6,556.25	812.5	1,194	0.680486
2/24/86	206.25	1,718.75	1,331	1.291322
9/22/86	1,062.5	343.75	806	0.426489
12/19/86	5,350	125	325	0.384615
2/23/87	8,962.5	0	558	0
10/14/87	643.75	0	588	0
10/26/87	9,906.25	312.5	1,531	0.204115
6/28/88	7,531.25	1,118.75	938	1.192697
10/12/88	7,550	87.5	748	0.116979
3/1/89	350	312.5	1,068	0.292603
5/8/89	6,012.5	537.5	798	0.673559
12/20/89	6,800	50	613	0.081566
5/15/90	7,912.5	962.5	645	1.492248
7/18/90	6,937.5	1,075	1,140	0.942982
10/5/90	3,000	100	1,418	0.070522
1/24/91	12.5	556.25	1,253	0.443935
3/15/91	5,475	112.5	1,250	0.09
9/6/91	1,350	387.5	978	0.396217
11/7/91	7,875	0	1,598	0
5/1/92	1,450	137.5	660	0.208333
/5/92	4,762.5	150	820	0.182927
8/21/92	787.5	525	950	0.552632
9/15/92	19,962.5	212.5	2,305	0.092191
Averages	**5,200.26**	**401.5625**	**1,065.75**	**0.409017**

Losing Trades

Date	Loss	Maximum Adverse Excursion		
		In $	ATR	in ATR
9/23/85	1,168.75	2,781.25	1,781	**1.561623**
11/21/85	250	281.25	650	0.432692
1/22/86	1,462.5	1,462.5	1,006	1.453777
4/17/86	693.75	750	1,074	0.698324
5/20/87	1,875	1,875	531	**3.531073**
8/3/87	93.75	93.75	575	0.163043
9/1/87	925	925	725	1.275862
2/5/88	2,781.25	2,781.25	844	**3.29532**
3/2/88	262.5	262.5	950	0.276316
2/18/88	2,181.25	2,375	1,194	**1.989112**
1/19/89	1,812.5	1,925	1,088	**1.769301**
9/15/89	3,150	3,150	2,255	1.396896
12/24/90	2,737.5	2,737.5	1,268	**2.158912**
6/12/91	81.25	137.5	853	0.161196
3/4/92	1,287.5	1,437.5	953	**1.508395**
Averages	**1,384.167**	**1,531.667**	**1,049.8**	**1.44479**

241

you should get such a move, it will give you a much bigger *R*-multiple profit.

However, tight stops have some serious drawbacks as well. First, they will decrease the reliability of your system. You will have to make many more trades in order to make a profit. And if you cannot tolerate a lot of small losses, which many traders and investors cannot, then tight stops will be your downfall.

Second, tight stops dramatically increase your transaction costs. Transaction costs are a major part of doing business. In fact, I seldom see a system that over a number of years produces profits that are much bigger than the transaction costs it generates—that is, if a system generates a million dollars in net profits, then it probably generates more than a million dollars in transaction costs. If you are in and out of the market all the time, then such transaction costs can eat your profits down to nothing. This becomes a major factor if you are trading small size, so that your cost per trade is much higher than it should be.

> ...I seldom see a system that over a number of years produces profits that are much bigger than the transaction costs it generates—that is, if a system generates a million dollars in net profits, then it probably generates more than a million dollars in transaction costs.

Losing much less money when you abort a trade is probably an exciting prospect to most of you. However, the worst thing a trader can do is miss a major move. Consequently, you must be willing to get right back in the position should it again give you a signal. Many people cannot tolerate three to five losses in a row, which this strategy will regularly produce. However, let's say that each exit only produces a loss of $100. You lose on five of these exits in a row and then the market suddenly gives you the move you expected. A week later you exit with a 20 *R* profit of $2,000. You've had five losers and one winner. You've been "right" less than 17 percent of the time—which most people would have problems with—but your total profit from six trades is $1,500 less any commissions and slippage.[6]

In such a situation, you have to understand what is happening. Let's suppose you used a wide stop such as three times the ATR. Let's also suppose that in this situation, the three-times-ATR stop was $600. If you predicted the move correctly, you might not have been stopped out at all. As a result, you would have only made one trade with a 3.33-R profit of $2,000. But your total profit would be $1,900, including the $100 for slippage and commissions. Remember that in the previous example, you only made $900 after subtracting your losses and your slippage and commissions.

When you have a $600 stop, if it takes two attempts to make the profit, the situation is still a little better than with the $100 stop. You make $2,000 on the profitable trade, but you lose $600 on the one loss—for a net profit of $1,400. If you subtract $200 for slippage and commissions, you now have $1,200 net profit. This is still better than the first example in which we needed to make six trades to get the profit. However, you might not have concluded that if you had not made the adjustment for slippage and commissions.

With the $600 stop, your profitability drops off dramatically when you have multiple failures. If you are stopped out twice before you get your $2,000 profit, then you will only have a net profit of $500. If you are stopped out three times before you get your $2,000 profit, then you'll have a net loss of $200.

My point in giving you these examples is that your protective loss stop must not be taken lightly. It must be chosen carefully with respect to your objectives and your temperament.

USING A STOP THAT MAKES SENSE

The most important factor in determining the nature of your stop is to determine if it makes sense given your objectives, the nature of the concept you are trading, and your temperament. You must use something that makes sense. Let's look at some of the other types of protective stops that you might use and examine the issues involved.

Dollar Stops

Many traders advocate the use of dollar stops. These have somewhat of a psychological advantage—you figure out how much you are willing to lose on a trade and set that as a stop beforehand. In addition, they also have several technical advantages. First, such stops are not that predictable. Most people are not likely to figure out where you got into the market, so they are not likely to figure out that your stop is $1,500 or $1,000 away. Second, when such stops are beyond the MAE, they end up being very good stops. Simply determine, in dollars, what your MAE is likely to be in a given contract and set your stop a little beyond that.

However, some people confuse such stops with money management and ignore what we are calling position sizing. These people believe that if you want to risk 1 percent of your equity and you have $100,000, then just put your stop $1,000 away and call it a money management stop. This is naïve.

If this is how you set your stop, don't confuse it with position sizing. Position sizing is the most important part of your system in determining how much you are likely to make trading the system. Don't give up that most important component by doing something so naïve as to set such money management stops.

Percent Retracement

Some people set stops by allowing the price to retrace a certain percentage of the entry price. This is a very common practice among stock traders. For example, you might buy a stock at $30 and sell it if it retraced by 10 percent to $27. Using this same methodology, you would sell a stock you bought at $10 at $9 and you'd sell a $100 stock at $90.

This practice is fine if your retracement method is based upon some sort of MAE analysis. But if you just picked some number out of the air—which is a common practice—then you could be throwing away a lot of potential profits with your stop.

Volatility Stops

Volatility stops are based upon the assumption that the volatility, to some extent, represents noise in the market. Consequently, if you set a stop at some multiple of the ATR (we used the example of three times the ATR previously), then you probably have a good stop that is beyond the immediate noise of the market. My experience is that volatility stops are among the best stops you could select.

Dev-Stops[7]

Cynthia Kase coined the term "dev-stop" in her book, *Trading with the Odds*, and devotes an entire chapter to the topic. If you have a normal distribution of prices, then 1 standard deviation of price change in either direction would account for about 67 percent of the prices. Two standard deviations will encompass about 97 percent of the prices. Market prices are not normal—they tend to be skewed to the right—so some correction is needed in the standard deviation to take into account this skew. This amounts to about a 10 percent correction on the first standard deviation and a 20 percent correction on the second standard deviation.

While it's not appropriate to go into calculations of the standard deviation in this chapter, you might find the standard deviation of the average true range to be quite useful as a stop. Take the average true range for the last 30 days and calculate the standard deviation. The average true range plus 1 standard deviation plus a 10 percent correction factor would be one level of stop. The average true range plus 2 standard deviations plus a 20 percent correction factor would be another level of stop.

Channel Breakout and Moving-Average Stops

Just as the channel breakout and moving-average concepts can be used as entries, they can also be used as stops. My personal bias is that these sorts of stops are not nearly as good as stops based upon the average true range or MAE. In addition, they are both stops and profit-taking exits. Nevertheless, they are worthy of a brief discussion for the sake of completeness.

A common entry technique that has been used for many years is the moving-average crossover. These were discussed extensively in Chapter 8. When you have two moving averages, you basically have a reversal exit. When you are in a position and the short average crosses the longer, you have both a stop to get you out of your current position and a reversal entry signal to go the other way (long or short, depending upon the direction of the cross). Of course, the problem with such systems is that you are always in the market and get whipsawed many times.

R. C. Allen[8] popularized the three-moving-averages system in which you get an entry signal when both the shorter averages have crossed the longer. This would mean, by definition, that the shortest average was now on top (or on the bottom). When the shortest signal crosses the medium signal, you now get your stop signal. However, you do not get a reversal signal to enter a short position until both the short and medium averages cross the longer average.

Channel breakouts were also discussed in Chapter 8. You might enter the market, for example, when prices make a new high for the last 40 days. Your stop might also be a channel breakout—when prices make a new low for the last 10 days. This method has the advantage of giving prices a lot of room, being well beyond the noise, and has been used by many well-known traders. However, it has the tremendous disadvantage of giving back a lot of profits because your stop is both the worst-case protective stop and your profit-taking exit.

Support and Resistance Stops

Support and resistance stops have also been mentioned earlier. Typically, the trader will enter the market and look for areas of support and resistance on the chart. Stops will typically be placed at the extremes of these levels. Some traders may be paranoid about such stops because they seem so obvious. If so, you may want to add a constant to the stop. Thus, you might have a stop at a support area below your entry plus some constant.

Time Stops

Many traders and investors say that if a position does not go in your favor fairly quickly, then it probably will not. As a result, another common stop-loss method is the time stop. The time stop simply takes you out of a position after a fixed amount of time if you haven't made a profit (or made a profit above some arbitrary level).

One great trader said that he treated each day in a trade as an entirely new day. If he could not justify getting into that trade on that day, then he would simply close it out. This is effectively a time stop.

The choice to use a time stop is very personal. Don't use one if you are a long-term trader and have no way to get back in the market should your big expected move suddenly occur. Don't use one if you have trouble getting back into a position you have exited. However, if you like short-term trading, then time stops are probably an excellent addition to your arsenal.

Before using time stops, however, check out their effectiveness within the framework of your methodology. If you decide to use a 3-day time stop, for example, determine the effectiveness of such a stop. How often will a position do nothing for 3 days and then take off? If you find enough examples to suggest that you could miss a major move, then avoid such stops. However, if you find that they only cut your losses faster, then by all means include them.

Discretionary and Psychological Stops

If you have a good intuitive sense of the market, then you might also consider discretionary stops—of which one might be a time stop. Many of the best professional traders use discretionary stops, but I would not recommend them for the amateur or beginning trader.

The psychological stop, in contrast, is great for most market players. Unless you are in the market for the long haul, i.e., you don't ever plan to sell, you should consider psychological stops. Long-term trend followers could have a problem with such stops as well, since one good trade can make a whole year of trading. Unless you are psychologically well balanced, you'll probably decide it's time to take a vacation or use a psychological stop right about the time the big trade comes along.

There are certain time periods when the most important factor in your trading—you, the human being—is nowhere near 100 percent. These are the times you should just consider getting out of the market. The times that almost predict certain disaster are (1) when you are going through a divorce or separation from a significant person, (2) when a significant person in your life dies or is in the hospital, (3) when a child is born, (4) when you move your home or office, (5) when you are psychologically exhausted or burnt out, and (6) when you are so excited about the market that you see your position doubling overnight—even when it hasn't moved. These are probably periods when you should just close down all your active positions.

You might also consider using psychological stops when you go on a trip. For example, if you take a vacation, allow that vacation to be a time away from the market and close out all your positions. When you take a business trip and cannot follow the market in a normal way, I'd also suggest closing out all your positions. These psychological stops are among the most important you can have. I'd strongly recommend that you start using them.

SUMMARY: PRESERVING CAPITAL

- Your protective stop is like a red light. You can go through it, but you're not very likely to do so safely.
- Your protective stop has two main functions: (1) It sets up the maximum loss that you'll likely take in your position (R), and (2) it sets a benchmark against which to measure subsequent gains.
- Your primary job as a trader or investor should be to devise a plan that will get you profits that are large multiples of R, your initial risk.
- Consider going beyond the noise when you set your stops. This can be done by setting stops that are several times the ATR, by using dev-stops, or by determining the MAE and going beyond that.
- Tight stops have the advantage of creating large-R-multiple winners and minimizing losses. However, they have the disadvantage of reducing reliability and greatly increasing your transaction costs. As a result, you should probably only use tight stops if you have really planned your entry well.
- Other types of stops include dollar stops, percent retracement stops, volatility stops, channel breakout stops, moving-average stops, support and resistance stops, time

stops, and discretionary stops. Each has its own particular merit, and selecting the right one for you is part of the job of designing a trading system that is right for you.

STOPS USED BY COMMON SYSTEMS

Stock Market Systems

William O'Neil's CANSLIM Method

William O'Neil does not promote market-related stops, but instead argues that you should never let a stock go against you by more than 7–8 percent. This is a version of the "percent retracement" stop discussed earlier. Essentially, O'Neil's 7–8 percent refers to a 7–8 percent retracement in the price of the stock—it has nothing to do with your equity. Thus, if you buy a stock at $20, you should never let it go against you by more than 7–8 percent of $20, or $1.40 to $1.60. If you buy a stock at $100, then you should never let it go against you by more than $7 to $8. O'Neil cautions that 7–8 percent should be the maximum loss you should tolerate. He actually recommends that your overall average of all losses be around 5 to 6 percent.

Although O'Neil's guidelines are some of the best provided by anyone recommending methods to trade stocks, in my opinion they can be improved upon. You would be much better off with a market-based stop. Determine your MAE using the O'Neil system. This probably should be calculated with respect to various price ranges. If you find that low-priced stocks, i.e., under $25, seldom move more than $1 against you if they are good purchases, then your stop might be $1. You might find that even $100 stocks seldom move against you by more than $2 if they were good purchases. If that's the case, then your potential for big R gains on high-price stocks would be tremendous.

Since O'Neil recommends that you enter when the market breaks out of the base, you probably should exit if it returns to the base—or at least if it goes to the bottom of the base. Another possible exit would be to abort the position if it moves three times the average daily price volatility against you.

The Warren Buffett Approach to Investing

Warren Buffett, according to most of the books on him, considers most of his holdings to be lifetime holdings. He feels that his returns will be large enough over the long term to weather the psychological ups and downs of the market. In addition, he has no desire to pay the transaction costs of getting in and out—to say nothing of the tax consequences. As a result, Warren Buffett considers his main job to be that of buying companies that he is willing to own forever. As a result, Warren Buffett doesn't seem to have any protective stops:

> I never attempt to make money on the stock market. I buy on the assumption that they could close the market the next day and not reopen it for five years.[9]

However, Buffett has been known to sell an investment occasionally. Remember that a protective stop is something that you use in a worst-case scenario to protect your capital. As a result, I'm sure Buffett must go through some regular review of his investments to determine if they still meet his criteria. The more wisely you select your investments, understand how the companies operate, and can evaluate whether or not they are managed well, the more you can use this sort of approach. However, I would strongly recommend that even the most die-hard long-term investor have a worst-case bailout signal for every investment at the time it is purchased.

Motley Fool Foolish-Four Approach

This approach also has no real protective stops except to reassess the portfolio each year on the anniversary date. Since high-yield approaches generally work only on very high capitalization stocks that are highly respected (such as the Dow 30), there is probably little chance of having a serious problem[10] with these stocks.

Nevertheless, when you research this method, you'll find that most of the time the quarterly return is because of the performance of one or two of the four stocks that really ran. However, quite often one of the stocks will have gone down considerably. Thus, in my opinion, this method could be improved upon with a stop. Compare the losing years with the winning years in this technique. How much did you lose (at most) during winning years? How much did you lose during losing years? In other words, determine the MAE of this technique. You might find that the MAE technique will have little effect on the downside risk in winning years and limit the downside risk in losing years.

Futures Market Systems

Kaufman Adaptive Moving-Average Approach

Kaufman in discussing the nature of stop losses makes an interesting observation. He says that the size of the erratic price move against you times the number of times that move is likely to occur is always about the same. For example, you might have 20 occurrences of a 5-point move, 10 occurrences of a 10-point move, and 5 occurrences of a 20-point move. All these would add up to 100 points of loss plus slippage and transaction costs. As a result, he argues that larger stops are generally better because they minimize transaction costs.

When Kaufman tests a system in his book, he only uses a few simple ideas with respect to stops. First, a trade is exited at the close if the loss exceeds a preset percentage level. This is much like the O'Neil concept. Second, a trade is exited when a reversal signal is given, including when the trade is losing money.

Many of the concepts discussed in this chapter, in my opinion, would greatly improve the adaptive moving-average system. For example, consider using a volatility stop, a MAE stop, or the dev-stop.

Gallacher's Fundamental Trading

If you recall from Chapter 18, Gallacher is a fundamental trader. He uses fundamentals to trade commodities and enters the market on a 10-day channel breakout when the fundamentals are setups for the market to move in a particular direction. His stop loss is simple. It's a 10-day channel breakout in the opposite direction.

Although many of the ideas behind Gallacher's trading are very sound, readers of this book, in my opinion, would find that many of the stop-loss approaches recommended in this book could greatly improve upon this simple method of trading.

Ken Roberts' 1-2-3 Methodology

Remember that Roberts' setup is that the market makes a 9-month high or low and then makes a 1-2-3 pattern. The entry signal is when the market hits a new price extreme in the opposite direction of the old high or low—in other words, when the market again passes point 2 on the 1-2-3 pattern you enter. The stop loss is simply putting the stop at a logical point on the chart—just beyond point 3.

Once again, in my opinion, users of this approach would be much better off with a stop that was based on a statistical extreme. Several such stops might include (1) three times the ATR, (2) the ATR plus three times the standard deviation of the ATR, (3) a dev-stop, or (4) an estimate of the MAE in this particular case and a stop put just beyond that.

NOTES

1. This kind of trading is difficult due to the very large commissions charged even by discount stockbrokers. However, discount Internet trading has changed that.
2. The stock exchange promotes this by having margin calls at only 50 percent and teaching people that they could lose it all. Furthermore, they are justified in doing so because most people don't have a plan to trade and are psychologically wired to lose money.
3. Suggested by J. Wells Wilder in *New Concepts in Technical Trading Systems*. See the Recommended Readings in Appendix I.
4. Sweeney, *Campaign Trading*. See the Recommended Readings in Appendix I.
5. Refer to *Campaign Trading* for more details about MAE.
6. If slippage and commissions are $100 per trade, you have to subtract $600 from your $1,500 profit. It basically makes your 20-R profit now seem like a 9-R profit. This is why short-term traders must always consider the transaction cost factor in their trading. It's probably the major factor influencing short-term success.
7. Dev-stop is a copyrighted indicator of Cynthia A. Kase.
8. LeBeau and Lucas have an excellent discussion of this topic. See the Recommended Readings in Appendix I.

9. W. Buffett, quoted in *Fortune* by Jeremy Gain, "The Bull Market's Biggest Winners," *Fortune,* August 8, 1983, p. 36.

10. You won't lose all your money with such a strategy, but if a major bear market started, you could easily lose 30 percent or more in a short period of time.

CHAPTER 10

How to Take Profits

You've got to know when to hold 'em; know when to fold 'em;
know when to walk away; and know when to run.
Kenny Rogers
From The Gambler

Several years ago Ed Seykota, who is featured in Jack Schwager's
Market Wizards book, remarked at one of our seminars that if you
wanted to learn how to trade, you should go down to the beach and
watch the waves. Soon you'd notice that waves wash ashore and
then turn around and go back to sea. He then suggested that you
start moving your hands in rhythm with the waves—moving them
toward you as the wave approaches and moving them away from
you as the wave withdraws. After doing that for a while, you'll
notice that you will soon be in touch with the waves. "When you
reach that state of being in tune with the flow," he said, "you'll
know a lot about what it takes to become a trader." Notice that to
be able to get in touch with the waves, it's important for you to
know when the wave has finished its movement.

Another man came to visit me from Australia. He'd made a lot
of money in the computer software business, and he now wanted
to research trading systems. He'd been visiting people all over the
United States to learn the essence of trading. We had dinner
together, and he carefully explained all his trading ideas to me.
When I finished hearing his ideas, which were all good, I was a lit-

tle perplexed. All his research had to do with discovering entry techniques into the market. He'd done no research into what exits to use or how to control his position size. When I suggested to him that he now needed to spend at least as much time developing his profit-taking exits as he had on entry and an equal amount of time, if not more, on position sizing, he seemed upset.

People just seem to want to ignore exits—perhaps because they cannot control the market on the exit. Yet for those who want control, exits do control two important variables—whether or not you'll make a profit and how much profit you will make. They are one of the major keys to developing a successful system.

PURPOSE BEHIND PROFIT-TAKING EXITS

There are a lot of problems to solve with exits. If the worst case does not happen (i.e., so you don't get stopped out), then the job of your system is to allow you to make the most profit possible and give the least amount of it back. Only your exits do this!

Notice that I use the word "exits"—the *plural* version of the word—because most systems need several exits to do the job properly. As a result, consider using different exit strategies for each of your system objectives. As you design your system, keep in mind how you want to control your risk-to-reward ratio and maximize your profits using the types of profit-taking exits described in this section.

There are many different classifications of exits other than your initial stop loss. These include exits that produce a loss but reduce your initial risk, exits that maximize profits, and exits that keep you from giving back too much money and psychological exits. The categories are somewhat overlapping. Several techniques for you to consider are provided with each type of exit. As you peruse each, think about how it could be adapted to your system. Most exit strategies are incredibly accommodating to special system objectives.

Exits That Produce a Loss, But Reduce Your Initial Risk

Your initial stop loss, discussed in Chapter 9, was designed to be your worst-case loss that protects your capital. However, this class of exit will also produce a loss, but these exits are designed to make sure you lose as little as possible.

The Timed Stop

Generally, people enter the market because they expect the price to move in their favor shortly after entry. As a result, if you have a meaningful entry signal, then a potentially useful exit is one that will get you out after a period of time when you are not profitable. For example, such an exit might be "get out of the market at the close in 2 days if this position is not profitable." Such an exit would cause one to lose money, but not as much as if one's worst-case stop were hit.

The Trailing Stop

The trailing stop is one that is adjusted on a periodic basis according to some sort of mathematical algorithm. The random entry system (described in Chapter 8) used a three-times-volatility trailing stop that was adjusted from the close on a daily basis only when it moved in favor of the trade. For example, after the first day of trading, if the price moves in your favor or if volatility shrinks, then the trailing stop is moved in your favor. It might still be at a loss, but it is moved in your favor. Thus, if the market moves against you enough to stop you out, you would still take a loss, but it would not be as big as your initial stop. Figure 10–1 shows an example of a volatility trailing stop. Such trailing stops could be based upon any number of factors—volatility, a moving average, a channel breakout, various price consolidations, etc.—and each could have any number of different variables controlling them. See the next section for some specific examples.

The important point about trailing stops is that your exit algorithm will continually make adjustments that will move the exit in your favor. That movement might not be profitable, but it would reduce your potential loss.

You must give careful consideration, through testing and examining your results, whether or not you want to do this. For example, quite often by reducing your initial risk as you move up your trailing stop, you merely give up your chance for a profit. Instead, you just take a smaller loss. Be careful in this area of your

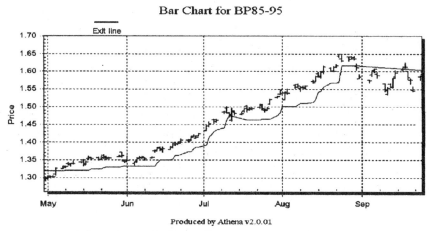

Bar Chart for BP85-95

Produced by Athena v2.0.01

Figure 10–1 A three-times-volatility trailing stop

system development, and if your system does utilize tight stops, be aware that a reentry strategy could be used.

Exits That Maximize Your Profits

In order to maximize your profits (let them run), you must be willing to give some of them back. In fact, the ironic part of system design is if you want to maximize profits, you must be willing to give back a great deal of the profits you have already accumulated. As a wise and very wealthy trader once said, "You can't make money if you're not willing to lose. It's like breathing in, but not being willing to breathe out." Various types of exits will help you do this (i.e., breathe fully), including trailing stops and the percent retracement stop.

The Trailing Stop

The trailing stop also has the potential to help you gain large profits, but it will always give some of your profits back. Let's look at some examples of trailing stops that you might want to use.

The **volatility trailing stop,** which has already been mentioned, is a multiple of the daily volatility of the market. J. Wells

Wilder, who first promoted the concept, suggests that it should be a number somewhere between 2.7 and 3.4 times the average true range of the last 10 days. We used 3.0 in the random entry system. The point of the volatility stop is keep your stop out of the noise of the market, and 3 times the daily volatility certainly does that. Others have looked at the weekly volatility. If you use the weekly volatility, then you probably can get by with a stop somewhere between 0.7 to 2 times the weekly volatility.

The **dollar trailing stop** is another possibility. Here you would decide some number such as $1,500, and keep a trailing stop at that amount behind yesterday's close. Dollar stops are excellent if they have some rational basis. However, using a $1,500 stop in an S&P contract, a corn contract, a $150 stock, and a $10 stock is madness. The amount of your dollar stop should be adjusted for what is reasonable for each market. The best way to determine what is reasonable for each market is to check the volatility of that market. As a result, you might as well use a volatility-based stop instead.

A **channel breakout trailing stop** is also quite useful. You might decide that you will get out at the extreme price of the last X days (you fill in the number). Thus, in a long position, you might decide to sell if the price hits the low of the last 20 days, whereas in a short position you might decide to sell if the price hits the high of the last 20 days. As the price moves in your favor, this number is always adjusted in your favor.

> ...a 200-day moving average would have kept you actively involved in the stock market over the last 3 years (1995–1997) and allowed you to make significant profits.

A **moving-average trailing stop** is another common trailing stop. If price is moving in any particular direction, then a slow moving average will trail behind that price and could be used as a stop. However, you will have to determine the number of periods involved in that moving average. For example, a 200-day moving average would have kept you actively involved in the stock market over the last 3 years (1995–1997) and allowed you to make significant profits.

There are many different types of moving averages—simple,

exponential, displaced, adaptive, etc.—and all these could be used as trailing stops. Your job is simply to find the one or several that best help you meet your objectives. Different types of moving averages were discussed extensively in the entry chapter, Chapter 8, of this book.

There are also other kinds of **trailing stops based upon consolidations or chart patterns.** For example, every time the market moves beyond a consolidation pattern, that old consolidation pattern could become the basis of a new stop. This amounts to a discretionary trailing stop, and it will give back a lot of profits. Nevertheless, it may have some merits in combination with other types of exits.

The Profit Retracement Stop

This kind of stop makes an assumption that you must give back a percentage of your profits in order to allow them to grow. As a result, it just assigns a number to the amount of retracement allowed and makes it part of your system. However, in order to use a profit retracement stop, you must reach a certain level of profitability such as a 2-R profit.

Here's how this kind of stop might work. Suppose you purchase 100 shares of Micron at $52. You initially assume a 1-R risk of $6, by assuming that you will get out if the stock drops to $46. Once you obtain a 2-R profit of $12 by having the stock move up in price to $64, you decide to begin a profit retracement stop. Let's say that you decide to put on a 30 percent profit retracement stop. Since you now have $12, you are willing to give up 30 percent of that, or $3.60.

When the profit moves up to $13, a 30 percent retracement now becomes $3.90. And at $14, a 30 percent retracement becomes $4.20. Since the actual dollar amount as a fixed percent continues to grow as the profit grows, you may want to change the percentage as the profit gets bigger. For example, you might start out at a 30 percent retracement, but move the amount down to 25 percent at a 3-R profit and to 20 percent at a 4-R profit. You could continue to decrease the amount until you only allowed a 5 percent retracement at 7-R, or you might allow it to remain at 20 percent once you reach 4-R. This would depend entirely upon your objectives in designing your system.

Exits That Keep You from Giving Back Too Much Profit

If you are managing other people's money, it is more important to minimize drawdowns than it is to produce large returns. As a result, you might want to consider exits that keep you from giving back too much profit. For example, if you have open positions on March 31 that put your client's account up 15 percent in his March statement, then that client is going to be upset when you give back much of that profit. Your client will consider that open profit to be his money. As a result, you need some sort of exit that will lock in most of that profit once you reach a particular objective or after a reporting period to the client.

As I mentioned earlier, many of the exits presented overlap categories. For example, the percent retracement exits combined with an objective is an excellent exit to keep you from giving back too much profit. However, there are others that also work well.

The Profit Objective

Some people use trading systems that tend to predict profit targets (e.g., Elliott Wave). If you use such a system, then you probably can target specific objectives.

However, there is a second way to target objectives. You might determine, based upon historical testing, that your method produces the kind of reward-to-risk ratio you desire if you take a profit at some specific multiple of your initial risk. For example, you might find that four times your initial risk (4–R) is a great objective. If you can achieve that, then you might want to take your profit or institute a much closer stop. All the methods discussed below can be tightened in some way once a profit objective is reached.

The Profit Retracement Exit

One excellent idea for an exit that was mentioned previously is to only be willing to give back a certain percentage of your profit and to tighten that percentage after some important milestone (such as a report to clients or a profit objective) is reached. For example, after you have a 2–R profit, you might be willing to give back 30 percent of that profit in order to allow it to grow. When you have a much greater profit, say 4–R, you might only be willing to give back 5 to 10 percent of it before you exit.

For example, let's say you bought gold at $400 with a stop at $390. Thus, your initial risk is 10 points, or $1,000. Gold moves to $420 so that you have a 20-point profit (2–R). That might be a trigger to only allow a 30 percent retracement of your profit, or $600. If gold moves down to $414, you'll take your profit.

Gold continues to move up and reaches $440, so that you now have a 4–R profit of $4,000. Until you reached the 4–R profit, you were willing to give up 30 percent of your profit, which was $1,200 at the $4,000 level. However, the 4–R level is now your signal to risk only 10 percent of your profit. Your stop is now moved to $436—allowing just over a $400 decline.

My intention is not to suggest specific levels (such as a 10 percent retracement at 4–R), but merely to suggest a methodology for you to attain your objectives. It is up to you to determine what levels will help you best attain your objectives.

A Large Volatility Move against You

One of the best exits you can have is a large volatility move against you. In fact, this type of move is also a very good entry for a system—commonly known as a volatility breakout system.

What you need to do is keep track of the average true range. When the market makes an abnormally large move (let's say two times the average daily volatility) against you, you would exit the market. Let's say you have 200 shares of IBM trading at $145. The average daily volatility is $1.50, and you decide that you will get out if the market moves twice that volatility against you in a single day. In other words, since the market closed at $145 and twice the daily volatility is $3, you'll exit the market if it moves to $142 tomorrow. This would be a tremendous move against you, and you don't want to stay in if this sort of move occurs.[1]

It should be obvious why this cannot be your only exit. Suppose you continue to keep this two-times-volatility stop. The market is at 145 today, so your volatility exit is 142. The market closes down 1 point to 144. Your new volatility exit is now 141. The next day the market closes down 1 point to 143. Your new volatility exit is now 140. This could keep on going until the price goes to zero. Thus, you need some other type of exit—such as your protective stop and some sort of trailing stop—to get you out to preserve your capital.

Parabolic Stops

Parabolic exits were first described by J. Wells Wilder, and they are very useful. The parabolic curve starts out at a previous low point and has an accelerating factor in upward-moving markets. As the market trends, it gets closer and closer to the price. Thus, it does a great job of locking in profits. Unfortunately, it is quite far from the actual price at the beginning of your trade. Also, the parabolic stop may sometimes come a little too close to the prices, and you can get stopped out while the market continues to trend.

There are a few ways of working around these setbacks. One possibility is adjusting the acceleration factor of the parabolic stop to rise faster or slower compared with the true prices of the market. In this way, parabolic stops can be well customized to your particular system and to the market you're trading.

To better control your risk at the start of a trade, you could set a separate dollar stop. For example, if the parabolic stop offers a $3,000 risk at the purchase of the position, you could set a simple $1,500 stop until the parabolic comes within $1,500 of the true contract price; a $3,000 risk might be too much for your particular objectives.

Furthermore, if you are using a parabolic exit, you should consider designing a reentry technique. If the parabolic stop gets too close to the actual price, you might stop out before the end of a certain trend that you are following. You don't want to miss out on the rest of the trend, so you may want to get back into a trade. While parabolic stops may not be as exceptional as other exit techniques for risk control, they are excellent for protecting profits.

Psychological Exits

One of the smartest exits anyone can have is a psychological exit. These depend more upon you than upon what the markets do. Since you are the most significant factor in your trading, psychological exits are important.

There are certain times in which your probability of losing money in the market goes up greatly—no matter what the markets do. These include periods when you just don't feel well because of health or mental problems, when your stress is high, when you are going through a divorce, when you've just had a new child, or when you are moving. Your chances of doing something that will cause market losses are greatly increased during these periods. As a result, I strongly recommend that you use a psychological exit and pull yourself out of the market.

Another good time for a psychological exit is when you must be away from the market due to business or a vacation. Those also are not good times to remain in the market. Again, I recommend the psychological exit during these periods.

Some people would argue that one trade might make your entire year and you don't want to miss that trade. *I agree with that philosophy if you are disciplined and fairly automated in your trading. However, most people are not.* During any of the periods I mentioned, the average person would lose money despite being in a good trade. Consequently, it is important to know yourself. If it is likely that you will blow out even on a good trade, then you must employ psychological exits.

JUST USING YOUR STOP AND A PROFIT OBJECTIVE

One of your objectives in designing a trading system might be to maximize the probability of high-R-multiple trades. You might decide, for example, to use tight stops with the objective of getting a 20-R multiple trade. To do so, you might decide to use the break-out-retracement strategy described in Chapter 8 to develop a tight stop. Let's say that your stop is only $1 on a high-priced stock, so you'll only lose $100 on 100 shares. This would be a very tight stop, for example, in a $100 stock undergoing a sharp breakout. You could be stopped out five times in a row with just a $100 loss each time—for a total loss of $500. One $20 move in the underlying stock would give you a $2,000 profit, or a $1,500 net profit. You are "right" one time out of six, but you make a $1,500 net profit,[2] less commissions.

In order for this strategy to work, you must avoid trailing stops, or those stops must be very large. Your only exits will be your initial 1-R stop and your profit objectives. This will give you the maximum opportunity for a 20-R profit. You may have to tolerate drops of $1,000 or more in your profit, but never more[3] than a 1-R loss or $100 to your starting equity. Remember, your goal is a 20-R profit which you might achieve regularly.

SIMPLICITY AND MULTIPLE EXITS

What works best in system design are simple concepts. Simplicity works because it tends to be based upon understanding rather than optimization. It works because one can generalize simple concepts across a number of markets and trading instruments.

However, you can still have multiple exits and make them simple. Don't confuse the two concepts. Simplicity is necessary so that your system will work, while multiple exits are usually necessary to meet your objectives. Each of your multiple exits can be simple, of course.

Let's look at an example. Suppose you have a goal of simply using a trend-following system and you'd like to be in the market a long time. You believe that there is nothing magical about your entry signal, so you want to give your position plenty of room. You believe that a large move against you might be a trigger for potential disaster, so you want to get out when it occurs. Lastly, you decide that since your initial risk will be quite wide, you will have to capture as much as possible once you get a 4-R profit. Consequently, let's design some simple exits based upon these beliefs.

First, you want a wide initial stop to give the position plenty of room without whipsawing you out of the market and causing you to have to get in several times with resulting transaction costs. Consequently, you decide to use the three-times-volatility stop that you read about earlier. That will be your worst-case stop, and it will also be your trailing stop because you will trail it from the close each day—always moving it in favor of your position.

Second, you believe that a strong move against you is a good warning sign. Consequently, you decide that whenever the market moves twice the daily volatility from yesterday's close against you in a single day, you will get out. This stop will float on top of the other one.

Lastly, a 4-R profit will trigger a much tighter stop so that you will not give back much profit and can be assured of capturing what you already have. As a result, after a 4-R profit is triggered, your trailing volatility stop moves up to 1.6 times the average true range (i.e., instead of 3 times).

Notice that all these stops are simple. They all came out of my head from thinking about what kind of stops would meet the objectives. No testing was involved, so they are not overoptimized. No rocket science is involved—they are simple. You do have three distinct exits which help meet your trading system goals, but only one of these will be in the market at one time—the one closest to the current price.

WHAT TO AVOID

There is one kind of exit that is designed to get rid of losses, but it totally goes against the golden rule of trading of cut your losses short and let your profit run. Instead, it produces large losses and small profits. This type of exit is one in which you enter the market with multiple contracts and then scale out with various exits. For example, you might start with 300 shares and sell 100 of them when you can break even on all 300 shares. You might then sell another 100 shares at a $500 profit and keep the last 100 shares for a huge profit. Short-term traders use this type of strategy frequently. On a gut level, this sort of trading makes sense because you seem to be "insuring" your profits. But if you step back from this sort of exit and really study it, you'll see how dangerous this type of trading is.

What you are actually doing with this sort of exit is practicing reverse position sizing. You are making sure that you will have multiple positions when you take your largest losses. In our example, you'd lose on all 300 shares. You are also making sure that you only have a minimal-sized position when you make your largest gains—100 shares in our example. It's the perfect method for people with a strong bias to be right, but it doesn't optimize profits or even guarantee profits. Does it make sense now?

If it doesn't make sense to you why you should avoid this sort of trading, work out the numbers. Imagine that you only take either a full loss or a full profit. Look at your past trades and determine how much of a difference this sort of trading would have made. In almost every instance when I've asked clients to do this, they become totally amazed at how much money they would have made holding on to a full position.

S U M M A R Y

People avoid looking for good exits because exits do not give them control over the market. However, exits do control something. They control whether you make a profit or a loss, and they control just how big that profit or loss will be. Since they do so much, perhaps they are worthy of a lot more study on the part of most people.

We reviewed four general categories of exits—exits that make your initial loss smaller, exits that maximize your profits, exits that minimize how much profit you give back, and psychological exits. Various exit strategies were presented for each category with a great deal of overlap.

The reader would do best to consider simple multiple exits. Simple exits are easy to conceptualize and don't require extensive optimization (if any). Multiple exits are recommended because they will help you most fully meet the objectives that you have stated for your trading system.

We have examined how to set up a high-expectancy system by itself that can return good profits. The next chapter will discuss how the opportunity factor interacts with expectancy.

EXITS USED BY COMMON SYSTEMS

Stock Market Systems

William O'Neil's CANSLIM System
William O'Neil's fundamental profit-taking rule is to take a 20 percent profit whenever you achieve it. Since his stop loss is about 8%, this means a 2.5-R profit. As a result, his fundamental profit-taking exit is an objective.

However, O'Neil then tempers his basic profit-taking rule with *36 other selling rules.* Some of these rules are exceptions to the basic selling rule, while others are reasons to sell early. In addition, he also adds eight more rules concerning when to hold onto a stock. I'll refer the reader to O'Neil's wonderful book for the specific details since my intention is explain how various systems fit into the framework outlined in the chapter. It is not my intention to give you every detail of the system.

Warren Buffett's Business Approach

Warren Buffett generally does not sell for two reasons. First, when you sell, you must pay capital gains tax. As a result, if you determine that the company has good returns for the amount you have invested, why sell it? You would automatically be turning over some of your profits to the U.S. government.

Second, why should one sell a company that is fundamentally sound and bringing in excellent returns? If a company has invested its capital in such a way that it is bringing in excellent returns, then you should get an excellent return on your money.

Third, when you do sell, you will also incur transaction costs. Thus, if the market is just going through psychological ups and down, why sell a good investment?

In my opinion, however, it is more myth than fact that Buffett doesn't sell. That myth is probably created by the fact that Buffett himself has not written about his own investment strategy. Instead, other people, who probably have the typical bias toward emphasizing entry, have tried to decipher what Buffett really does do.

If the business situation in a stock Buffett owned changed dramatically, then he would have to sell. Let me give you an example: Buffett announced in early 1998 that he owned about 20 percent of the world's silver supply. Silver does not pay dividends. If you own as much as Buffett does, you actually have costs involved with storing the commodity and protecting it. If Warren Buffett does not have a planned exit strategy for that silver, then, in my opinion, he is making one of the biggest mistakes of his investing career. On the other hand, if he does have a planned exit strategy, then I would guess that he has a planned exit strategy for most of his stock purchases as well. When other people have written about him, they have simply reflected their own biases and focused on his entry and setup strategies, while ignoring his exit strategies.

Motley Fool Foolish-Four Method

The Motley Fool Foolish-Four method involves a once-a-year adjustment to one's portfolio. You readjust your positions so that you are now taking positions in the second, third, fourth, and fifth best dividend-paying stocks in the Dow Jones Industrials Average. If those stocks are the same as the prior year's, there is no exit.

However, if any of the stocks no longer qualify, then you would exit out of those and enter into the stocks that do qualify.

If the second highest-paying dividend stock from the prior year is no longer in that position, then you would also make an adjustment of either cutting the position in half (if it were still in the top five) or exiting it entirely (if it no longer was part of the foolish four stocks). You would also exit some stocks in order to do an equal-size adjustment of stocks. However, that is a topic for the position sizing chapter.

Futures Market Systems

Kaufman's Adaptive Methods

Kaufman cautions that his basic trend-following system should not be confused with a complete strategy. He simply presents it as a sample method with no subtleties in the selection of either entry or exit.

The adaptive moving average was presented in Chapter 8 as a basic entry technique. You simply enter a long position when the moving average turns up by more than the amount of a predetermined filter. You enter a short position when the moving average turns down by more than the amount of a predetermined filter.

Kaufman comments that one should take profits whenever the efficiency exceeds some predetermined level. For example, he states that a high efficiency ratio cannot be sustained, so that it usually drops quickly once a high value is obtained. Thus, Kaufman has two basic exit signals: (1) when there is a change in the adaptive moving average in the opposite direction (perhaps when it exceeds some threshold in the opposite direction) and (2) when the efficiency average hits a very high value such as 0.8.

I think adaptive exits have more potential than any other form of exits. Some of my clients have developed exit strategies that move up with the market, giving the position plenty of room while it moves. However, as soon as the market starts to turn, these exits take you right out. They are incredibly creative and yet simple. And if the market resumes a trend, their basic trend-following system would be able to enter them right back into the market. I would strongly suggest that you spend a lot of time in this area in your system development.

Gallacher's Fundamental Trading

Gallacher's system, as you will recall from Chapter 8, has you entering the market (1) when fundamental setups are in place and (2) when the market makes a new 10-day high (i.e., a 10-day channel breakout). The system is a reversal system—so it is always in the market. It essentially closes out the position (and reenters in the opposite direction) when the 10-day low is breached (i.e., a 10-day channel breakout).

However, remember that Gallacher only takes positions in the direction of the fundamentals. Consequently, unless the fundamentals change dramatically, he will only exit a long position (i.e., not reverse it) on a 10-day low, and he will only exit a short position (i.e., not reverse it) on a 10-day high. This is a very simple exit that probably won't get you into a lot of trouble. However, my guess is that this system could be improved dramatically with more sophisticated exits.

Ken Roberts' 1-2-3 Methodology

Ken Roberts' profit-taking approach, in my opinion, is very subjective. It amounts to a consolidation trailing stop approach. If Roberts' method is correct and has gotten one into a long-term move, then Roberts would simply recommend that one raise one's stop and place it below (or above) a new consolidation once it is formed.

This is an old trend-following approach that worked exceptionally well in the 1970s. Its main drawback is that one may give back a lot of profits. It still will work now, but Roberts' methodology would probably work better with many of the exits discussed in this chapter. I would particularly recommend a multiple-exit strategy.

NOTES

1. These are hypothetical numbers and not necessarily a recommended exit for IBM. You need exits that meet your own criteria and that you test.
2. Once again this points out the importance of deep discount commissions.
3. Your loss will never be more than 1-R unless the market gets away from you, which is quite probable from time to time.

CHAPTER 11

The Opportunity and Cost Factors

You have the essence of trading system design in the first 10 chapters of this book. Most people would be happy with just the material so far, because it covers the areas that most people give all their focus to. But the two most important areas involving making money in the market still remain—the opportunity factor (along with the cost per opportunity) and the position-sizing factor.

The material we've covered to this point is really about expectancy—how to create the best possible expectancy. It's about how to obtain the most money per trade per dollar risked. Using our snow fight metaphor from Chapter 6, we've shown you how to make sure that the total volume of "white" or winning snow arriving at any given time (on the average) is larger than the total volume of "black" or losing snow.

Figure 11–1 shows one possible way of illustrating expectancy. Basically you have created a two-dimensional diagram. The x-axis refers to the reliability of trading—the percentage winning trades. The y-axis refers to the size of the average reward compared with the average risk—how big are your average winning compared with your average losing trades?

SEVERAL APPROACHES TO TAKE

If you've done a great job with the material in the first 10 chapters, you should be able to come up with a system that has a positive

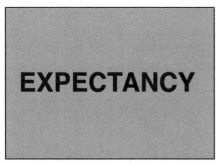

EXPECTANCY   Relative Size of Profits to Loses

Reliability of Your Trading System

Figure 11–1 Expectancy illustrated as a two-dimensional figure relating the reliability of your system to the relative size of profits and losses. It is hoped that the area is a large positive number.

expectancy. You might take any number of routes to get to that system. Here are some possible examples.

Long-Term Trend Following with a Large R-Multiple Objective

Let's say that you decide you want to be a long-term trend follower and go for big-R-multiple trades. You decide to use a 40-day channel breakout as a setup. You then enter after a retracement, putting your stop just below the retracement. You have an initial profit objective of at least a 10-R profit. This means that either you get stopped out at a loss or you reach your 10-R profit. Once your 10-R profit is attained, you then have a 30 percent retracement stop—meaning that you are now willing to give back 30 percent of your profit before you'll get out.

This type of trading means that a 1-R risk is very small for you. It means that you'll be stopped out frequently (i.e., have lots of losses), but that your gains will usually be 20-R multiples or bigger. When you test your system, you find that you make money on 18 percent of your trades, but that your average gain is about 23 times the size of your average loss. If you put these values into Formula 6–1, it gives you a positive expectancy of $3.32 per dollar risked—an excellent expectancy.

After transaction costs are taken into consideration, you find that your expectancy drops down to $2.90 per dollar risked. You decide that this level is great. However, the critical question that now remains is, how often will you get one of the 23-*R* profits? Will it come once a year or once a week?

The Standard Long-Term Trend Follower with a 40 Percent Reliability and 2:1 Reward to Risk Ratio

Others might decide that they cannot tolerate the number of losses generated by the high-*R*-multiple approach just described. Instead, they decide to take more of a standard trend-following approach to the market. They decide to use an adaptive moving average as an entry and a three-times-volatility trailing stop—both to protect one's initial capital and to serve as a profit-taking exit.

In this case, your initial risk is much greater because it is three times the average daily range in prices. However, you discover after a lot of testing that your average loss is only 0.5-*R*. You also discover that your average gain is 2.4-*R* and that you make money on about 44 percent of your trades. When you work out your expectancy using Formula 6–1, you discover that your expectancy is a respectable 77.6 cents per dollar risked. And after transaction costs, you determine that your expectancy is more like 63 cents per dollar risked.

Again, you now have a critical question to answer. How often will you be able to trade this system, and will you be satisfied with those results?

High-Probability, Low R-Multiple Trading

You've decided that you really cannot tolerate the possibility of long losing streaks. Consequently, you need to be "right" at least 60 percent of the time. Furthermore, you are willing to sacrifice the size of your profits in order to be correct more often.

As a result, you decide to use a volatility breakout for an entry. You know that when you get a large move, it's likely to continue for a while. You decide that when the market moves either up or down by 0.7 times the average true range of the last 5 days, you'll enter.

You also test a lot of such entries and notice that the maximum adverse excursion against you is seldom more than 0.4 times the average true range. As a result, you decide to use that as your initial stop. You also are perfectly happy with 0.6 times the average true range as a profit objective, because you determine that that objective is reached at least 60 percent of the time. In other words, either you get out at your stop with a loss or you take your profit objective.

When you plug these numbers into Formula 6–1, you determine that you have an expectancy of 50 cents per dollar risked. However, when you add in transaction costs, the number reduces to 30 cents per dollar risked.

The question you must now ask is can you survive with only a 30 cent expectancy? Do you generate enough trades, compared with the long-term trend followers, to compete with them for investment profits?

The Market Maker Who Gets the Bid-Ask Edge on Each Trade, But Occasionally Gets Swept Along by the Market

Our last trader, who represents an extreme, is the market maker. This person tries to get the bid-ask spread on every trade that comes along. Let's say that the bid-ask spread represents a gain of about 8 cents per trade and that our trader gets it about 90 percent of the time. Another 5 percent of his trades are small losses of about 8 cents per trade. However, the last 5 percent of his trades represents the big losses (for him) that he sometimes needs to take when he gets swept along by the market. These losses might amount to $1 per trade.

When our last trader applies these data to the expectancy formula, he arrives at a figure of about 1.8 cents per dollar risked. After transaction costs, he clears about 1.2 cents per dollar risked. How does this particular person make a living? He probably does not have much chance compared with the person who knows how to make more than a dollar for every dollar risked. Or does he?

FACTORING IN OPPORTUNITY

Table 11–1 shows our four traders with their various expectancies. Initially, the trader with the largest expectancy seems clearly to be the trader that one would expect to have the most success. Indeed,

TABLE 11-1

Expectancy, Cost, and Opportunity Factors for Our Four Traders

	Trader 1	Trader 2	Trader 3	Trader 4
Expectancy	$3.32	$0.776	$0.50	$0.018
After costs	$2.90	$0.630	$0.30	$0.012
Opportunity	0.05	0.5	5	500
Volume, $/day	$0.145	$0.315	$0.15	$6.00

this trader's expectancy is far better than that of most long-term trend followers, so we would expect him to have a great track record. However, as we've shown previously, the opportunity factor clearly changes the element of expectancy. This is also illustrated in Table 11-1 in the dollar volume generated each day by the system.

Let's say that trader 1 generates one trade on the average every 20 days. Trader 2 gets a trading opportunity every other day, while traders 3 and 4 generate 5 and 500 trades per day, respectively.

With this perspective in mind, trader 1 and trader 3 seem to generate about an equal volume of potential profit each day—although trader 3 is less likely to have extensive drawdown periods. However, the total advantage clearly belongs to the market maker. The market maker, if he is smart, should seldom have a losing day.

One of the people in my supertrader program is a floor trader. He starts each year with $100,000 in trading capital with the goal of making a living plus as much money as he can. Just because of his wisdom and knowledge of his edge, he was able to make $1.7 million in trading capital in just over 3 months in 1997. Is that an edge?[1]

Are you beginning to understand how profits are a function of the expectancy times the opportunity? The result amounts to a dollar volume in expectancy generated each day. That dollar volume is the most important factor in determining how much money you will make on a daily basis.

Figure 11-2 is the expectancy figure with opportunity as a third dimension. What you now have, as illustrated in the diagram, is a three-dimensional solid equaling the dollar volume generated by your trading system each day. The new dimension, in dark gray,

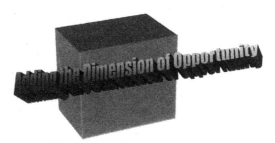

Figure 11–2 Expectancy plus opportunity
becomes three-dimensional

is the dimension of opportunity. The resulting profits no longer
depend upon a two-dimensional surface, but rather on a three-
dimensional solid.

THE COST OF TRADING OPPORTUNITY

There is a definite cost of trading. The market maker has to get his
edge. Your broker has to get her cost. And your profit is what
remains, if anything, when these costs are deducted.

The cost per trade is really a part of the expectancy equation,
but it is so important that I wanted to add a little more about cost
reduction. The fewer trades you make, the less the cost per trade
becomes a factor. Many long-term trend followers spend little time
thinking about their trading cost, because it is so insignificant compared with the potential profit to be made. For example, if you are
thinking about making $5,000 per trade, then you probably are not
paying much attention to trade costs of $100.

However, if you are short term in your orientation and make
lots of trades, then trade cost is a lot bigger consideration for you—
at least it should be. For example, if your average profit per trade
was $50, then you would pay much more attention to a $100 trading cost.

Look for Low Commissions

Unless you need a specific service from your broker, you should pay
attention to getting the best possible execution at the lowest possi-

ble cost. For example, stock traders can now do unlimited Internet trading for under $10. This is a big drop from so-called discount brokers who used to charge $50 just to buy 100 shares of stock plus another $50 to sell those same 100 shares. However, you must be sure that (1) you are getting good execution at a reasonable price and (2) that your Internet broker will be available to you during highly volatile periods when you need to make a trade immediately.

Futures traders have long been able to get great commissions. Typically, a futures broker only charges you one price per "round turn," which means getting in and getting out of a position. You can typically negotiate rates of $30 and under—sometimes much better depending upon your volume of trading.

Execution Costs

The term "execution costs" typically refers to the costs of getting into and out of a trade that are beyond the broker's commissions. These are typically the difference between the bid and the ask price (i.e., the market maker's edge) and the cost of high volatility. When the market maker isn't sure he can get your position done at a profit (because the market is moving), your cost of execution will typically go up to cover his risk.

Some traders go to great lengths to control execution costs. For example, Monroe Trout, interviewed in Jack Schwager's *The New Market Wizards*,[2] needed very low slippage in his trading methodology. Originally, he executed through many brokers and kept track of the slippage he got on each trade through each broker. When the slippage got too high, a broker was typically replaced. Eventually, Trout decided that he needed to buy his own brokerage company just to be sure his orders were executed correctly.

If you are a short-term trader, then you probably need to give the same sort of attention to execution costs. What does it cost you to execute a trade? How can you lower those costs? Interview your broker carefully. Make sure that anyone who will handle your orders understands exactly what you are trying to accomplish. Proper execution for short-term traders could mean the difference between a solid profit and no profit.

The Cost of Taxes

There is a third kind of cost on profits—the cost that the government imposes. The government regulates the trading business and there is a cost of the government's involvement. Thus, there are exchange fees added to each transaction and to the cost of getting data. In addition, there is also the very real cost of the government taxing your profits.

Real estate investors have long been able to avoid some of these taxes on profits by filling out a Form 1031 and then buying another, more expensive piece of property. Furthermore, long-term stock investors (who seldom sell) such as Warren Buffett also avoid these taxes, because you don't pay taxes on unrealized profits on your stock. Consequently, a major cost of doing business in the market can be avoided by sticking to real estate or being a long-term stock investor.

However, short-term traders must pay full taxes on their profits, and these taxes can be a significant cost. Futures traders, for example, have their open positions marked to the market at the end of the year and are required to pay taxes on their unrealized profits. Thus, you might have $20,000 on unrealized profits on December 31 that you get taxed on by the government. You might end up giving back $15,000 of those open profits, but you will not get your taxes back until the next year when your actual profit on that trade is less.

Tax considerations obviously are an important part of the costs of a trading business. The overall topic is way beyond the scope of this book. Nevertheless, it is a real cost and it should go into your planning.

Psychological Costs

Short-term trading, which gives you lots of opportunity, can have a large psychological cost. You always have to be in peak form; otherwise you will fail to open a potentially huge trade or you will make a mistake that could cost you years of profits.

A number of times, short-term traders have called me up with a statement that goes something like: "I'm a day trader. I'm in and out a number of times each day. And I almost always make money each day. It's great! However, yesterday I gave back nearly a year's worth of profits and I'm really upset." This is definitely a psychological problem. Such mistakes come either from big psychological blunders trading or from the psychological blunder of playing a negative expectancy game that wins most of the time but has huge R multiples against you occasionally.

We've been talking throughout this book about numbers. You've learned about the numbers involved in expectancy. You've learned how important it is for you to multiply expectancy times the opportunity factor. However, the psychological cost factor can be the most significant factor of all. And the more you trade, the more it comes into play.

Even long-term traders have a psychological factor. Long-term traders are usually successful because of a few high-R-multiple trades that they make each year. This kind of trader cannot afford to miss those good trades. When you miss your biggest trade of the year, quite often you might not have a profitable year. Again, the psychological factor comes into play!

One of my good friends, who is a professional trader, once told me that psychological factors didn't come into play when he and his partner were trading. They had a game plan worked out and everything was very mechanical. I said the factors do come into play because you have to execute those trades. He agreed, but still didn't think psychology was that important for their trading. Several years later, however, his partner got discouraged because they never made money trading the British pound. When a trade came up, they didn't take it. That trade turned out to be the one big trade that would have made their year. The moral is that psychological factors always come into play in any sort of trading.

SUMMARY

Most of this book has been about developing a high-expectancy trading system. Expectancy is a two-dimensional surface related to the reliability of your trading system and the relative size of profits and losses.

Opportunity to trade makes a third dimension that gives "volume" to your dollars in profits or losses. You must multiply the opportunity factor by the expectancy factor to get your potential volume of dollars that you could reap each day. Thus, a high expectancy doesn't necessarily translate into a high dollar volume each day if you don't make many trades.

Lastly, there is a cost to trading which must be subtracted from the dollar volume each day. This cost is usually figured into the expectancy. However, there are a number of costs to trading, and each should be given some consideration. Reducing any one of them could have a major effect on your bottom line.

The four major types of costs are brokerage commissions, execution costs, tax costs, and psychological costs. Each was discussed briefly.

N O T E S

1. Most floor traders never make it. They go bankrupt (or at least lose their capital) within a year or two, because they don't understand what their edge is or they don't know how to capitalize upon it.
2. See the Recommended Readings in Appendix I.

CHAPTER 12

What Do You Mean Position Sizing?
I Only Have $10,000 in My Account!

> When I get a 30 percent profit, I take a third. When I get a 50 percent profit I take another third. When I get a pattern to the reverse, I'll take the rest of the profit.
>
> *Quoted from a lecture on money management*
> *at a seminar on stock trading*

The instructor made the above quote at a stock market seminar, telling me that it was his formula for money management. However, in my opinion, it has nothing to do with money management. Instead, it has everything to do with exits.[1] Later, after the seminar, I approached him to ask him what he meant by "money management"—which was the topic of his talk. His response was, "That's a very good question. I think it's how one makes trading decisions."

Money management is the most important aspect of system development, other than psychology, and yet virtually every book on the market that talks about trading or system development totally neglects the topic. In fact, even books that are devoted to money management say little about the most important aspect of the topic—position sizing. As a result, few people really understand the implications of money management.

Money management (position sizing) is **not** any of the following:

- It is **not** that part of your system that dictates how much you will lose on a given trade.
- It is **not** how to exit a profitable trade.
- It is **not** diversification.
- It is **not** risk control.
- It is **not** risk avoidance.
- It is **not** that part of your system that maximizes performance.
- It is **not** that part of your system that tells you what to invest in.

Money management is that part of your trading system that answers the question "how much?" throughout the course of a trade. How much essentially means how big a position you should have at any given time throughout the course of a trade. As a result, I've elected to call it "position sizing" throughout this book.

> Money management is the most important aspect of system development, other than psychology, and yet virtually every book on the market that talks about trading or system development totally neglects the topic....As a result, few people really understand the implications of money management.

In the process of answering the question "how much?" you may have to consider some of the issues mentioned above, but those issues are not your position-sizing algorithm. For some of you, elements like risk control may seem more important than deciding how much. But the question of how much accounts for most of the variability in the performance of various professional traders.

Remember the snow fight model described in Chapter 6. Well, position-sizing models include two factors from that metaphor. Those factors are the size of the initial protection (i.e., the size of the snow wall or your starting equity) and the number of snowballs that come at the wall at one time (i.e., how many positions you have on at one time).

Figure 12–1 gives an illustration of how position sizing adds one more step in determining the total dollar volume that you must

Figure 12–1 Position sizing has the effect of adding *many* simultaneous three-dimensional boxes to a situation at one time.

consider. Recall that Figure 11–2 created a three-dimensional box that added opportunity to expectancy. Figure 12–1 shows that with position sizing a fourth dimension must be added—the dimension of multiple, simultaneous positions in the market. Since drawing four dimensions is rather difficult, Figure 12–1 illustrates the effect of position sizing by showing that you can have many three-dimensional boxes affecting your position at one time.

Remember the Ralph Vince study described in Chapter 2. In that study, 40 Ph.D.s played a money management game with a positive expectancy. However, 95 percent of them lost money. Why? The reasons had to do with their psychology and with poor position sizing.

Let's say you started the game risking $100. In fact, you do that three times in a row and you lose all three times—a distinct possibility in this game. Now you are down to $700 and you think, "I've had three losses in a row, so I'm really due to win now." That's the gambler's fallacy because your chances of winning are still just 60 percent. Anyway, you decide to bet $300 because you are so sure you will win. However, you again lose and now you only have $400. Your chances of making money in the game are slim now, because you must make 150 percent just to break even. Although the chances of four consecutive losses are slim—0.0256—it still is nearly certain to occur at least once in a 100-trial game.

Here's another way the doctorates could have gone broke. Let's say they started out betting $250. They have three losses in a row totaling $750. They are down to $250. They now must make 300 percent just to get back to even, and they probably won't be able do that before they go broke.

In either case, the failure to profit in this easy game occurred because the person risked too much money. The excessive risk occurred for psychological reasons—greed, failure to understand the odds, and, in some cases, even the desire to fail. However, *mathematically their losses occurred because they were risking too much money.* For example, if one black snowball that is bigger than the wall is thrown at the wall, then the wall will be destroyed. It does not matter how favorable the ratio of white to black snow is—one black snowball bigger than the wall will destroy the wall.

The size of your equity is equivalent to the size of the wall in the snow fight metaphor. What typically happens is that the average person comes into most speculative markets with too little money. An account under $50,000 is small, but the average account is only $1,000 to $10,000. As a result, many people are practicing poor money management just because their account is too small. *Their mathematical odds of failure are very high just because of their account size.*

Look at Table 12–1. Notice how much your account has to

T A B L E 12–1

Recovery after Drawdowns

Drawdowns	Gain to Recovery
5%	5.3% gain
10%	11.1% gain
15%	17.6% gain
20%	25% gain
25%	33% gain
30%	42.9% gain
40%	66.7% gain
50%	100% gain
60%	150% gain
75%	300% gain
90%	900% gain

recover from various-sized drawdowns in order to get back to even. For example, losses up to 20 percent only require a moderately larger gain (i.e., no more than 25 percent bigger) to get back to even. But a 40 percent drawdown requires a 66.7 percent gain to break even, and a 50 percent drawdown requires a 100 percent gain. Losses beyond 50 percent require huge, improbable gains in order to get back to even. As a result, when you risk too much and lose, your chances of a full recovery are very slim.

POSITION-SIZING STRATEGIES

Professional gamblers have long claimed that there are two basic position-sizing strategies—martingale and anti-martingale. Martingale strategies increase one's bet size when equity decreases (during a losing streak). Anti-martingale strategies, on the other hand, increase one's bet size during winning streaks or when one's equity increases.

If you've ever played roulette or craps, the purest form of martingale strategy might have occurred to you. It simply amounts to doubling your bet size when you lose. For example, if you lose $1, you bet $2. If you lose the $2, then you bet $4. If you lose the $4, then you bet $8. When you finally win, which you will eventually do, you will be ahead by your original bet size.

Casinos love people who play such martingale strategies. First, any game of chance will have losing streaks. And when the probability of winning is less than 50 percent, the losing streaks could be quite significant. Let's assume that you have a streak of 10 consecutive losses. If you had started betting $1, then you will have lost $2,047 over the streak. You will now be betting $2,048 to get your original dollar back. Thus, your win-loss ratio at this point—for less than a 50:50 bet—is 1 to 4,095. You will be risking over $4,000 to get $1 in profits. And to make matters worse, since some people might have unlimited bankrolls, the casinos have betting limits. At a table that allows a minimum bet of $1, you probably couldn't risk more than $100. As a result, martingale betting strategies generally do not work—in the casinos or in the market.

If your risk continues to increase during a losing streak, you will eventually have a big enough streak to cause you to go bankrupt. An even if your bankroll was unlimited, you would be committing yourself to risk-to-reward strategies that no human being could tolerate psychologically.

Anti-martingale strategies, which call for larger risk during a winning streak, do work—both in the gambling arena and in the investment arena. Smart gamblers know to increase their bets, within certain limits, when they are winning.[2] And the same is true for trading or investing. Position-sizing systems that work call for you to increase your position size when you make money. That holds for gambling, for trading, and for investing.

The purpose of position sizing is to tell you how many units (shares or contracts) you are going to put on, given the size of your account. **For example, a position-sizing decision might be that you don't have enough money to put on any positions because the risk is too big.** It allows you to determine your reward and risk characteristics by determining how many units you will risk on a given trade and in each trade in a portfolio. It also helps you equalize your trade exposure in the elements in your portfolio. Lastly, certain position-sizing models equate a 1-R risk across all markets.

Some people believe that they are "doing an adequate job of position sizing" by having a "money management stop." Such a stop would be one in which you get out of your position when you lose a predetermined amount of money—say $1,000. However, *this kind of stop does not tell you "how much" or "how many," so it really has nothing to do with position sizing.* Controlling risk by determining the amount of loss if you are stopped out is not the same as controlling risk through a position-sizing model that determines "how many" or if you can even afford to hold one position at all.

There are numerous position-sizing strategies that you can use. In the remainder of this chapter, you'll learn different position-sizing strategies that work well. Some are probably much more suited to your style of trading or investing than others. Some work best with stock accounts, while others are designed for a futures account. **All of them are anti-martingale strategies in that the formula for "how much" goes up as your account size grows.**

The material is somewhat complex. However, I've avoided the use of difficult mathematical expressions and given clear examples of each strategy. As a result, you simply need to read the material carefully. Go over it until you understand it thoroughly.

The System Used

In presenting the results of all these strategies, I've elected to use a single trading system, trading the same commodities over the same time period. The system is a 55-day channel breakout system. In other words, it enters the market on a stop order if the market makes a new 55-day high (long) or a new 55-day low (short). The stop, for both the initial risk and profit taking, is a 21-day trailing stop on the other side of the market.

To illustrate, if you go long and the market hits a 21-day low, you exit. If you are short and the market makes a new 21-day high, you exit. This stop is recalculated each day, and it is always moved in your favor so as to reduce risk or increase your profits. Such breakout systems produce above-average profits when traded with sufficient money.

This system was tested with a million dollars in start-up equity with a basket of 10 commodities in the years 1981 through 1991. Whenever futures data are presented in this chapter, they are based upon this same 55-/21-day breakout system tested over the same commodities over the same years. The only difference between the tables is the position-sizing model used.

MODEL 1: ONE UNIT PER FIXED AMOUNT OF MONEY

Basically, this method tells you "how much" by determining that you will trade one unit for every X dollars you have in your account. For example, you might trade one unit (i.e., 100 shares, one contract, etc.) per $50,000 of your total equity.

When you started trading or investing, you probably never heard about position sizing. At most, you probably thought something like "I can only afford one unit." If you knew something about it, your knowledge probably came from some book by an author who didn't understand it either. Most books that discuss money management are not about position sizing. Instead, they tell you about diversification or about optimizing the gain from your trading. Books on systems development or technical analysis don't even begin to discuss position sizing adequately. As a result, *most traders and investors have no place to go to learn what is probably the most important aspect of their craft.*

Thus, armed with your ignorance, you open an account with $20,000 and decide to trade one contract of everything in which you get a signal to trade (an equity investor might just trade 100 shares). Later, if you're fortunate and your account moves to $40,000, you decide to move up to two contracts (or 200 shares) of everything. As a result, most traders who do practice some form of position sizing use this model. It is simple. It tells you "how much" in a straightforward way.

The one unit per fixed amount of money has one "advantage" in that you never reject a trade because it is too risky. Let me give you an example of an experience of two traders I know. One of them trades one contract per $50,000 in equity, while the other limits his risk to 3 percent of equity and won't open a position in which his exposure is more than that. Each was presented with an opportunity to trade the Japanese yen by his respective trend-following system. The person trading one contract, no matter what, took the trade. The subsequent move in the yen was tremendous, so this person was able to produce the biggest monthly gain that his firm had ever experienced in its history—a monthly 20 percent gain.

On the other hand, the second trader couldn't take the trade. His account size was $100,000, but the risk involved exceeded his 3 percent limit if the trade went against him. The second trader did not have a profitable month. *Of course, this factor of always taking a trade also works in reverse.* The first trader could have taken a large loss if the yen trade had gone against him, which the second trader would have avoided.

Table 12–2 shows the results with this system using the first position-sizing model. Notice that the system breaks down at one contract per $20,000 in equity. At $30,000, you'd have to endure an 80 percent drawdown and you'd have to have at least $70,000 if you wanted to avoid a 50 percent drawdown.

To really evaluate this position-sizing method, you'll have to

T A B L E 12–2

55-/21-Day Breakout System with One Contract per $X in Equity
(Starting Equity Is $1 Million)

1 Contract per $X in Equity	Profits1	Rejected Trades	Annual % Gain	Margin Calls	Maximum Drawdown
$100,000	$5,034,533	0	18.20%	0	36.86%
$90,000	$6,207,208	0	20.20%	0	40.23%
$80,000	$7,725,361	0	22.30%	0	43.93%
$70,000	$10,078,968	0	25.00%	0	48.60%
$60,000	$13,539,570	0	28.20%	0	54.19%
$50,000	$19,309,155	0	32.30%	0	61.04%
$40,000	$27,475,302	0	36.50%	0	69.65%
$30,000	$30,919,632	0	38.00%	0	80.52%
$20,000	($1,685,271)	402	0.00%	1	112.00%

compare it with the tables developed from the other models (see Tables 12–4 and 12–6).

Despite its advantage of allowing you to always take a position, I believe that the one-unit-per-fixed-dollars type of position sizing is limited, because (1) not all investments are alike, (2) it does not allow you to increase your exposure rapidly with small amounts of money, and (3) you'll always take a position even when the risk is too high. In fact, with a small account, the units-per-fixed-amount model amounts to minimal position sizing. Let's explore these reasons.

Not all investments are alike. Suppose you are a futures trader and you decide you are going to be trading up to 20 different commodities with your $50,000. Your basic position-sizing strategy is to trade one contract of anything in that portfolio that gives you a signal. Let's say you get a signal for both bonds and corn. Thus, your position sizing says you can buy one corn contract and one bond contract. Let's assume that T-bonds are at $112 and corn is at $3.

With T-bonds futures at $112, you are controlling $112,000 worth of product. In addition, the daily range at the time (i.e., the volatility) is about 0.775, so if the market moved three times that amount in one direction, you would make or lose $2,325. In contrast, with the corn contract you are controlling about $15,000 worth of product. If it moved three daily ranges with you or against you, your gain or loss would be about $550. Thus, what happens with your portfolio will depend about 80 percent on what bonds do and only about 20 percent on what corn does.

One might argue that corn has been much more volatile and expensive in the past. That could happen again. But you need to diversify your opportunity according to what's happening in the market right now. Right now, based on the data presented, one corn contract has about 20 percent of the impact on your account that one bond contract would have.

It does not allow you to increase your exposure rapidly. The purpose of an anti-martingale strategy is to increase your exposure when you are winning. When you are trading one contract per $50,000 and you only have $50,000, you will have to double your equity before you can increase your contract size. As a result, this is not a very efficient way to increase exposure during a winning streak. In fact, for a $50,000 account it almost amounts to no position sizing.

Part of the solution would be to require a minimum account size of a million dollars. If you did that, your account would only have to increase by 5 percent before you moved from 20 contracts (1 per $50,000) to 21 contracts.

You'll always take a position even when the risk is too high. The one-unit-per-X-dollars model will allow you to take one unit of everything. For example, you could buy one S&P contract, controlling $225,000 worth of stock with a **$15,000** account.[3] Let's say the daily volatility in the S&P is **10 points and you have a three-times-volatility stop, or 30 points. Your potential loss is $7,500, or half your equity.** That is tremendous risk for just one position, but you could take that risk with the one-unit-per-X model of position sizing.

One reason to have a position-sizing strategy is to have equal opportunity and equal exposure across all the elements in one's portfolio. You want an equal opportunity to make money from each element of your portfolio. Otherwise, why trade those elements that are not likely to give you much profit? In addition, you also want to spread your risk equally among the elements of your portfolio.

Having equal opportunity and exposure to risk, of course, makes the assumption that each trade is equally likely to be profitable when you enter into it. You might have some way to determine that some trades are going to be more profitable than others. If so, then you would want a position-sizing plan that gives you more units on the higher-probability-of-success trades—perhaps a discretionary position-sizing plan. However, for the rest of this chapter, we're going to assume that all trades in a portfolio have an equal opportunity of success from the start. That's why you selected them.

The units-per-fixed-amount-of-money model, in my opinion, doesn't give you equal opportunity or exposure. But there are some position-sizing methods whereby you can equalize the elements of your portfolio. These include model 2—equating the value of each element in the portfolio; model 3—equating the amount of risk (i.e., how much you'd would lose when you got out of a position in order to preserve capital) in each element of the portfolio; and model 4—equating the amount of volatility of each element in the portfolio. Model 3 also has the value of equating what 1 R means to each market.

MODEL 2: EQUAL VALUE UNITS FOR STOCK TRADERS

The **equal units model** is typically used with stocks or other instruments that are not leveraged. The model says that you determine "how much" by dividing your capital up into five or ten equal units. Each unit would then dictate how much product you could buy. For example, with our $50,000 capital, we might have five units of $10,000 each. Thus, you'd buy $10,000 worth of investment A, $10,000 worth of investment B, $10,000 worth of investment C, and so forth. You might end up buying 100 shares of a $100 stock, 200 shares of a $50 stock, 500 shares of a $20 stock, 1,000 shares of a $10 stock, and 1,428 shares of a $7 stock. The position-sizing model involved in this strategy would be to determine how much of your

T A B L E 12–3

Distribution of Funds as Shares in Equal Units Model
(Each Unit Represents $10,000)

Stock	Price per Share	Total Shares	Total Dollar Amount
A	$100	100	$10,000
B	$50	200	$10,000
C	$20	500	$10,000
D	$10	1,000	$10,000
E	$7	1,428	$9,996

portfolio you might allocate to cash at any given time. Table 12–3 shows how many shares would be purchased of each of the five stocks, each with a $10,000 investment.

Notice that there is some inconvenience in this procedure. For example, the price of the stock may not necessarily divide evenly into $10,000—much less into 100-share units. This is shown with stock E in which you end up buying 1,428 shares. This still does not equal $10,000. Indeed, with this example, you might want to round to the nearest 100-share unit and purchase 1,400 shares.

In futures, the equal units model might be used to determine how much value you are willing to control with each contract. For example, with the $50,000 account you might decide that you are willing to control up to $250,000 worth of product. And let's say you arbitrarily decide to divide that into five units of $50,000 each.

If a bond contract is worth about $112,000, then you couldn't buy any bonds under this position-sizing criterion because you'd be controlling more product than you can handle with one unit. On the other hand, you could afford to buy corn. Corn is traded in units of 5,000 bushels. A corn contract, with corn at $3 per bushel, is valued at about $15,000. Thus, your $50,000 would allow you to buy three units of corn, or $45,000 worth. Gold is traded in 100-ounce contracts in New York, which at a price of $390 per ounce gives a single contract a value of $39,000. Thus, you could also trade one gold contract with this model.

The equal units approach allows you to give each investment an approximate equal weighting in your portfolio. It also has the advantage in that you can see exactly how much leverage you are carrying. For example, if you are carrying five positions in your $50,000 account, each worth about $50,000, you would know that you had about $250,000 worth of product. In addition, you would know that you had about 5-to-1 leverage, since your $50,000 was controlling $250,000.

When you use this approach, you must make a decision about how much total leverage you are willing to carry before you divide it into units. It's valuable information, so I would recommend that all traders keep track of the total product value they are controlling and their leverage. This information can be a real eye-opener.

The equal units approach also has the disadvantage in that it would only allow you to increase "how much" very slowly as you make money. In most cases with a small account, equity would again have to double to increase your exposure by one unit. Again, this practically amounts to "no" position sizing for the small account.

MODEL 3: THE PERCENT RISK MODEL

When you enter a position, it is essential to know the point at which you will get out of the position in order to preserve your capital. This is your "risk." It's your worst-case loss—except for slippage and a runaway market going against you.

One of the most common position-sizing systems involves controlling your size as a function of this risk. Let's look at an example of how this position-sizing model works. Suppose you want to buy gold at $380 per ounce. Your system suggests that if gold drops as low as $370, you need to get out. Thus, your worst-case risk per gold contract is 10 points times $100 per point, or $1,000.

You have a $50,000 account. You want to limit your total risk on your gold position to 2.5 percent of that equity, or $1,250. If you divide your $1,000 risk per contract into your total allowable risk of $1,250, you get 1.25 contracts. Thus, your percent risk position sizing will only allow you to purchase one contract.

Suppose that you get a signal to sell short corn the same day. Gold is still at $380 an ounce, so your account with the open position is still worth $50,000. You still have $1,250 in allowable risk for your corn position based upon your total equity.

Let's say that corn is at $4.03, and you decide that your maximum acceptable risk would be to allow corn to move against you by 5 cents to $4.08. Your 5 cents of allowable risk (times 5,000 bushels per contract) translates into a risk of $250 per contract. If you divide $250 into $1,250, you get 5 contracts. Thus, you can sell short 5 corn contracts within your percent risk position-sizing paradigm.

How does the percent risk position sizing compare with the other position-sizing models? Table 12–4 shows the same 55-/21-day breakout system with a position-sizing algorithm based upon risk as a percentage of equity. The starting equity is again $1 million.

T A B L E   12–4

55-/21-Day Breakout System with Risk Position Sizing

% Risk	Net Profits	Rejected Trades	% Gain per Year	Margin Calls	Maximum Drawdown	Ratio
0.10%	$327	410	0.00%	0	0.36%	0
0.25%	$80,685	219	0.70%	0	2.47%	0.28
0.50%	$400,262	42	3.20%	0	6.50%	0.49
0.75%	$672,717	10	4.90%	0	10.20%	0.48
1.00%	$1,107,906	4	7.20%	0	13.20%	0.54
1.75%	$2,776,044	1	13.10%	0	22.00%	0.6
2.50%	$5,621,132	0	19.20%	0	29.10%	0.66
5.00%	$31,620,857	0	38.30%	0	46.70%	0.82
7.50%	$116,500,000	0	55.70%	0	62.20%	0.91
10.00%	$304,300,000	0	70.20%	1	72.70%	0.97
15.00%	$894,100,000	0	88.10%	2	87.30%	1.01
20.00%	$1,119,000,000	0	92.10%	21	84.40%	1.09
25%	$1,212,000,000	0	93.50%	47	83.38%	1.12
30.00%	$1,188,000,000	0	93.10%	58	95.00%	0.98
35.00%	($2,816,898)	206	0.00%	70	104.40%	0

Notice that the best reward-to-risk ratio occurs at about 25 percent risk per position, but you would have to tolerate an 84 percent drawdown in order to achieve it. In addition, margin calls (*which are set at current rates and are not historically accurate*) start entering the picture at 10 percent risk.

If you traded this system with $1 million and used a 1 percent risk criterion, your bet sizes would be equivalent to trading the $100,000 account with 10 percent risk. Thus, Table 12–3 suggests that you probably should not trade this system unless you had at least $100,000 and then you probably should not risk more than about ½ percent per trade. And at ½ percent, your returns with the system would be very poor. Essentially, you should now understand why you need at least a million dollars to trade this system.

Just how much risk should you accept per position with risk position sizing? **Your overall risk using risk position sizing depends upon the size of the stops you've set to preserve your capital and the expectancy of the system you are trading.** For example, most long-term trend followers use trailing stops that are fairly large, several times the average daily range of prices. In addition, most trend followers are usually using a model that makes money 40 to 50 percent of the time and has a reward-to-risk ratio of 2.0 to 2.5. If your system does not fall into these ranges, then you need to determine your own position-sizing percentages.

With the above criteria (and precautions) in mind, if you are trading other people's money, you probably should risk less than 1 percent per position. If you are trading your own money, your risk depends upon your own comfort level. Anything under 3 percent is probably fine. If you are risking over 3 percent, you are a "gunslinger" and had better understand the risk you are taking for the reward you seek.

If you trade a system that sets very small stops, then you need to adopt much smaller risk levels. For example, if your stops are less than the daily range of prices, then you probably need guidelines that are about half (or less) of what we present here. On the other hand, if you have high expectancies in your system (i.e., your reliability is above 50 percent and your reward-to-risk ratio is 3 or better), then you can probably risk a higher percentage of your equity fairly safely. People who use very tight stops might want to consider using a volatility model (see below) to size their positions.

Most stock market traders don't consider this sort of model at all. Instead, they tend to think more in terms of the equal units model. But let's look at how risk position sizing would work with equities.

Let's say you want to purchase IBM and you have a $50,000 account. Suppose IBM's price is about $141 per share. You decide that you would get out of this position at $137, or a drop of $4 per share. Your position-sizing strategy tells you to limit your risk to 2.5 percent, or $1,250. Dividing 4 into 1,250 results in 312.5 shares.

If you bought 312 shares at $141, it would cost you $43,392— over 80 percent of the value in your account. You could only do that two times without exceeding the marginable value of your account. This gives you a better notion of what a 2.5 percent risk really means. In fact, if your stop was only a $1 drop to $140, you could purchase 1,250 shares based upon the model. But that 1,250 shares would cost you $176,250—which you couldn't do even by fully margining your account. Nevertheless, you are still limiting your risk to 2.5 percent. The risk calculations, of course, were all based upon the starting risk—the difference between your purchase price and your initial stop loss.

The percent risk model is the first model that gives you a legitimate way to make sure that a 1-R risk means the same for each item you are trading. Let's say that you are trading a million dollar portfolio in the stock market and are willing to use full margin. You are using a 1 percent risk model, and thus risking $10,000 for each position.

Table 12–5 shows how this is done. The stop shown is arbitrary and represents a 1-R risk. You might think that the stops are tight for such high-priced stocks. However, they might not be if you were going for big-R-multiple trades. Table 12–5 shows that we can only buy five stocks, because the dollar value of the stocks comes close to our $2 million margin limit—it may even exceed it with transaction costs. Nevertheless, our risk is only $10,000 per position if we are able to rigidly follow our predetermined stops. Thus, our total portfolio risk, on a million dollar portfolio, is only $50,000 plus slippage and costs. If you are an equity trader, study

T A B L E 12–5

Using a 1 Percent Risk in a Stock Portfolio

Stock	Price	Stop (1-*R* Risk)	Number Shares with $10,000 Risk	Equity Value
ATT	61.625	2 points	5,000	$308,125
Lucent	106.250	3 points	3,300	$350,625
K-Mart	14.750	0.5 point	20,000	$295,000
Merck	124.875	2.5 points	4,000	$499,500
Dell Computer	139.0	3 points	3,300	$458,700
Total				**$1,911,950**

Table 12–5. It might change the way you think about trading a portfolio of stocks.

MODEL 4: THE PERCENT VOLATILITY MODEL

Volatility refers to the amount of daily price movement of the underlying instrument over an arbitrary period of time. It's a direct measurement of the price change that you are likely to be exposed to—for or against you—in any given position. If you equate the volatility of each position that you take, by making it a fixed percentage of your equity, then you are basically equalizing the possible market fluctuations of each portfolio element to which you are exposing yourself in the immediate future.

Volatility, in most cases, simply is the difference between the high and the low of the day. If IBM varies between 141 and 143½, then its volatility is 2.5 points. However, using an average true range takes into account any gap openings. Thus, if IBM closed at 139 yesterday, but varied between 141 and 143½ today, you'd need to add in the 2 points in the gap opening to determine the true range. Thus, today's true range is between 139 and 143½—or 4½ points. This is basically Wells Wilder's average true range calculation as shown in the definitions at the end of the book.

Here's how a percent volatility calculation might work for

position sizing. Suppose that you have $50,000 in your account and you want to buy gold. Let's say that gold is at $400 per ounce and during the last 10 days the daily range is $3. We will use a 10-day simple moving average of the average true range as our measure of volatility. How many gold contracts can we buy?

Since the daily range is $3 and a point is worth $100 (i.e., the contract is for 100 ounces), that gives the daily volatility a value of $300 per gold contract. Let's say that we are going to allow volatility to be a maximum of 2 percent of our equity. Two percent of $50,000 is $1,000. If we divide our $300 per contract fluctuation into our allowable limit of $1,000, we get 3.3 contracts. Thus, our position-sizing model, based on volatility, would allow us to purchase 3 contracts.

Table 12–6 illustrates what happens with our 55/21 system in our portfolio of 10 commodities over 11 years when you size positions based upon the volatility of the markets as a percentage of your equity. Here volatility was defined as the 20-day moving average of the average true range. This is the same system and the same data described with the other models. The only difference among Tables 12–2, 12–4, and 12–6 is the position-sizing algorithm.

T A B L E 12–6

55/21 Breakout System with Volatility-Based Position Sizing

% Volatility	Net Profits	Rejected Trades	% Gain per Year	Margin Calls	Maximum Drawdown
0.1	$411,785	34	3.30%	0	6.10%
0.25	$1,659,613	0	9.50%	0	17.10%
0.5	$6,333,704	0	20.30%	0	30.60%
0.75	$16,240,855	0	30.30%	0	40.90%
1	$36,266,106	0	40.00%	0	49.50%
1.75	$236,100,000	0	67.90%	0	69.70%
2.50	$796,900,000	0	86.10%	1	85.50%
5.00	$1,034,000,000	0	90.70%	75	92.50%
7.5	($2,622,159)	402	0.00%	1	119.80%

Notice in Table 12–6 that a 2 percent volatility position-sizing allocation would produce a gain between 67 and 86 percent per year and drawdowns of 69 to 86 percent per year. The table suggests that if you used a volatility position-sizing algorithm with the system, you probably would want to use a number somewhere between 0.5 and 1.0 percent per position, depending upon your objectives. The best reward-to-risk ratio in this system occurs at a 2.5 percent allocation, but few people could tolerate the drawdown of 86 percent.

If you compare Table 12–4 with Table 12–6, you'll notice the striking difference in the percentages at which the system breaks down. These differences are the result of the size of the number that you must take into consideration before using the equity percentages to size positions (i.e., the current 21-day extreme against you versus the 20-day volatility). Thus, a 5 percent risk based upon a stop of the 21-day extreme appears to be equivalent to about 1 percent of equity with the 20-day average true range. **These numbers, upon which the percentages are based, are critical.** They must be considered before you determine the percentages you plan to use to size your positions.

Volatility position sizing has some excellent features for controlling exposure. Few traders use it. Yet it is one of the more sophisticated models available.

THE MODELS SUMMARIZED

Table 12–7 gives a summary of the four models presented in this chapter, along with their respective advantages and disadvantages. Notice that the model with the most disadvantages is the one that most people use—the units-per-fixed-amount-of-money model. Let's reemphasize those disadvantages because they are so important.

First, assume that you are opening an account with $30,000. That's probably not enough to trade futures with unless you just trade a few agricultural markets. However, many people will do it. In that account, you could probably trade a corn contract, an S&P contract, and a bond contract—although the margin requirements might prevent you from doing them simultaneously. However, the model has some flaws because it does allow you to trade all of

T A B L E   12–7

Four Position-Sizing Models Compared

Model	Advantages	Disadvantages
Units-per-fixed-amount-of-money model	You don't reject a trade because it's too risky. It might also be a disadvantage. You can open an account with limited funds and use this model. It does give you minimum risk per trade.	It treats unequal investments alike. It cannot increase exposure rapidly for small units. Small accounts could be over-exposed.
Equal units model	It gives each investment an equal weighting in your portfolio.	Small investor would only be able to increase size slowly. Exposure is not necessarily alike for each unit. Investments frequently do not divide well into equal units.
Percent risk model	It allows both large and small accounts to grow steadily. It equalizes performance in the portfolio by the actual risk.	You will have to reject some trades because they're too risky. May be a disadvantage. The amount risked is not the actual risk, and Gallacher would say exposure is unequal.
Percent volatility model	It allows both large and small accounts to grow steadily. It equalizes performance in the portfolio by volatility. It can equalize trades when using tight stops without putting on large positions. The amount risked is not the actual risk, and Gallacher would say that the exposure is unequal.	You will have to reject some trades because they are too risky. The daily volatility is not the actual risk. May be a disadvantage.

them. A percent risk model or a percent volatility model, in contrast, might reject both the S&P and the bond trades because they were too risky.

Second, this model would allow you to buy one of each of the contracts. That's ridiculous because you would be giving all your attention to the S&P contract because of its volatility and risk. All investment units are not alike, and one should probably reject any sort of position-sizing algorithm that does treat them alike. This model does because you have one unit of each.

Third, if your position-sizing model is to take one contract per $30,000, then you would have two problems. If your account dropped by $1, you couldn't take any positions. Most people wouldn't follow this because they would assume that they could take one contract per "however much money was in their account." In addition, if you were lucky enough for your account to go up, the account would almost have to double in size before you could take another contract. That's basically no position sizing!

Notice that the last three models do a much better job of balancing your portfolio. Why not select one of them?

EXAMPLES OF THE IMPACT OF POSITION SIZING

I'm currently consulting for a company that is producing position-sizing software that will do all the models we recommend and much more. The software, called Athena,[4] has millions of possibilities for position sizing, so you can test almost anything. It works with Trade Station[5] signals, and it has a few built-in systems.

Let's use Athena to see how several position-sizing paradigms perform in a complex trading environment. In addition, since stock traders are the least likely people to consider the role of position sizing, we will use a portfolio consisting of the current 30 Dow Jones Industrial Average stocks.

All stocks will be traded with the same system on the same data (i.e., from January 1992 through June 1997). We'll use a very simple system—a channel breakout, long-only system that enters a position on the high of the last 45 days and uses a three-times-volatility trailing stop to exit (either as a stop or as a profit-taking exit). Thus, the system is quite simple.

We used a million dollar portfolio with a 0.5 percent cost of trading. The system took 595 trades during the 5.5-year period. The system had 273 winning trades and 322 losing trades, meaning that 45.9 percent of the trades made money.

We ran one version of each of the position-sizing models presented in this chapter, plus a comparison model that only took 100 shares of stock on each trade. Once again, in each case, the same trades were used. The only difference in the results, therefore, was a function of the position-sizing model that was selected.

The first model used was the baseline, which just takes 100 shares of stock whenever the system signaled a trade. This model made a total of $32,567 over the 5.5 years, which translates to a compounded annual return of only 0.58 percent. It had a maximum drawdown during the 5.5 years of 0.75 percent.

Figure 12–2 shows the equity curve, plus the drawdowns, over the 5.5 years of trading. Nothing is very spectacular about Figure 12–2. You might as well leave your money in a savings

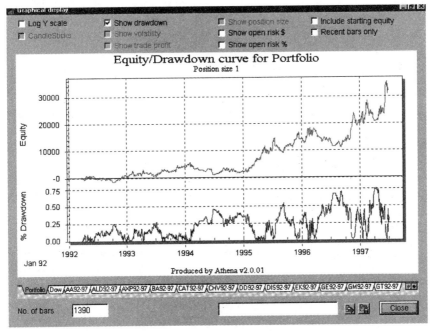

Figure 12–2 Dow stocks with baseline model of 100 shares each time

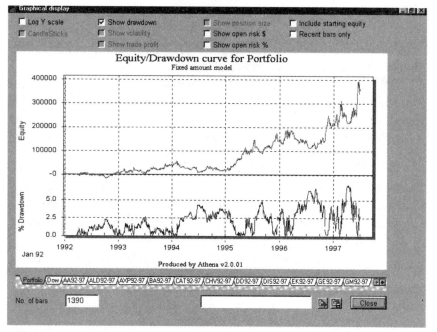

Figure 12–3 Dow Jones stocks traded with fixed-amount model,
100 shares/$100,000

account. However, remember it was included just as a baseline comparison.

The next model to look at was the fixed-amount model. This is a model typically used by futures traders in which you buy one unit per so much equity. In this case, we elected to purchase 100 shares per $100,000 in equity. Essentially, this means that when our equity is at a million, we would buy 1,000 shares of each position. When it reaches 2 million, we would have positions of 2,000 shares.

Figure 12–3 illustrates the equity curve with the fixed-amount model. It makes $237,457 over the 5.5 years. That translates into a compounded annual rate of return of 5.75 percent. However, it also produced a maximum drawdown of 7.13 percent—hardly spectacular performance, but better than our baseline.

Our next model is the equal leverage model that is typically

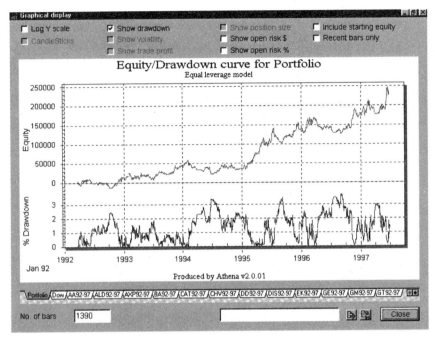

Figure 12–4 Position sizing using the equal leverage model with Dow stocks at 3 percent

used by equity traders. Here we will devote 3 percent of our equity to each position. Since we are trading a million dollars, no position will be larger than $30,000. Thus, you would buy 1,000 shares of a $30 stock, but only 300 shares of a $100 stock.

Obviously, the results of this model are not great at the leverage levels used. However, I simply picked an arbitrary level to show you the effect of position sizing. There are very large numbers of levels that could be selected with each model. All of them would produce different results.

Figure 12–4 shows the results of the equal leverage model. It produces 5.5-year profits of $231,121. That translates into an annual return of 3.86 percent with a maximum drawdown of 3.72 percent.

The next model gets a little more interesting. We'll use the percent risk model and size our positions at 1 percent risk. Since 1 percent of a million dollars is $10,000, this model simply means

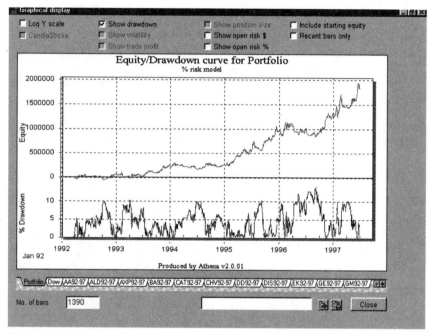

Figure 12–5 Dow stocks with a 1 percent risk position-sizing model

that our initial risk exposure will be no more than $10,000 on each stock. It says nothing about the value of the stocks, only the risk exposure.

Figure 12–5 shows that the 1 percent risk model made a profit of $1,840,493 over the 5.5 years. This translates into a 20.92 compounded annual rate of return. Its maximum drawdown during the 5.5 years was 14.14 percent. Clearly, this performance is beginning to be more interesting.

The last model we'll use is the percent volatility model. Here we are using the average true range of the stock over the last 10 days to determine the stock's volatility. We are sizing our positions at 0.5 percent volatility. This means that we are limiting our exposure to current market volatility to $5,000 for each position. Thus, if a stock's average true range has been $5 (or $500 for 100 shares), it

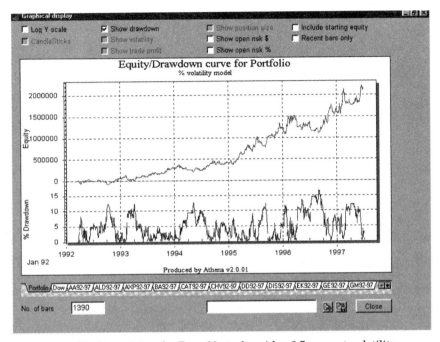

Figure 12–6 Position-sizing the Dow 30 stocks with a 0.5 percent volatility model

means that we initially can purchase 1,000 shares. Again, this has nothing to do with the value of the underlying security.

Figure 12–6 shows the equity curve for this last model. The model has a compounded annual return of 22.93 percent over the 5.5 years. The total return is $2,109,266. During the 5.5 year period, the maximum drawdown was 16.61 percent.

Lastly, Figure 12–7 shows a comparison of the five models presented. *Remember that each model used the same trading signals. The only difference was position sizing.* Look at the tremendous difference that the question of "how much" makes on the return! The baseline model made $32,567, while the 0.5 percent volatility model made over $2 million. If you are beginning to understand how important position sizing is, then you are beginning to understand one of the great secrets of trading.

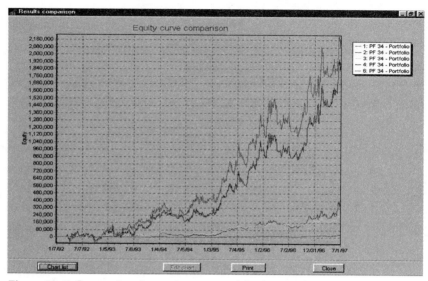

Figure 12–7 Comparing the equity curves of the five models

One could invent as many position-sizing algorithms as people have entry algorithms. There are millions of possibilities, and we have only touched the surface of the topic in this chapter.[6] Nevertheless, if you are beginning to understand the impact of position sizing, then I have accomplished my objective.

S U M M A R Y

In my opinion, the most significant part of trading system design is the part that has to do with money management. However, the term "money management" has been so misused over the years, that no one can agree upon a common meaning. As a result, I've elected to use the term "position sizing" in this chapter.

Position sizing basically adds a fourth dimension to the dimensions of reliability, reward-to-risk ratio, and opportunity. It dramatically adds to the potential profits or losses that can occur throughout the course of trading. In fact, position sizing, in my opinion, accounts for most of the variation in performance of various money managers. In essence, expectancy and opportunity form a solid that determines your volume of profits. Position sizing determines how many solids contribute to your profits at one time.

Position sizing also points out how important your underlying equity is. With large amounts of equity, you can do a lot with position sizing. With small amounts of equity, it is very easy to get wiped out.

Anti-martingale systems in which you increase your bet size as your equity increases are the primary models that work. Several anti-martingale position-sizing models were given, including:

Units per fixed amount of money. This model allows you to take one position per so much money. It basically treats all investments alike and always allows you to take one position.

Equal units model. This model gives an equal weighting to all investments in your portfolio according to their underlying value. It's commonly used by investors and equity traders.

The percent risk model. This model is recommended as the best model for long-term trend followers. It gives all trades an equal risk and allows a steady portfolio growth.

The percent volatility model. This model is best for traders who use tight stops. It can provide a reasonable balance between risk and opportunity (expectancy).

Several examples of money management were shown using new professional software that allows for quick, reasonable position sizing. These models, despite using the same system signals for entry and exit, showed returns that varied from $32,567 to $2,109,266. The difference in returns was due entirely to position sizing.

POSITION SIZING USED BY OTHER SYSTEMS

The performance of the world's greatest traders, in my opinion, has been driven by position sizing. However, let's look at the systems we've been discussing throughout this book and at the position sizing that they use. In most cases that will be quite easy, because they don't even talk about position sizing.

Stock Market Models

William O'Neil's CANSLIM Method

William O'Neil does not address the issue of "how much" to own in any given position. He only addresses the issue of how many stocks to own. He says that even a multimillion dollar portfolio should only own six or seven stocks. People with a portfolio of $20,000 to $100,000 should limit themselves to four or five stocks. People with $5,000 to $20,000 should limit themselves to three stocks, while people with even less should probably only invest in two.

This discussion sounds like the equal units approach with a slight twist. It suggests that you divide your capital into equal units, but that the number of units should depend upon the amount of money you have. A very small account should probably only have two units of perhaps $1,500 each or less. When you have about $5,000, then move to three units. Now you want each unit to grow to approach at least $4,000 per unit (i.e., you could afford to buy 100 shares of a $40 stock). When you can do this with five units ($20,000), then do so. At this point, you keep the same number of units until you can grow the size of a unit to about $25,000 to $50,000. At $50,000, you might want to move to as many as six or seven units.

The Warren Buffett Approach to Investing

Buffett is only interested in owning a few of the very best businesses—those that meet his exceptional criteria. He wants to own as much of those few businesses as he can, since it should give him excellent returns and he never plans to sell. Now that he has billions of dollars at his disposal, he can afford to own multiple companies. As a result, he simply adds more companies to his portfolio as they meet his criteria.

This is a rather unique style of position sizing. However, Buffett is the richest professional investor in the United States (and the second richest man, after Bill Gates). Who can argue with that kind of success? Perhaps you should consider this style of position sizing!

Motley Fool Foolish-Four Approach

In this approach you are only buying four stocks. As a result, the position-sizing methodology is an equal units approach—but again with a twist. This time the twist is to make one unit twice as big as the rest. This unit is used to purchase the stock with the best odds of giving you the biggest gain—the stock that has the second highest yield in the Dow 30 industrials. The remaining units are equal and only half as big. Since this method doesn't have an exit point, it would be difficult to improve upon it through position sizing.

Futures Market Models

Kaufman Adaptive Moving-Average Approach

Kaufman doesn't really discuss position sizing in his book, *Smarter Trading*. He does discuss some of the results of position sizing such as risk and reward. By risk he means the annualized standard deviation of the equity changes and by reward he means the annualized compounded rate of return. He suggests that when two systems have the same returns, the rational investor will choose the system with the lowest risk.

Kaufman also brings up another interesting point in his discussion—the 50-year rule. He says that levees were built along the Mississippi River to protect them from the largest flood that has occurred in the last 50 years. This means that water will rise above the levee, but not very often—perhaps once in a lifetime. Similarly, professional traders who design their systems properly may be faced with a similar situation. They may design their system carefully, but once in a lifetime they may be faced with extreme price moves that have the potential to wipe them out.

Safety, as we have indicated by the various position-sizing models, relates directly to the amount of equity you have and the amount of leverage you are willing to risk. As your capital grows, if you diversify and deleverage, then your capital will be safer. If you continue to leverage your profits, then you risk the chance of a complete loss.

Kaufman suggests that you can control your worst-case risk by looking at the standard deviation of your risk when testing at the selected leverage level. For example, if you have a 40 percent return and the variability of your drawdowns suggests that 1 standard deviation is 10 percent, then you know that in any given year:

- You have a 16 percent chance (1 standard deviation) of a 10 percent drawdown[7]
- You have a 2.5 percent chance (2 standard deviations) of a 20 percent drawdown
- You have a 0.5 percent chance (3 standard deviations) of a 30 percent drawdown

These results are excellent, but if you believe you will be in serious trouble if you lose 20 percent or more, Kaufman suggests that you only trade a portion of the funds allocated to you.

Kaufman also talks about asset allocation,[8] which he defines as "the process of distributing investment funds into one or more markets or vehicles to create an investment profile with the most desirable return/risk ratio." Asset allocation may simply amount to trading half of your capital with one active investment (i.e., a stock portfolio) while the rest of your capital is in short-term yield-bearing instruments such as government bonds. On the other hand, asset allocation may involve combining many investment vehicles in a dynamic approach—such as actively trading stocks, commodities, and the forex market.

It's clear from Kaufman's discussion, although he doesn't state it directly, that he is used to using the first position-sizing model—the one unit per so much capital. His form of reducing risk is simply to increase the capital required to trade one unit.

Gallacher's Fundamental Trading

Gallacher actually has an extensive chapter on position sizing in his book, *Winner Take All*. He says that risk is directly related to exposure in the market and he appears to detest the percent risk model presented here because it does not control exposure. For example, 3 percent risk on any size account could be 1 unit or 30 units depending upon where your stop is. There is no way, Gallacher argues, that the risk with 1 unit is not less than the risk in 30 units. For example, he states, "an account trading one contract of a commodity and risking $500 is a much less risky proposition than an account trading two contracts of that same commodity and risking $250 on each." Gallacher's statement is true, and everyone accepting the percent risk model should understand it. The stop is only the price at which your broker is told to sell. It does not in any way guarantee that price. This is one reason we recommend the percent volatility model for anyone who wants to trade tight stops.

Gallacher also points out that your risk increases not only with exposure, but also with time. The longer you trade the market, the greater the opportunity you have to be exposed to a tremendous price shock. A trader, trading one unit with all the money in the world, could eventually lose everything, Gallacher believes. That belief probably is true for most traders, but not all traders.

Trading different investments, Gallacher contends, only speeds up the effects of time. He argues that trading N positions for 1 year is the same as trading one position for N years in terms of the potential equity drawdown.

Gallacher recommends that you find the largest expected equity drop (LEED) that you will tolerate—perhaps 25 percent or perhaps 50 percent. He asks that you assume that this LEED will occur tomorrow. It probably won't, but you need to assume that it will occur.

He goes on to calculate a distribution of potential drawdowns by using the system's expectancy and the possible distribution of daily ranges for various commodities. He then recommends a minimum trading amount for various commodities so as not to experience a 50 percent drawdown. In other words, Gallacher is recommending a version of the typical one unit per so much equity in your account, but that amount varies depending upon the daily volatility of the investment.

The amount needed per unit of trading also differs depending upon whether you are trading one, two, or four simultaneous units. For example, he would recommend one unit per $40,000 for each $1,000 in daily range traded if the instrument is traded by itself. He recommends one unit per $28,000 for each $1,000 in daily range traded if the instrument is traded with one other. And, lastly, he recommends one unit per $20,000 for each $1,000 in daily range when traded with three other instruments.

Let's look at an example by looking at corn. Suppose the current price of corn varies by 4 cents per day. This amounts to a daily price variation of $200 (since one unit is 5,000 bushels). Based on Gallacher's model, since $200 is 20 percent of $1,000, you could trade one unit with 20 percent of $40,000 or one unit per $8,000. If you were trading corn with one other instrument, you could trade one unit per $5,600. And if you were trading with three other simultaneous instruments, you could trade one unit per $4,000.

Gallacher's method is an excellent variation of the one-unit-per-so-much-equity model, because it equates the various instruments according to their volatility. Thus, his method overcomes one of the basic limitations of that model. It does so by adding some complexity, but nevertheless it's an interesting way to trade.

Ken Roberts' 1-2-3 Methodology

Roberts' first position-sizing principle is that you don't need much money to trade commodities.[9] He answers the question of how much by saying only trade one contract. Unfortunately, he's catering to people who only have $1,000 to $10,000 in their account. Thus, the primary position-sizing rule is only trade one contract.

Roberts does say that one shouldn't take any risk over $1,000, which means that he avoids certain commodities like the S&Ps, deutschemark, yen, and perhaps even coffee—because the risk involved would typically be greater than $1,000. This statement makes Roberts sound conservative. Roberts does not include a position-sizing algorithm in his system. This can be dangerous, in my opinion, because you might still take a position in the market when most position-sizing algorithms would indicate that you should not do so.

NOTES

1. It's not even a good exit methodology, as explained in the exit chapter, because you take losses with a full position and you take your maximum profits with only a partial position.
2. See William Ziemba, "A Betting Simulation, the Mathematics of Gambling and Investment, *Gambling Times,* 1987, 80, pp. 46–7.
3. When this chapter was first written, an S&P contract amounted to about $450,000 worth of stock. However, the contract has since been reduced in size by 50 percent.
4. Athena is a trademark of Athena Management Systems. Athena is the goddess of wisdom, and the software, in my opinion, is indeed wise. You can see a demonstration of Athena at our web site at http://www.iitm.com.

5. TradeStation is a registered trademark of Omega Research.

6. I originally used a random entry study with various futures contracts in this chapter. In that study, with over 10 years of data, we showed returns ranging from $382,853 to nearly 1,700 times that amount at $640 million. Again, those returns were all achieved on the same signals and the only difference was the position-sizing algorithm. I elected not to include those results in this chapter because I felt people would complain that they were not realistic. Again, my purpose was not so much to show spectacular results as it was to show how much impact position sizing can have. As a result, I substituted those results in this chapter with the results using the Dow 30 stocks. You can still see the other study on our web site at http://www.iitm.com.

7. You can figure it this way: 68 percent of the variability falls between + 1 and −1 standard deviation, so 32 percent remains. This also means that there is 16 percent (half of 32 percent) beyond 1 standard deviation of 10 percent. In the same way, 95 percent of the returns will fall between + 2 and −2 standard deviations. Thus, half of 5 percent leaves 2.5 percent outside of −2 standard deviations. Lastly, 99 percent falls between + 3 and −3 standard deviations. Thus, by the same logic, only 0.5 percent of the results will be worse than −3 standard deviations. However, Kaufman is making the assumption that returns are normally distributed. Since market prices are not, returns may not be either.

8. Asset allocation was shown by Brinson, Singer, and Beebower ("Determinants of Portfolio Performance II: An Update." *Financial Analysts Journal*, 1991, 47, 40–49) to account for 91.5 percent of the variability of returns of 82 pension plans over a 10-year period. Stock selection and other types of decision making had very little influence on the returns. Brinson et al.'s definition of "asset allocation" was really position sizing—since it just indicated what percentage of the capital was in stocks, bonds, and cash. Professionals then became very excited about asset allocation, but its meaning was changed to reflect the lotto bias—it now seems to mean "selecting the right assets."

9. In my opinion, this assumption allows a lot of people to trade and makes it seem as if there is little risk involved. Readers of this book should be able to judge the risk of this assumption for themselves at this point.

CHAPTER 13

Conclusion!

To be a money master, you must first be a self-master.

J. P. Morgan

If you understand the psychological foundation for system design, then I've accomplished a major objective in writing this book. The source of the Holy Grail is inside you. You must assume total responsibility for what you do and for what happens to you. You must determine what you want from a system and detail a plan with the appropriate objectives. You must have a way to "cut your losses short and let your profits run," which is all about exits. Exits are a major part of developing a high positive expectancy system.

If you understand the six key elements of making money in the market and their relative importance, then I've met a second objective in writing this book. Those six key elements include (1) system reliability, (2) reward-to-risk ratio, (3) cost of trading, (4) your trading opportunity level, (5) the size of your equity, and (6) your position-sizing algorithm. You should understand the relative importance of each of these factors and why successful trading isn't about "being right" or "being in control" of the market.

Lastly, if you have a good plan in mind about how to develop a trading system that will meet your objectives, then I've met my third key objective in writing this book. You should understand the parts of a trading system and the role that each part plays. If not, then review Chapter 4. You should know how setups, timing, protective stops, and profitable exits combine to create a high expectancy system. You should understand the key role that opportunity plays and how it relates to trading cost. And most importantly, you should understand how important the size of your trading equity is and how it relates to various anti-martingale position-sizing algorithms.

If you have met those three key objectives, then you have a wonderful start. However, there is still much to learn in your trading journey that is beyond the scope of this book. As a result, I want to provide a brief overview of some of those areas in this final chapter. Since there is so much material to cover, I've elected to cover it in a question-and-answer format, which allows me to be extremely focused and to the point.

So if someone understands everything covered in this book, then what's left? It seems quite extensive.

A number of areas remain. We've talked about what's involved in a trading system and the relative importance of each element. However, we haven't extensively discussed data, software, testing procedures, order execution, portfolio design, and managing other people's money. We've touched on those topics, but not in depth. Most importantly, we haven't discussed the process of trading at all and all of the psychological elements that are involved with discipline and the day-to-day details of trading or investing.

Okay, so let's take each of those topics one by one. Where can readers get more information, and what information do they need to know? Let's start out with data.

The topic of data is a broad one and could be the basis for a mini-book. First of all, you must understand that data only represent the market. The data are not the actual market. Second, data may not really be what they appear to be. By the time the average person gets market data, there are usually a number of sources of potential errors. Consequently, if you get data from two different vendors and run the exact same system over the exact same markets and years, you can come up with different results. The reason will be differences in the data. Obviously, this affects both your historical testing and your day-to-day trading.

There are basically two conclusions you will eventually make about data. First, nothing in this business is that exact. Second, you need to find reliable vendors and be certain that they stay reliable. We've written a newsletter about data which I'll be happy to send you for free. The address and phone number are in the back of the book.

Okay, what about software? What should people look for in software?

The news is not that great. Most software is designed to appeal to people's psychological weaknesses. Most of it optimizes results to make you think that you have a great system when you may not even have a profitable system. The software typically tests one market at a time over many years. That's not the way professionals trade. But it will allow you to get very optimistic results because those results are curve-fitted to the market.

I would strongly recommend that you at least be aware that this is what most of the software does. In addition, you need software that will help you concentrate on the more important elements of trading or investing—such as position sizing. I strongly recommend the Athena software in this regard. I helped initiate the development of this software because we were unable to find other software to help people size their positions, and adequately test the results of various position-sizing algorithms.

What about testing? What do people need to know about testing?

Testing is not exact. We used a well-known software program and ran a simple program that entered the market on a two-day breakout and exited after one day. The program was really simple because we were just looking at the accuracy of collecting on-line data. However, we were using some well-known, very popular software to do the data collection and run the simple system. Yet when that software was run in real time, it got one set of results. When that software was run again in a historical mode on the same data it had collected, it got a different set of results. That shouldn't happen, but it did. And in my opinion, that's quite scary.

If you approach the world of trading and investing as a perfectionist, you will be frustrated over and over again. Nothing is exact. You can never know how it will really turn out. Instead, trading is very much a game of discipline, of being in touch with the flow of the markets, and of being able to capitalize upon that flow. People who can do that can make a lot of money in the markets.

That sounds very pessimistic. Why test at all?

So you can get an understanding of what works and what doesn't work. You shouldn't believe everything I've told you. Instead, you need to prove to yourself that something is true. When something seems reasonably true, then you can develop some confidence in using it. You must have that confidence or you'll be lost when you are dealing with the markets.

You probably cannot be exact. But no science is exact. People used to think that physics was exact, but now we know that the very act of measuring something changes the nature of the observation. Whatever it is, you are a part of it. You cannot help that because it is probably the nature of reality. And it again illustrates my point about the search for the Holy Grail System being an inner search.

Are there any more issues around testing?

Yes, there are a lot of issues around robustness, knowing what you want, statistics. These are way beyond the scope of this book, but we do tend to cover them in our newsletter. In fact, we periodically take people through the process of designing a system around a particular concept.

Okay, let's talk about order execution.

Order execution is important from the viewpoint of communication. You must have a broker who understands what you want and what you are trying to do. When you can communicate that, you will get help in what you are trying to do.

So what does that mean?

Well, first you must know your system inside out. You must understand your concept. Then you must convey what you are doing to your pit broker and what you expect from him or her. For example, if you are a trend follower and you are trading breakouts, you will want to trade real breakouts. Communicate that to your broker. You can find someone who will act with a little discretion on your order. If the market is really moving, you'll be executed. But if a few traders are just testing new high prices, then you don't want to be executed because the market won't have any follow-through. If you communicate that to your broker, you can get the kind of service that will put you only in the kind of markets you want. If you don't communicate what you want, you won't get that kind of service.

Your broker also needs to know what you will pay for execution. What I just talked about is great for a long-term trend follower, but is terrible for a day trader. A day trader just needs good execution with a minimum of cost and a minimum of slippage. However, you will never get minimum costs unless you communicate that to your broker.

What about portfolio testing and multiple systems?

Again, we have a potential topic for a book. But think about the opportunity factor that we've discussed in this book. You have a chance, when you trade a portfolio of markets, to open up many more trading opportunities. That means you will get your big trade—perhaps several of them in a year. It means you might have enough opportunity to never have a losing quarter or perhaps a losing month.

Multiple systems give you the same advantage—more opportunity. Multiple systems can be particularly good if they are non-correlated. It means that you will always have some winners. Your drawdowns will be less or nonexistent. And if that occurs, you will have a much greater capital base to come from (for position sizing) when a giant winner comes along.

I think that people who understand these principles can easily make 50 percent per year. I already have some supertraders in my program who are doing much better than that, and we are going to prove the point much more extensively in the future. However, one of the keys to making all this happen is having sufficient funds. If your snow wall is too small, you'll get wiped out by the first big black snowball that comes along. And that will occur no matter how good your system is or how well prepared you are.

Okay, what about discipline and process of trading?

This is the area I first modeled. If you understand this area, you have a real chance of success. But if you don't understand it, you have little chance of success.

I first started the process of finding out about good trading by asking a lot of good traders what they did. My assumption was that the common answers were the "real" secrets of success.

Most traders would tell me something about their methods. After interviewing 50 traders, I had 50 different methodologies. As a result, I concluded that methodology wasn't that significant to trading success. These traders all had low-risk ideas, but there were a lot of different types of low-risk ideas and that was just one of the keys. I'd now express that in terms of having a high positive expectancy, with lots of opportunity and with plenty of understanding of how to use position sizing to realize that expectancy over the long run. However, doing that requires a lot of discipline.

I've developed a complete course on peak performance trading, and there is very little overlap between that course and this book.

Give us a synopsis. How about some steps people could follow on a regular basis to be more disciplined in their trading?

- Okay, step 1 is to have a trading plan and test it. You should know how to do most of that from the information contained in this book. Your basic goal is to develop confidence and a strong understanding of the concept you are trading.

- Step 2 would be to assume total responsibility for everything that happens to you. Even if someone runs off with your money or a broker rips you off, assume that you were somehow involved in creating that situation. I know that sounds a bit strong. But if you do that, you can correct your role in what happens. When you stop committing the same mistakes over and over, you have a chance to be successful.

- Step 3, find your weaknesses and work on them. I have several coaches to help me as a businessperson. In addition, I act as a coach for a number of people in our supertrader program. And the key to that program is to find weaknesses and eliminate them. Develop a diary of what happens to you. Notice common emotional patterns and make the assumption that they are you.

- The fourth step is to do some global planning. Make a list of everything that could go wrong in your business and determine how you will respond to that situation. That will be the key to your success—knowing how to respond to the unexpected. For everything you can think of that might go wrong, develop several courses of action. Rehearse those action plans until they become second nature to you. This is a critical step to success.

- Step 5, on a daily basis analyze yourself. You are the most important factor in your trading and investing. Doesn't it make sense to spend a little time analyzing yourself? How are you feeling? What is going on in your life? The more aware you are of these issues, the less control they will have over your life.

- The sixth step is to determine what could go wrong in your trading at the beginning of the day. How will you react to that? Mentally rehearse each option until you have it down pat. Every athlete does extensive mental rehearsal and it is important for you to do the same.

- Step 7, at the end of the day do a daily debriefing. Ask yourself a simple question: Did I follow my rules? If the answer is yes, then pat yourself on the back. In fact, if you followed your rules and lost money, pat yourself on the back twice. If the answer is no, then you must determine why! How might you get yourself into a similar situation in the future? When you find that similar situation, then you must mentally rehearse the situation again and again to make sure you know how to respond appropriately in the future.

Those seven steps should have a gigantic influence on anyone's trading.

What do you think the most important thing is that traders or investors can do to improve their performance?

That's an easy question, but the solution is not easy. Take total responsibility for everything that happens to you—in the market and in your life.

Let me give you an example from one of the marble games we play at seminars. Let's say the audience has $10,000 in play equity and the audience members can risk any amount of that on each marble that is drawn (and replaced). Let's also say 40 percent of the marbles are losers and one of them loses 5 to 1 (i.e., it's a −5–R multiple). The game goes on for 100 draws so that some large losing streaks will occur. In 100 draws, we'll probably have 6 or 7 losses in a row at some point in time. Moreover, that losing streak might include the 5-to-1 loss.

I'm a little sneaky. When someone draws out a losing marble, I ask that person to continue drawing until he or she eventually draws a winning marble. That means that someone in the audience will draw all of the long losing streak.

At the end of the game, usually half the audience loses money and many of them go broke. When I ask them, "How many of you think this person (i.e., the person who pulled the losing streak) is responsible for your losses?" many of them raise their hands. If they really believe that, it means that they didn't learn anything from the game. They went bankrupt because of poor money management, but they'd rather blame it on someone else (or something else) such as the person who picked the losing marbles.

> In life and in trading, there will always be someone who picks the losing marbles. Only when you finally realize that the result somehow depends upon you will you start learning to correct your mistakes. In life and in trading…correct your mistakes.

The most astute traders and investors are the ones who learn this lesson early. They are always looking to themselves to correct mistakes. This means they will eventually clear out the psychological issues that prevent them from making a lot of money. As a result, they will also continue to profit from their mistakes.

Thus, my first advice to anyone is to look to yourself as the source of everything that happens in your life. What are the common patterns and how can you fix them? When you do this, your chances of success go up dramatically.

Great, any last words of wisdom?

I'd like to mention something about beliefs, because I think they are so important. First, you cannot trade the markets—you can only trade your beliefs about the market. As a result, it is important for you to determine exactly what those beliefs are.

Second, certain key beliefs, which have nothing to do with the market, will still determine your success in the markets. Those are your beliefs about yourself. What do you think you are capable of doing? Is trading or success important to you? How worthy of success do you believe yourself to be? Weak beliefs about yourself can undermine trading with a great system.

At this point, I'd like to mention something that will help you to move to the next step. We have a game on our web site at http://www.iitm.com. That game gives you a positive expectancy and only emphasizes position sizing and letting your profits run. What I'd suggest that you do is use that game as a training ground for your trading. See if you can make money playing the game. We give prizes for being in the top 10, and playing the game is free. Develop a plan for getting into the top 10 without taking a lot of risk. It's possible. In fact, if you read the briefings, you'll even see an example of how to do it. It's not that difficult, but few people can do it.

Prove to yourself that you can do it. Games reflect behavior. If you cannot do it in our game, then you have no chance in the market. You will also have most of the psychological issues playing the game that you will have when you face the market. The game is an inexpensive place to learn.

As my final words of advice, I'd suggest that you read this book over four or five times. My experience is that people filter things according to their belief systems. There is probably a lot of material that you overlooked. A second reading may pick up some new gems for you. And multiple readings will make it second nature for you.

Recommended Readings

Balsara, Nauzer J. *Money Management Strategies for Futures Traders*. New York: Wiley, 1992. Good money management book, but it is more about risk control than position sizing.

Barach, Roland. *Mindtraps*, 2d ed. Raleigh, NC: International Institute of Trading Mastery, 1996. Good book about the psychological biases we face in all aspects of trading and investing. Call 1-919-362-5591 for more information.

Campbell, Joseph (with Bill Moyers). *The Power of Myth*. New York: Doubleday, 1988. One of my all-time favorite books.

Chande, Tushar. *Beyond Technical Analysis: How to Develop and Implement a Winning Trading System*. New York: Wiley, 1997. One of the first books to really go beyond just emphasizing entry.

Colby, Robert W., and Meyers, Thomas A. *Encyclopedia of Technical Market Indicators*. Homewood, IL: Dow-Jones Irwin, 1988. Excellent just for its scope.

Connors, Laurence, and Raschke, Linda-Bradford. *Street Smarts*. Malibu, CA: Gordon Publishing Group, 1995 Great book of short-term trading techniques.

Gallacher, William. *Winner Take All: A Top Commodity Trader Tells It Like It Is*. Chicago: Probus, 1994. One of the systems mentioned in the text comes from this witty and straightforward book.

Gardner, David, and Gardner, Tom. *The Motley Fool Investment Guide: How the Fool Beats Wall Street's Wise Men and How You Can Too*. New York: Simon & Schuster, 1996. Simple investment strategies most people can follow.

Hagstrom, Robert, Jr. *The Warren Buffett Way: Investment Strategies of the World's Greatest Investor*. New York: Wiley, 1994. Probably the best book on Buffett's strategy. However, this is not Buffett writing about his strategy, and the author seems to have all the normal biases that most people have—it makes it seem as if all Buffett does is pick good stocks and hold onto them.

Kase, Cynthia. *Trading with the Odds: Using the Power of Probability to Profit in the Futures Market.* Chicago: Irwin, 1996. I believe there is more to this book than even the author knows.

Kaufman, Perry. *Smarter Trading: Improving Performance in Changing Markets.* New York: McGraw-Hill, 1995. Great ideas and contains another of the systems discussed throughout this book.

Kilpatrick, Andrew. *Of Permanent Value: The Story of Warren Buffett.* Birmingham, AL: AKPE, 1996. Fun reading.

LeBeau, Charles, and Lucas, David. *The Technical Traders' Guide to Computer Analysis of the Futures Market.* Homewood, IL: Irwin, 1992. One of the best books ever written on systems development.

LeFevre, Edwin. *Reminiscence of a Stock Operator.* New York: Wiley, 1993. New edition of an old classic.

Lowe, Janet. *Warren Buffett Speaks: Wit and Wisdom from the World's Greatest Investor.* New York: Wiley, 1997. Fun reading with great wisdom.

Lowenstein, Roger. *Buffett: The Making of an American Capitalist.* New York: Random House, 1995. A good book to round out your Buffett education.

Mitchell, Dick. *Commonsense Betting: Betting Strategies for the Race Track.* New York: William Morrow & Company, 1995. A must for people who really want to stretch themselves to learn position sizing.

O'Neil, William. *How to Make Money in Stocks: A Winning System in Good Times and Bad,* 2d ed. New York: McGraw-Hill, 1995. A modern classic that includes one of the systems reviewed in this book.

Roberts, Ken. *The World's Most Powerful Money Manual and Course.* Grant's Pass, OR: 1995. Good course and good ideas. However, be careful if you don't have enough money. Call 503-955-2800 for more information.

Schwager, Jack. *Market Wizards.* New York: The New York Institute of Finance, 1988. A must read for any trader or investor.

Schwager, Jack. *The New Market Wizards.* New York: HarperCollins, 1992. Continues the tradition, and it again is a must read. William Eckhardt's chapter alone is worth the price of the book.

Schwager, Jack. *Schwager on Futures: Fundamental Analysis.* New York: Wiley, 1996. Great book for anyone who wants to understand fundamentals in the futures market.

Schwager, Jack. *Schwager on Futures: Technical Analysis.* New York: Wiley, 1996. Solid background on many topics related to learning about markets.

Sloman, James. *Nothing.* Durham, NC: Dana Institute, 1981. Call 1-919-362-5591 for more information. A great book about flow. This has nothing to do with trading, but I think all traders and investors should read this book.

Sloman, James. *When You're Troubled: The Healing Heart.* Raleigh, NC: Mountain Rain, 1993. Call 1-919-362-5591 for more information. Great book about helping yourself through life. The author calls this book his life's purpose, and I tend to agree.

Sweeney, John. *Campaign Trading: Tactics and Strategies to Exploit the Markets.* New York: Wiley, 1996. Great book that emphasizes the more important aspects of trading.

Tharp, Van. *The Peak Performance Course for Traders and Investors.* Raleigh, NC: International Institute of Trading Mastery, 1988–1994. Call 1-919-362-5591 for more information. This is my model of the trading process, presented in such a way as to help you install the model in yourself.

Tharp, Van. *How to Develop a Winning Trading System That Fits You: A 3-Day Seminar on Tape.* Raleigh, NC: International Institute of Trading Mastery, 1997. Call 1-919-362-5591 for more information. This is our original systems seminar, which is great information for all traders and investors.

Vince, Ralph. *Portfolio Management Formulas: Mathematical Trading Methods for the Futures, Options, and Stock Markets.* New York: Wiley, 1990. Difficult reading, but most professionals should tackle it.

Vince, Ralph. *The New Money Management: A Framework for Asset Allocation.* New York: Wiley, 1995. An improvement from *Portfolio Management Formulas* and again a book that most professionals in the field of investing and trading should read.

Wilder, J. Wells, Jr. *New Concepts in Technical Trading.* Greensboro, NC: Trend Research, 1978. One of the classics of trading and a must read.

Key Terms Defined

Adaptive Moving Average A moving average that is either quick, or slow, to signal a market entry depending upon the efficiency of the move in the market.

Algorithm Rules for computing, i.e., procedures for calculating mathematical functions.

Anti-Martingale Strategy A position sizing strategy in which position size is increased when one wins. Any position sizing strategy based upon one's equity will be an anti-martingale strategy.

Arbitrage Taking advantage of discrepancies in price or loopholes in the system to make consistent low-risk money. Usually involves the simultaneous purchase and sale of related items.

Average Directional Movement (ADX) An indicator that measures how much a market is trending. Both bullish and bearish trends are shown by positive movement.

Average True Range (ATR) The average over the last "X" days of the true range which is the largest of the following: (1) today's high minus today's low; (2) today's high minus yesterday's close; or (3) today's low minus yesterday's close.

Backwardation Usually, future prices are above today's cash prices. However, in times of shortages nearby prices will rise above the price of future prices. This is the phenomenon called *"backwardation."*

Bearish The opinion that the market will be going down in the future.

Best-case example Many books show you illustrations of their key points about the market (or indicator) that appear to perfectly predict the market. However, most examples of these points are not nearly as good as the one that is selected, which is known as a best-case example.

Bias   The tendency to move in a particular direction. This could be a market bias, but most of the biases discussed in this book were psychological biases.

Bullish   The opinion that the market will be going up in the future.

Candlesticks   A type of bar chart, developed by the Japanese, in which the price range between the open and the close is either a white rectangle (if the close is higher) or a black rectangle (if the close is lower). These charts have the advantage of making the price movement more obvious visually.

Capitalization   The amount of money in the underlying stock of a company.

Chaos Theory   A theory about physical systems which suggests that one moves from stability to chaos. This theory has recently been used to explain explosive moves in the markets and the nonrandomness of the markets.

Commodities   Physical products that are traded at a futures exchange such as grains, foods, meats, metals, etc.

Consolidation   A pause in the market during which prices move in a limited range and do not seem to trend.

Contract   A single unit of a commodity or future. For example, a single unit or contract of corn is 5,000 bushels.

Degree of Freedom   A statistical term equal to the number of independent observations less the number of parameters to be estimated. More degrees of freedom generally helps in describing past price movement and hurts in predicting future price movement.

Dev-stop©   A stop loss criterion developed by Cynthia Kase which depends on the standard deviation of price movement.

Directional Movement   An indicator attributed to J. Wells Wilder which uses the largest part of today's range that is outside of yesterday's range.

Disaster Stop   A stop loss order to determine your worst case loss in a position.

Discretionary Trading   Trading that depends upon the instincts of the trader as opposed to a systematic approach. The best discretionary traders are those who develop a systematic approach and then use discretion in their exits and position sizing to improve the performance.

Divergence   A term used to describe two or more indicators failing to show confirming signals.

Diversification   Investing in independent markets to reduce the overall risk.

Drawdown   A decrease in the value of your account because of losing trades or because of "paper losses" which may occur simply because of a decline in value of open positions.

Elliott Wave   A theory developed by R. N. Elliott which holds that the market moves in a series of five up-waves followed by a series of three correction down-waves.

Equities   Refers to stocks secured by ownership in the company.

Equity   The value of your account.

Equity Curve   The value of your account over time, illustrated in a graph.

Expectancy   How much you can expect to make on the average over many trades. Expectancy is best stated in terms of how much you can make per dollar you risk. Two formulas are given in Chapter 6 that show you how to calculate expectancy.

False Positive   Something that gives a prediction which then fails to happen.

Filter   An indicator which selects only data which meet specific criteria. Too many filters tend to lead to overoptimization.

Floor Trader   Person who trades on the floor of a commodities exchange. Locals tend to trade their own account, while pit brokers tend to trade for a brokerage company or a large firm.

Forex   Stands for Foreign Exchange. A huge market in foreign currencies made by large banks worldwide.

Fundamental Analysis   Analysis of the market to determine the supply and demand characteristics. In equities markets, fundamental analysis determines the value, the earnings, the management, and the relative data of a particular stock.

Futures   When commodity exchanges added stock index contracts and currency contracts, the term "futures" was developed to be more inclusive.

Gambler's Fallacy   The belief that a loss is due after a string of winners and/or that a gain is due after a string of losers.

Hit Rate   The percentage of winners you have in your trading or investing. Also known as the "reliability of your system."

Holy Grail System   A mythical trading system that perfectly follows the market and is always right, producing large gains and zero drawdowns. No such system exists, but the real meaning of the Holy Grail is right on track. It suggests that the "secret" is inside you.

Indicator   A way of summarizing data in a "meaningful" way to help traders and investors make decisions.

Inside Day   A day in which the total range of prices falls between the range of prices of the prior day.

Investing   Refers to a buy-and-hold strategy that most people follow. If you are in and out frequently or you are willing to go both long and short, then you are trading.

Judgmental Heuristics   Shortcuts that the human mind uses to make decisions. These shortcuts make our decision making quite quick and comprehensive, but they lead to biases in decision making that often cause people to lose money. A number of these biases are discussed in Chapter 2.

Largest Expected Equity Drop (LEED)   A term used by Gallacher to assist in limiting risk. It refers to the largest drop in equity that you will tolerate.

Leverage   The relationship between the amount of money one needs to put up to own something and its underlying value determines the amount of leverage one has. High leverage increases the potential size of profits and losses.

Limit Move   A change in price that reaches the limit set by the exchange in which the contract is traded. Trading usually is halted when a limit move is reached.

Liquidity   The ease and availability of trading in an underlying stock or futures contract. When the volume of trading is high, there is usually a lot of liquidity.

Long   Owning a tradable item in anticipation of a future price increase. Also see *Short*.

Low-risk Idea   An idea which has a positive expectancy and which is traded at a risk level that allows for the worst possible situation in the short-term so that one can realize the long-term expectancy.

Marked to Market   A term used to describe the fact that open positions are credited or debited funds based upon the closing price of that open position during the day.

Market Maker   A broker, bank, or firm that makes a two-way price to either buy or sell a security, currency, or futures contract.

Martingale Strategy   A position-sizing strategy in which the position size increases after you lose money. The classic martingale strategy is where you double your bet size after each loss.

Maximum Adverse Excursion (MAE)   The maximum loss attributable to price movement against the position during the life of a particular trade.

Mental Rehearsal   The psychological process of preplanning an event or strategy in one's mind before actually doing it.

Modeling   The process of determining how some form of peak performance is accomplished and then passing on that training to others.

Momentum   This refers to an indicator which represents the change in price now from some fixed time period in the past. Momentum is one of the few leading indicators. Momentum as a market indicator is quite different from momentum as a term in physics which equals mass times acceleration.

Money Management   A term that was frequently used to describe position sizing, but has so many other connotations that people fail to understand its full meaning or importance. For example, it also refers to: (1) managing other people's money; (2) risk control; (3) managing one's personal finances; (4) achieving maximum gain; and many other concepts.

Moving Average   A method of representing a number of price bars by a single average of all the price bars. When a new bar occurs, that new bar is added, the last bar is removed, and a new average is then calculated.

Negative Expectancy System   A system in which you will never make money over the long-term. For example, all casino games are designed to be negative expectancy games. Negative expectancy systems also include some highly reliable systems (i.e., with a high hit rate) which tend to have occasional large losses.

Neural Network   This term refers to an artificial intelligence program that learns through feedback and a trial-and-error process.

> **Back Propagation Network**   A multilayered neural network in which errors are fed back to adjust the weightings of the neurons.
>
> **Hidden Neuron**   Elements in a neural network that lie between the input and output layers.
>
> **Normalization**   A process in the neural network in which the data are put into a specific range, such as 0 to 100.
>
> **Transformation**   The process of changing from one state to another in a neural network. Also converting input data to a more suitable form (e.g., variations in stock prices might be best expressed in a logarithmic form).

NeuroLinguistic Programming (NLP)   A form of psychological training developed by systems analyst Richard Bandler and linguist John Grinder. It forms the foundation for the science of modeling excellence in human behavior. However, what is usually taught in NLP seminars are the techniques that are developed from the modeling process. For example, we have modeled top trading, system development, and money management at IITM. What we teach in our seminars is the process of doing those things, not the modeling process per se.

Optimize   Optimization is the process of finding those parameters and indicators that best predict price changes in historical data. A highly optimized system usually does a poor job of predicting future prices.

Option   The right to buy or sell an underlying asset at a fixed price up to some specified date in the future. The right to buy is a *call option,* and the right to sell is a *put option.*

Oscillator   This term refers to an indicator that de-trends price. Most oscillators tend to go from 0 to 100. Analysts typically assume that when the indicator is near zero, the price is "oversold," and that when the price is near 100, it is "overbought." However, in a trending market, prices can be overbought or oversold for a long time.

Parabolic   This term refers to an indicator that has a U-shaped function, based upon the function ($y = ax^2 + bx + c$). Because it rises steeply, it is sometimes used as a trailing stop that tends to keep one from giving back profits.

Peak-to-Trough Drawdown   A term that is used to describe one's maximum drawdown from the highest equity peak to the lowest equity trough prior to reaching a new equity high.

Position Sizing   The most important of the six key elements of successful trading. This element determines how large a position you will put on throughout the course of a trade. In most cases, algorithms for determining position size are based upon one's current equity.

Positive Expectancy   This term is used to describe a system (or game) that will make money over the long term if played at a low-enough risk level.

Post-dictive Error   This term refers to an error that is made when you take into account future data that you should not know. For example, if you buy on the open each day if the closing price is up, you will have the potential for a great system, but only because you are making a post-dictive error.

Prediction   Most people want to make money through the process of prediction. Analysts are employed to predict prices. However, great traders make money by "cutting losses short and letting profits run," which has nothing to do with prediction.

Relative Strength Indicator (RSI)   This refers to a futures market indicator described by J. Wells Wilder, Jr., that is used to ascertain overbought and oversold conditions. It is based upon the close-to-close price change.

R-value   The initial risk taken in a given position, as defined by one's initial stop loss.

R-multiple   All profits can be expressed as a multiple of the initial risk (R). For example, a 10-R multiple is a profit that is 10 times the initial risk. Thus, if your initial risk is $10, then a $100 profit would be a 10 R-multiple profit.

Random   A number determined by chance. A number which cannot be predicted.

Reliability   Refers to how accurate something is or how often it wins. Thus, a 60% reliability means that something wins 60% of the time.

Retracement   A price movement in the opposite direction of the previous trend. A retracement is usually a price correction.

Reward-to-Risk Ratio   The average return on an account (on a yearly basis) divided by the maximum peak-to-trough drawdown. Any reward-to-risk ratio over three that is determined by this method is excellent. It also might refer to the size of the average winning trade divided by the size of the average losing trade.

Round Turn   This terms refers to the process of both getting into and exiting a futures contract. Futures commissions are usually based upon a round-turn as opposed to charging for both getting in and getting out.

Scalping This term refers to the actions, usually of floor traders, who buy and sell quickly to get the bid and ask price or to make a quick profit.

Seasonal Trading Trading based upon consistent, predictable changes in price during the year due to production cycles or demand cycles.

Set-up This terms refers to a part of one's trading system in which certain criteria must be present before you look for an entry into the market.

Short Selling an item in order to be able to buy it later at a lower price. When you sell before you have bought the item, you are said to be "shorting" the market.

Slippage The difference in price between what you expect to pay when you enter the market and what you actually pay. For example, if you attempted to buy at 15 and you end up buying at 15.5, then you have a half point of slippage.

Specialist A floor trader assigned to fill orders in a specific stock when the order has no offsetting order from off-the-floor.

Spreading The process of trading two related markets to exploit a new relationship. Thus, you might trade Japanese yen in terms of British pounds. In doing so, you are trading the relationship between the two currencies.

Stalking This term refers to the process of getting ready to get into a position. This is one of the ten tasks of trading from Dr. Tharp's model.

Standard Deviation The positive square root of the expected value of the square of the difference between some random variable and its mean. A measure of variability that has been expressed in a normalized form.

Stochastic An overbought-oversold indicator, popularized by George Lane, that is based upon the observation that prices close near the high of the day in an uptrend and near the low of the day in a downtrend.

Swing Trading This term refers to short-term trading designed to capture quick moves in the market.

System A system is a set of rules for trading. A complete system will typically have: (1) some setup conditions; (2) an entry signal; (3) a worst case disaster stop to preserve capital; (4) a profit taking exit; and (5) a position sizing algorithm. However, many commercially available systems do not have all of these criteria.

Tick A tick is the minimum fluctuation in price of a tradable item.

Trade Distribution This term refers to the manner in which winning and losing trades are achieved over time. It will show the winning streaks and the losing streaks.

Trade Opportunity This is one of the six keys to profitable trading. It refers to how often a system will open a position in the market.

Trading Opening a position in the market, either long or short, with the expectation of either closing it out at a substantial profit or cutting losses short if the trade does not work out.

Trailing Stop A stop loss order that moves with the prevailing trend of the market. This is typically used as a way of exiting profitable trades.

Trending Day   A day that generally continues in one direction, either up or down, from the open to the close.

Trend-following   The systematic process of capturing extreme moves in the market with the idea of staying in the market as long as the market continues its move.

"Turtle Soup"™   A trademarked entry technique that is based upon the assumption that markets typically reverse after 20-day channel breakouts.

Validity   A term that indicates how "real" something is. Does it measure what it is supposed to measure? How accurate is it?

Volatility   A term that refers to the range of prices in a given time period. A highly volatile market has a large range in daily prices, whereas a low-volatility market has a small range of daily prices. This is one of the most useful concepts in trading.

Volatility Breakout   An entry technique which enters when the market moves a specific amount from the open, based on the previous daily ranges of the market. For example, a 1.5 ATR volatility breakout would be one that enters if the market moves (up or down) more that 1.5 times the average true range of the last "X" days from today's open.

INDEX

A Personal Invitation from Van K. Tharp

Get a Free Newsletter:

We publish a monthly newsletter, *Market Mastery*, that includes tips on how to develop a system and how to improve your performance by changing your thinking One of the topics not covered extensively in this book is the subject of data — wha can go wrong and how to find good data. As a way of saying "thank you" for your interest, we're offering you a free issue of *Market Mastery* covering this topic. Thi issue also includes a book review and valuable information on how to protect yourself in today's market. You can have it for free by contacting our office at 800 385-IITM. When you call, let us know you saw this offer in this book.

Play a Free Market Simulation Game on our Website.

I believe that one of the best ways to learn to trade or invest well is through simulation games—especially if those games teach the most important factors first. We've designed a game on our website that teaches you position sizing and protecting your profits—the keys to success. Each game lasts about six months, costs nothing to play, and awards prizes to the winner and lots of education to the losers. Find out more about it on our web site at http://www.iitm.com. It's free, so try it now.

International Institute of Trading Mastery, Inc.

8308 Belgium Street
Raleigh, NC 27606

919-362-5591, Phone
919-362-6020, Fax
info@iitm.com, e-mail